OXFORD HISTORIES

A WAR OF PEOPLES 1914–1919

SERIES ADVISORS
Geoff Eley, University of Michigan
Lyndal Roper, University of Oxford

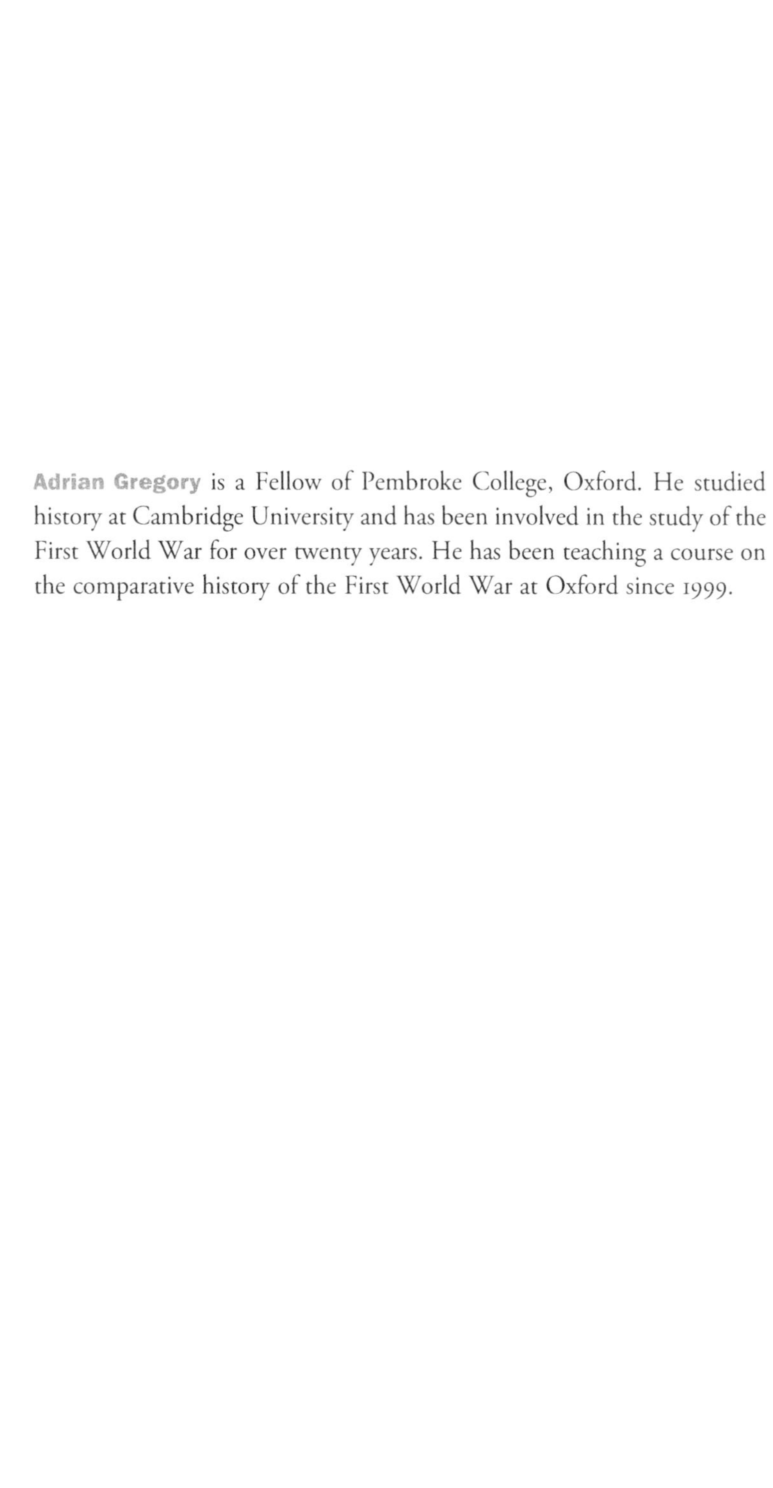

Adrian Gregory is a Fellow of Pembroke College, Oxford. He studied history at Cambridge University and has been involved in the study of the First World War for over twenty years. He has been teaching a course on the comparative history of the First World War at Oxford since 1999.

A War of Peoples 1914–1919

ADRIAN GREGORY

Great Clarendon Street, Oxford, OX2 6DP,
United Kingdom

Oxford University Press is a department of the University of Oxford. It furthers the University's objective of excellence in research, scholarship, and education by publishing worldwide. Oxford is a registered trade mark of Oxford University Press in the UK and in certain other countries

First Edition published in 2014

Impression: 1

Published in the United States of America by Oxford University Press
198 Madison Avenue, New York, NY 10016, United States of America

British Library Cataloguing in Publication Data
Data available

Library of Congress Control Number: 2013949229

ISBN 978–0–19–954257–4 (hbk)
978–0–19–954258–1 (pbk)

As printed and bound by
CPI Group (UK) Ltd, Croydon, CR0 4YY

CONTENTS

LIST OF MAPS AND SOURCES

Map 1. The Western Front.

Map 2. The Adriatic.

Map 3. Eastern Europe.

Map 4. The Ottoman Empire.

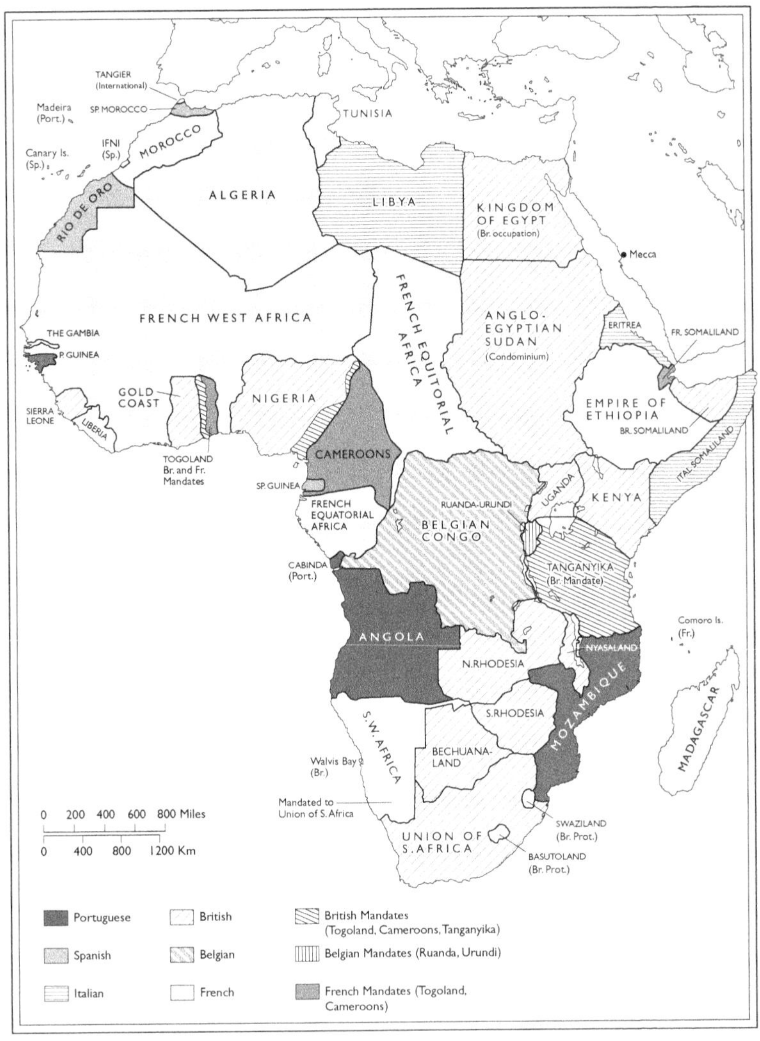

Map 5. Africa after the First World War.

INTRODUCTION

WHAT DO WE KNOW? HOW DO WE KNOW IT? WHAT DOES IT MEAN?

By 1914 mass literacy and the bureaucratic state ensured that the First World War would be massively documented. Furthermore the war would continue to generate important historical sources long after it finished, in the form of memoirs of the mighty and humble alike. The result is countless billions of pages of text in dozens of languages, far beyond the capability of any single historian to know anything but the tiniest fraction first hand. Beyond the written word there are vast quantities of visual representations and material relics.

Source 1: Still from the film *All Quiet on the Western Front*, 1930

The best-known death from a war that killed more than 10 million people is that of a fictional character. At the end of the 1930 American film *All Quiet on the Western Front*, the hero, Paul Baumer, is shot by a sniper whilst reaching from his trench for a butterfly. This image has come to define the meaning of the war for three generations (Source 1). It is estimated that the film has been seen in the cinema or on television by over a billion people since its first release.

Baumer is an invention; he neither lived nor died in the real past. His creator, the German author Erich Maria Remarque, had little actual experience of the front line in the war, and the character is not in any sense autobiographical but almost entirely based on his imagination as a novelist. Furthermore the plot of the book is altered in the film and the memorable scene at the end of the film does not occur in the novel.

The title of the film *All Quiet on the Western Front* is a very loose translation of the German title of the novel *Am Western Nichts Neu* (Nothing New in the West) using an anachronistic allusion to a famous headline from the American Civil War. The German protagonist was played by an American actor who was too young to have served in the war and even the hand that reaches for the butterfly is not that of the actor who plays Baumer, but the hand of the film's director. Given these multiple levels of fiction, distortion, and illusion, in what sense is this image historical evidence?

Historical knowledge is not generated purely from what occurred in the past; it is framed by narrative and analysis of what these events mean. Popular understandings of the war were created rather than simply emerging from collective memory and historians are not immune to framing their enquiries within popular understanding. So in his study of this *fictional* film, the critic Andrew Kelly makes the *historical* statement, 'The outcome of the First World War was not victory or glory, it was slaughter and waste.' He goes on to state, 'This is the view of the war today for which *All Quiet on the Western Front* is partly responsible.' For Kelly the fictional representation reveals the 'historical truth'—but arguably this fictional representation is not revealing but creating this 'truth'.

What then are the truths about the war, which are created by this film? They are that the war begins with illusion and enthusiasm and ends with despair and death. That the war destroys all the soldiers involved. That there is no meaning and no victory, all battles are pointless, the soldiers on each side bear no hatred towards those on the other side and have no interest in the national cause. That the real war is fought in the trenches of the Western Front in a predominantly male world and that civilians are irrelevant and ill-informed. It is a war about nothing, simply slaughter and waste, a dead hand reaching for a butterfly.

This narrative and analysis of the war has dominated not only the popular view of the First World War in the English-speaking world since the film was released in 1930, but also popular and professional historical writing. Yet the analysis and narrative is partly a contingent product of the fiction, first by a *German* novelist, who writing in a defeated nation could obviously see no point to any wartime sacrifices, and then by an *American* film crew who intensified the 'anti-war' message of the novel for both dramatic and political reasons.

What if the 'true meaning of the war' was seen as encapsulated in a different film?

The African Queen, a 1951 film adapted from the novel by C. S. Forrester, is no more nor less a work of fiction than *All Quiet on the Western Front.* Yet the truths about the First World War in that film are almost polar opposites of those in the 1930 film. This is a war that involves the active engagement of civilians and women, a war of hatred towards the enemy and real atrocities, of wide-ranging operations in exotic locales, of the strategic importance of naval power, and of the movement from neutrality to active participation. The male hero makes a journey from disillusionment and cynicism to redemption and commitment. It is a film that ends in survival, decisive victory, and triumph. The film defies so many expectations about the First World War that it is easy to forget it is a film about that war at all. Yet every one of the 'truths' it tells is just as supported by historical evidence from 1914 to 1919. It is also arguably a film that is much truer to the actual mentalities of that period than *All Quiet on the Western Front.*

In the end there is a difference between the evidence of historical fact and the inventions of such fictions. But we do well to remember that the facts we select out of the myriad available to us and the way we interpret those facts are patterned and shaped by narratives which have a distinctly fictional dimension. The central section of this book is a narrative of the war, but one which tries to remember that the ultimate meaning of events was and is contested.

Source 2: General Falkenhayn, 'The Christmas memorandum', December 1915

France has been weakened militarily and economically—almost to the limit of what it can stand—through the ongoing loss of coal fields in the northwest of the country. Russia's army has not yet been fully defeated, but its offensive ability has been so broken that it will not be able to regain anything like its old strength. Serbia's army can be considered destroyed. Italy has without a doubt recognized that it cannot count on its appetite for spoils being satisfied in the near future and would therefore probably be happy to escape from this adventure in any honourable way possible.

If conclusions are nowhere drawn from these facts then this is due to various phenomena which do not need detailed discussion. There is only one matter— the most important one—that cannot be passed over. That is the incredible pressure that England still exerts on its allies....

Thus it is all the more important that all the means suitable for harming England in what is properly its own territory are simultaneously brought to ruthless application. These means are submarine warfare and laying the groundwork for a political and economic alliance not only between Germany and its allies, but also between Germany and those states which are not yet fully constrained within England's sphere of influence. The formation of this alliance is not the topic of this exposition. Solving the task lies solely with the political leadership.

Submarine warfare, however, is a tool of war, just like any other tool. Those in charge of leading the war effort cannot avoid taking a position on this... An advance against Moscow would lead us nowhere. We do not have enough strength for any of these enterprises. As a result Russia is not a suitable object for attack. Only France remains....

There are targets lying within reach behind the French section of the Western Front to which the French leadership would need to use their very last man. Should they do this, then France would bleed to death, for there is no retreat, regardless of whether we ourselves reach the target or not. Should they not do this, and should targets fall into our hands, then the effect on morale in France would be enormous. For these operations which are limited in terms of territory, Germany will not be compelled to extend itself to a degree that would leave it seriously exposed on other fronts. Germany can confidently await the relief operations that can be expected at these fronts—and indeed can hope to have enough forces available to meet the attacks with counterstrikes. For Germany can conduct the offensive quickly or slowly, break off the offensive for a period of time or strengthen the offensive according to its objectives.

The targets being spoken of are Belfort or Verdun. What was said above applies to both of them. All the same Verdun is preferred.

Eric von Falkenhayn, *Die Oberste Heeresleitung 1915–1916 in ihren wichtigsten Entschliessungen* (Berlin 1920), p. 176 (The Supreme Command 1915–1916 and its Crucial Decisions). Translation by Jeffrey Verhey.

Any attempt to write the history of the war must consider the written statements, both contemporary and retrospective, of the political and military leadership. These are unavoidably the core of traditional narrative history. They can also be an interpretative minefield. All of the combatant nations experienced ferocious infighting between the military and civilian leadership, between allies, between political factions and military cliques. Many and perhaps most contemporary documents were written with at least half an eye to self-justification in the historical record, a problem that became infinitely worse after the war with accounts deliberately written to traduce enemies and claim retrospective wisdom.

General Falkenhayn's memorandum (Source 2), allegedly sent to the Kaiser in December 1915, is an extreme example of the slipperiness of some of the documentation. It quickly became a key document in interpreting the war; the German official history cites it (rather critically) as the explanation for the Battle of Verdun and as a result it enters into the wider historiography in most languages. Alastair Horne in his popular 1962 English-language book about Verdun, *The Price of Glory*, uses it as a key document, alongside a translation of the code name of the battle, *Gericht*, as 'place of execution', to argue that Falkenhayn's only objective was to kill and maim Frenchmen, 'to bleed France white'.

But there is no original document that can be produced to support this. The first appearance of the memorandum was in Falkenhayn's post-war book, which although it is titled to sound like an official history is in fact a memoir. The German official history, perhaps suspiciously, simply cites this work. If there was an original document, it is unlikely to exist after the destruction of the Prussian military archive by the RAF in 1945. This has led some sceptical historians, including Falkenhayn's biographer Holger Afflerbach, to question the authenticity of the memorandum. They would argue that the supposed document is a retrospective justification for Falkenhayn's failure to capture Verdun in 1916 and that the references to an attritional battle was a post-war attempt to suggest that the bloodbath on the Meuse was a deliberate strategy rather than a manifestation of strategic failure. Furthermore the stress on all-out submarine warfare against Britain, which was vetoed in 1916 by civilian politicians, adds a further level of excuse. The translation of *Gericht* as 'place of execution' is eccentric; it is more accurately a 'tribunal' or place of judgement, suggesting that the battle is intended to be just and decisive rather than simply murderous.

In his 2005 book *German Strategy and the Path to Verdun*, Robert Foley carefully avoids using this document. But he believes that it is probably real and that it certainly reflects with substantial accuracy what Falkenhayn was thinking in December 1915. There are a number of undoubtedly genuine and contemporary writings by Falkenhayn which express very similar ideas and the Christmas memorandum does seem consistent with his disposition of forces in early 1916, including the very limited number of infantry committed to the start of Verdun. Foley's interpretation would put particular stress on the maintenance of reserves to mount the counterstrikes mentioned towards the end of the document.

Other documents of this type can cause similar problems. For example, the typewritten version of Field Marshal Douglas Haig's diary sometimes shows signs of clear retrospective interference, and even the handwritten 'original' was sometimes altered. Its status as a 'private diary' is also called into question by the fact that during the war sections of it were selectively released by Lady Haig, with her husband's support, to influential politicians. The minutes of meetings are sometimes heavily edited and on occasion the most sensitive things were never written down. Perhaps worst of all is the sheer immensity of the records. No historian can hope to develop first-hand knowledge of any but a small portion of them. As a result any general history is reliant on the interpretations of experts, but at times an author must make choices on the basis of what is felt to be the balance of probabilities.

Source 3: 'The Song of Craonne'

When our eight days rest are up
We are going back to the trenches
Our place is useful
Because without us there would be a collapse
But we are done for good, we've had it
No one wants to march
With heavy hearts and a tear
We say goodbye to the civilians
All the same, without drums, without trumpets
We go up there with lowered heads.

(Chorus)
Farewell to life, farewell to love
Farewell to all the women.
That's it for good, that's it forever
In this infamous war
It's at Craonne, on the plateau
That we leave our skins
We've been condemned to death
We are the ones they sacrifice.

Eight days in the trenches
Eight days of suffering
Yet we still have hope
That this evening we will be relieved
That is what we wait for
Suddenly in the silent night
We hear someone coming
It's an officer of the riflemen
Who are coming to replace us
Quietly in the shadows, soaking in the rain
Those little riflemen pick out their graves.

(Repeat Chorus)

It is miserable to see on the *grands boulevards*
The fat cats having their fun
For them life is rosy
For us not so much
Instead of hiding, these shirkers
Would be better put in the trenches
To defend their cash
Because us poor sods have nothing
All of our comrades are being buried
To protect the wealth of these gentlemen.

(Repeat Chorus)

The sentiments of ordinary soldiers of the war are notoriously hard to establish. All sources have their problems. Letters were subject to censorship and perhaps more significantly to self-censorship. Early published letter collections were sometimes self-consciously propagandistic and the subsequent survival of unpublished letter collections tends to tilt towards the higher social classes. Some soldiers kept diaries, despite the fact that such items were usually a breach of military discipline as a possible source of intelligence if captured. But diarists are rarely typical or representative. Trench newspapers produced by the soldiers themselves in several armies provide an interesting and valuable source, but again there has to be a suspicion that they reflected the views of the more literate and articulate soldiers and that they were potentially subject to official scrutiny.

The experiences of the vast majority of soldiers who were less articulate are harder to uncover. Investigation of army disciplinary documents can reveal a great deal, but tends by its nature to emphasize discontent and resistance. In Britain and the Dominions there was an extensive oral history from the 1960s until the first decade of the twenty-first century. But it is clear that post-war experiences, including evolving understandings of the meaning of the war, shape and frame these recollections.

Contemporary soldiers' songs are interesting evidence, but they need to be handled with care. 'The Song of Craonne' is a classic example (Source 3). It has become forever associated with the 'mutiny' of French soldiers in 1917 after the failure of the Chemin des Dames offensive—fought in the vicinity of the small town of Craonne in the department of Aisne in Picardy. Ever since it has been regarded as a subversive and pacifist song of resistance to the war by the ordinary soldiers. Allegedly the French high command offered a huge reward for the identity of the song's composer, which was never claimed. Its performance was officially banned in France from 1917 until the 1970s, although it proved impossible to suppress.

But the association of the song with the mutineers is more questionable in detail. Earlier versions had appeared in 1915 as the 'Song of Lorrette' and in 1916 the lyrics in the chorus were 'It's at Verdun, in front of Vaux'. The song long pre-dated the collective indiscipline of 1917. The lyrics are as expressive of melancholic resignation as of rebellion. Different English translations can minimize or emphasize these aspects. Furthermore the most repeated version we have, with its particular emphasis on hatred of the 'fat cats', was written down in 1919 by Paul Vaillant-Couturier, a prominent left-winger who was later the editor of the Communist Party newspaper *Humanité.* It is likely that the song circulated with variant lyrics.

All armies sang songs that were subversive. Many of the British ones were collected together for the musical theatre production *Oh! What a Lovely War*. But what these songs meant to the men singing them is opaque. Some of the most apparently bitter and disillusioned songs appeared very early in the war and were sung cheerfully by men marching off to battle. Soldiers sang songs that were sentimental and even occasionally patriotic. Furthermore songs were not just lyrics, they were tunes, and the appeal of the 'Song of Craonne' was at least as much musical as political: it was and is hauntingly beautiful when sung in French.

Source 4: Food deliveries to Petrograd 1916–17 (railway wagons)

In the early twenty-first century readers tend to be impressed by numbers. Quantification has become central to the operation of modern society and this process was already well underway by 1914. Governments at war urgently sought statistical information for purposes of management and planning. But in using this material it is important to consider how the information was generated and it is worth remembering that numbers require interpretation; they do not speak for themselves.

The figures cited here ultimately derive from the surveys of the Special Committee on food supply (Source 4). In principle they ought to be reliable, as the organization had an interest in getting them right. But we should also be aware that there are things the figures don't tell us. We do not know whether the cattle were well fed or scrawny. Were the potato wagons full or had they been plundered en route? We also do not know whether food was illegally reaching the city by other means.

Other forms of economic data can be much more misleading. Inflation figures are usually based on the *official* prices of a basket of goods, indeed the modern measurement of inflation largely dates from the war. But official prices do not tell us anything about prices on the black market, and by definition black-marketeers and their customers do not inform governments of the prices. So any inflation figure needs to be modified by an estimate of the size and scope of black market activity, which is very hard for governments and subsequently historians to know.

The importance of the table below derives from the knowledge that the fall of the Tsarist regime in the 'February' revolution was precipitated by protests about food supply. But the causality implied is not entirely straightforward: total food deliveries declined sharply in January, but most of this decline was specific to the delivery of meat, whilst the food protests of February were primarily about bread. Yet even bread is a complicated issue. The supply of wheat flour may have been adequate, but the supply of the rye flour that produced the cheapest bread clearly was not. It is nevertheless conceivable that what ultimately triggered these protests was less a failure of supply to the city of Petrograd than

	Estimated average monthly needs	Actual arrivals: 1916 July	August	September	October	November	December	1917 January
Wheat	–	72	82	239	71	29	45	55
Wheat flour	1,500	1,433	484	552	807	1,248	719	1,131
Rye	900	496	1,096	891	262	278	141	121
Rye flour	1,200	1,013	709	210	–	449	417	112
Potatoes and cabbages	600	293	298	866	2,330	1,052	434	349
Cattle	3,000	1,477	3,437	4,068	2,364	3,282	2,594	1,625
Fowl	300	345	406	607	238	223	636	410
Fish	300	110	241	790	1,026	1,092	342	–
Eggs	300	819	465	628	631	210	55	48
Butter	150	190	227	137	289	230	196	257
Sugar	600	343	233	296	740	620	589	358
Tea and salt	150	1	62	88	134	81	116	119
TOTAL	12,150	8,297	11,594	12,639	14,168	11,332	8,654	6,556

Note: The figures for total monthly arrivals are greater than the addition of individual items, as certain products have been excluded from the table.

From Robert B. McKean, *St Petersburg between the Revolutions: Workers and Revolutionaries June 1907–February 1917* (New Haven, CT, 1990), table 11.viii, p. 345.

hoarding caused by rumours of imminent rationing. So when using tables of figures it is important to interrogate them and not take on faith that they prove the point that a historian claims they are making.

A final point of caution; all of the months in the table above are defined by the old Julian calendar which was used in Russia prior to the revolution. This means that Russian months began thirteen days later than those in the West. Any attempt to use this information in comparison with other nations needs to allow for this.

Source 5: Caproni CA 36 Bomber (Italian aircraft introduced into service 1916)

Speed: 137/kmh
Range: 599 km
Service ceiling: 4,864 m
Rate of climb: 125 m/min
2 x machine guns
800kg bombs
Surviving examples: USAF museum, Dayton, Ohio; Italian airforce museum, Lake Bracciano, Lazio
Websites:
<http://www.world%20war1.com/dbc/caproni3.htm>
<http://www.aerei-italiani-net/schedeT/aereoca.htm>

The Caproni bomber (Source 5) used by the Italians to bomb cities in Austria was a highly significant weapon of the war. The Americans also used it in 1918. Amongst those who flew it was Fiorello La Guardia, later a famous mayor of New York. The French Minister of War to the newly created republic of Czechoslovakia died in a Caproni that crashed in May 1919. Above all this was the aircraft that inspired the Italian General Douhet to claim after the First World War that wars of the future would be decided not by soldiers on the battlefield but by the strategic bombing of cities.

Tens of thousands of weapons from the First World War have been preserved in museums and technical data about weaponry is widely available on the internet. There are also thousands of enthusiasts who make available their detailed knowledge about weapons and tactics. Academic historians are frequently snobbish about such sources and are often reluctant to dwell on the details of weaponry. But the technical capabilities of the weapons available to the opposing armies had important consequences on the battlefield and this in turn helped determine the overall shape of the war.

At the same time it is important to avoid fetishization. Fascination with technical details is a widespread male tendency, but weapons are not the same as railway engines or racing cars in that they were designed and intended to kill. This is just as true of cavalry sabres as it is of mustard gas. Artefacts also require contextualization. We often need to know why certain things have been saved and collected whereas others were not.

Digitization is opening up many other topics. Maps and panoramas are widely and readily available, as are photographic collections. Posters for recruiting and war loans can be viewed on-line. There are major collections relating to war poetry and war memorials. The Commonwealth War Graves Commission has a searchable database listing every serviceman and woman of the British Empire known to have died by name. But the internet is also utilized for misinformation, conspiracy theories, and propaganda. There are sites dedicated to the claim that the war was begun by the Jesuits or the Bavarian Illuminati. The issue of the Armenian Genocide is a minefield of claim and counter-claim.

Source 6: The Edith Cavell memorial

St Martin's Place, opposite the National Portrait Gallery, London. 7.6m tall.

Commemorating the British nurse executed by the Germans in 1915, the memorial was sculpted by Sir George Frampton, RA, who worked for free on the commission (Source 6). It was unveiled in 1920 to a lukewarm critical reception. Other memorials to Cavell can be found in Brussels, Norwich, Washington DC, and Melbourne. A mountain in the Canadian Rockies was named after her as were streets in Lisbon (Portugal), Dunedin (New Zealand), Trenton (New Jersey), and Mauritius. Until November 2011 she was also commemorated in the name of a multi-storey car park in Peterborough.

The First World War produced more monuments than any other event in human history. In the United Kingdom alone there are over fifty thousand known memorials to the 'Great War'. The Cavell memorial belongs to the tiny number dedicated to a single individual. In this respect it stands in stark contrast with battlefield memorials such as the monument to the missing at Thiepval on the Somme, which commemorates 72,191 dead of the British Empire with no known grave, or the ossuary at Verdun which houses the bones of an estimated 130,000 unidentified French and German soldiers.

The Cavell memorial helps illustrate the way in which the meaning and context of memorials shifts and evolves. The 1920 ceremony of dedication can be seen at www.britishpathe.com/video/stills/nurse-cavell-memorial. The ceremony is conventionally patriotic. Initially the memorial was perceived primarily as an indictment of German brutality, extending the wartime propaganda surrounding the execution. This propaganda had been intense; the first film made about Cavell in 1918 had been crudely titled *The Woman the Germs Shot*. But the meaning of the memorial shifted very rapidly. Key to this process was the addition to the memorial in 1924 of Cavell's now famous last words: 'Patriotism is not enough. I must have no hatred or bitterness towards anyone.'

The memory of Cavell remained controversial through the 1920s. In 1928 a new film was made about her. Starring Sybil Thorndike and entitled *Dawn*, it drew a protest from the German ambassador and condemnation from the British Foreign Secretary. Margot Asquith, who had been the wife of the Prime Minister at the time of Cavell's execution, stated, 'When the efforts of every civilized nation are being directed to peace and goodwill, it can serve no good purpose to revive ugly memories of war.' It fell to the contrarian George Bernard Shaw to point out that if prominent people really wanted Cavell forgotten for diplomatic reasons, then logically they should demolish Frampton's memorial in central London.

In 1939 a new film was made entitled *Nurse Cavell*, starring Anna Neagle. This film was made in Hollywood and was ambiguous in tone. Although it could be regarded as a specific indictment of German militarism, it could also be seen as a pacifist statement ending with Cavell's 'Patriotism is not enough.'

Cavell remains a powerful symbolic figure. She can serve as an icon for both pacifists and feminists as well as a symbol of service and patriotism. Recently her statue has become a focal point for demonstrations by 'The women in black', a feminist peace movement that refers to Cavell as a 'legendary bad-ass' (www.badreputation.org.uk). It is strange and perhaps appropriate that this most solid of symbols has also proved the most flexible in its meaning.

CHAPTER 1
THE FIRST YEAR 1914–1915: ESCALATION

'The age of cabinet wars is behind us—now we only have people's war'

Helmuth von Moltke the Elder addressing the Reichstag, May 1890

At noon on 28 July 1914 the Dual Monarchy of Austria-Hungary declared war on Serbia. The first shots of the war were fired by Austrian gunboats on the river Danube into the adjacent Serbian capital of Belgrade following the expiry of an ultimatum. The government in Vienna had demanded that the Serbs should allow the occupation of their country while the Austrian authorities investigated the assassination on 28 June of the heir to the imperial throne, the Archduke Franz Ferdinand, by Bosnian Serbs in the Bosnian city of Sarajevo, which had recently been annexed by the Dual Monarchy. The assassins had been armed, trained, and encouraged by a renegade section of the Serbian secret service. The Serbian government, which had made a feeble attempt to warn Vienna of the possibility of an attack, had been willing to concede some Austrian demands, but Vienna had deliberately shaped the ultimatum in such a way as to make its rejection almost inevitable. Serbia would have effectively been placed under Hapsburg control whilst the murder was investigated.

Important figures in Vienna had sought a confrontation well before the assassination. The Austrian military leadership, in particular the commander of the Imperial army, Conrad von Hötzendorf, were determined to destroy Serbian independence, which they saw as an unacceptable threat to the future of an empire with a large and growing 'South Slav' population that might wish to break away and form a union with Serbia. Conrad was also willing to risk war with Serbia's traditional supporter, Russia, which he saw as irredeemably hostile to Vienna and which he confidently believed could be defeated with the support of Austria's ally Germany. Some civilian politicians, in particular Stefan Tisza, the Prime Minister of the Hungarian half of the Empire, were much more cautious, but the insult to the Imperial family represented by the assassination provided a powerful push to war.

The decision by the German leadership to back the Austrian demands completely and unconditionally stemmed from a willingness to risk war in order to break the 'encirclement' caused by the alliance of France and Russia. This could be achieved by driving a wedge between those powers during a Balkan crisis. The German leadership had probably made the stronger decision that in principle it was better to fight a pre-emptive war against these enemies sooner rather than later. The army leadership, particularly the Chief of Staff, Helmuth von Moltke, believed that the new French conscription law combined with the pace of Russian industrial growth and armament production meant that by 1916 Germany would be faced with opponents who could not be beaten. Germany might have responded by a massive programme of deterrent armaments, but such a programme would have required taxes that were politically too difficult. In December 1912 it had been agreed in a secret meeting of the German military and naval leadership in Potsdam that August 1914 would be the best date for starting a war, and although it cannot be proved that such a decision was irreversible, there was certainly a concerted effort to manipulate the July crisis in such a way that the German leadership could make it look as if Russia was responsible for war, a crucial consideration for domestic opinion.

The Russian leadership, traditionally supporters of Serbia for reasons of both religion and solidarity with the Slav 'race', faced a dilemma. The Tsar and his inner circle did not desire war, although the Foreign Minister was more aggressive. There was an acute awareness that Russia's relative backwardness made war a dangerous gamble; a humiliating defeat at the hands of Japan in 1904–5 had almost toppled the Imperial dynasty. For this reason Nicholas II had previously been a supporter of international peace initiatives and he also hoped that his personal relationship with his cousin Wilhelm II might serve to smooth things over.

On the other hand the precariousness of the monarchy would not allow further humiliation in foreign policy and Russia's French allies were sending encouraging signals. Indeed President Poincaré of France had been in St Petersburg on an official visit during the previous weeks and had indicated his firm support. Russia decided tentatively to support the Serbs whilst trying to negotiate a wider settlement.

France had suffered a humiliating defeat at German hands in 1870 and had lost territory in Alsace and Lorraine. But the desire for revenge had ceased to dominate French politics. During the crisis of 1914 the main French motivation was to make sure that the Russian alliance remained firm because this was seen as essential to French security. French leaders were only too aware that German population growth had far outstripped that of France and that all the efforts to persuade French men and women to have larger families had failed. In order to offset this German advantage in military manpower the French were counting on the masses of Russia, as well as conscripting a higher proportion of their own population. Some French generals also suggested that the French colonies in Africa might provide an inexhaustible pool of recruits, but this was largely untested in 1914. Like the Russians the French did not intend to initiate war, but they would stand by their ally.

Britain, worried by the expansion of the German navy, had drawn closer to France since the turn of the century. In turn this led to settlements of long-standing colonial rivalries with both France and then Russia. There had been secret military 'conversations' between the French and British armies, and French war plans had come to count on British support. But formally Britain remained uncommitted; the *Entente* with France was an understanding rather than an alliance. As the diplomatic crisis developed during 1914 the British Foreign Secretary, Sir Edward Grey, took the lead in trying to organize an international conference to settle it by traditional diplomatic means. Germany consistently blocked this effort.

Italy and Romania had both been in alliance with Germany and Austria-Hungary, but both used the manner of the Austrian attack on Serbia to claim that they were not bound to assist the Hapsburgs in a war of aggression. The alliances had been designed to neutralize claims that these nations might make on Hapsburg territories populated by Italians and Romanians, but the outbreak of war made both Italian and Romanian governments consider that they might be able to take better advantage of the situation by talking to the enemies of the Austrians and Germans.

Events now gathered pace. On Wednesday 29 July, President Poincaré arrived back in Paris. He was met by a demonstration organized by right-wing 'patriots' demanding support for Russia. But the French government hesitated, in part because they were unsure about the British stance. In Berlin, the Foreign Ministry were warned by their ambassador in London that Grey had communicated that it might not be possible for Britain to stand aside if France were attacked. Kaiser Wilhelm was furious, scribbling angry notes in the margins of the despatch.

On 30 July Russia finally ordered general mobilization. On the same day the leader of the French socialists, Jean Jaurès, was assassinated by a 'patriot' who feared that he would mobilize opposition to war. The French socialists, no friends of Russia, were indeed planning a massive counter-demonstration for the next day. But Jaurès had always supported the notion of national self-defence and if Germany attacked France it was unlikely that he would have opposed the government.

On 31 July Moltke sent a telegram to Vienna telling the Austrians that if they mobilized against Russia, Germany would follow suit. In fact Germany had already decided to mobilize and did so in the evening. On the morning of 1 August the Kaiser saw a chance to limit the war. A note from the German ambassador in London had suggested that if Germany refrained from attacking France, the British might be able to keep France from supporting Russia. Moltke responded immediately by informing his monarch that this was impossible. The German war plan was predicated on attacking France and it was not possible to switch these forces to the east. The Kaiser gave way. Germany declared war on Russia whilst the bulk of its army began to march towards France.

It is frequently stated that Germany went to war in 1914 committed to 'the Schlieffen Plan', which promised a victory in six weeks by means of a flanking attack on France through Belgium. It also became a dogmatic belief in post-war Germany that this plan failed because Moltke tinkered with it, misunderstanding its brilliance.

The so-called 'Schlieffen Plan' was in fact a short memorandum written after his retirement by the Prussian Chief of Staff, Alfred von Schlieffen, in 1905. It called for a rapid advance through both Holland and Belgium using a massively expanded army in order to deal quickly with France and free the German army for subsequent operations against Russia, which would be slower to mobilize. The memorandum was largely intended to make the political case for an expansion of the army, an expansion that had not fully occurred by 1914. Moltke's war plan in 1914 did contain elements of this Schlieffen concept. Crucially the basic logic still held that France, being more developed than Russia, would mobilize faster and that Russian size and backwardness would make a decisive result in the east difficult. So the bulk of the German army would be deployed to the west and would take the offensive. Belgian neutrality would be violated in order to attack the French left flank with a strong force. But Dutch neutrality would be respected. This meant that the awkward Maastricht salient of the Netherlands would cramp German deployment. This was not due to any moral qualms but because if Britain entered the war Dutch neutrality would act as a means for Germany to continue trading in the face of blockade. Moltke also kept strong forces on the German left to block a French offensive into Alsace and allocated larger forces against Russia. These cautious moves, much criticized later, were sensible because even the reduced German right wing was going to be stretched to the limit of its supply capacity in terms of the road and rail networks within Belgium.

On 2 August German troops crossed the frontiers of Luxembourg and Belgium. The German Foreign Minister had summoned the Belgian ambassador and presented him with an ultimatum demanding that Belgium allow German troops to occupy its territory, which would be restored after the war. In the evening King Albert of Belgium formally rejected this demand, as he was bound to do by international treaties. In London the French ambassador begged Sir Edward Grey for his support. Grey agreed that the Royal Navy would defend the French coast, but beyond that he was vague.

On 3 August Germany declared war on France. The violation of Belgian neutrality now provided a legitimate reason for British intervention. The treaty that had created Belgium in 1839 obliged the great powers including the United Kingdom and Prussia to respect and uphold Belgian neutrality. Such considerations of international law weighed heavily with liberal opinion in Britain and Ireland and helped resolve divisions at the highest political level. Senior figures in the government including the Prime Minister Herbert Asquith, the Foreign Secretary Sir Edward Grey, and in all likelihood the 'radical' Chancellor of the Exchequer David Lloyd George had been convinced for some time that in the event of a Franco–German war Britain would have to lend its support to France to prevent Germany, which appeared hostile to Britain, from dominating the continent. This was a conviction shared by the Conservative opposition. But a large section of the governing Liberal Party and their Irish Nationalist and Labour allies was unlikely to accept this. They were much more swayed by the moral argument of defending the rights of Belgium against German militarism. In this sense the German war plan was for the British government a 'gift from Mars'. It declared war at 11 p.m., midnight Berlin time, on 4 August.

All of the major powers envisaged fighting the war on enemy territory. The French war plan, Plan XVII, was for an offensive into the lost territories of Alsace and Lorraine. The French nevertheless initially held back from the frontier. The Russian war plan foresaw an early advance both into East Prussia and into Austria's Polish province of Galicia. The Hapsburg Empire had always assumed that it would mount an offensive against Russian Poland, and it now added a second offensive into Serbia as well.

The offensive plans of all these nations have been linked to a supposed 'short war illusion'. But expert military opinion varied widely as to the anticipated length of a war, and the desire to take the initiative and fight the war on enemy soil was even more logical for those who believed that the struggle might be long and attritional. Nor was the strategic offensive based upon an unrealistic view of the defensive tactical capabilities of modern firepower. Recent experience in South Africa, Manchuria, and the Balkans had amply demonstrated to commanders in all the armies that rifles, machine guns, and fast-firing field artillery could have devastating effects on troops in the open. Much of the tactical emphasis on the spirit of the offensive was not a demonstration of the primitive stupidity of commanders but an attempt to utilize psychology to overcome the inevitable fear and chaos of the modern battlefield. The temptation for soldiers to 'go to ground' under fire had been observed as far back as the American Civil War and the subsequently much derided emphasis on bayonets, and in the case of the French, colourful uniforms with red trousers, was an attempt to overcome this natural fear.

Politicians were probably more likely to believe in a short war than the military men, in part because the military, particularly in Germany, had led them to believe that the war could be won quickly despite their hidden uncertainty. Politicians were also prone to doubt the ability of domestic populations to sustain a long war. It was widely believed that the collapse of credit and trade combined with the disruptive effects of mass mobilization would simultaneously cause mass unemployment and shortages leading to inflation, and that in these circumstances the threat of socialist revolution amongst the working class would quickly be realized. Schlieffen himself had stated that a war could not last long due to the pacifist tendencies of the majority of the European people.

The outbreak of war did lead to massive rises in unemployment and increases in prices, amounting to one of the worst economic crises in modern history. In France the disruption caused by invasion meant that the crisis lasted for months. But popular unrest was limited and what little did occur was mostly directed against enemy aliens and minorities. Shop windows were smashed from the Urals to the Atlantic, but persecution was most virulent in Russia where dislike of the economic influence of German 'colonists', some of whom had lived in Russia for two centuries, quickly moved from rioting to state-supported expropriation and by early 1915 wholesale deportation. Inappropriate names were everywhere changed; St Petersburg was renamed Petrograd, German Shepherd dogs became Alsatians, Battenberg became Mountbatten, Berlin in Ontario became Kitchener.

Organized resistance to war was less apparent. The socialist Second International of 1889 had pledged itself to oppose a European war by a variety of means including general strikes. During the Second Moroccan Crisis of 1911 the German socialists, who ran the largest and best-organized political party in Europe, had sponsored massive protests against the prospect of a war with France, helping to tie the hands of the German government. In the 1914 crisis, early socialist protests faded quickly. As late as 31 July the socialist paper *Vörwarts* had warned that the war would turn all of Europe into a 'vast battlefield, a vast hospital' and bring 'unemployment, hunger, sickness, death and misery'. But the German government had deliberately manipulated the crisis in such a way that it appeared as if it was responding to Russian aggression, and the German socialists feared Tsarism more than their own government. This was not in itself irrational. Although the German elites were intensely hostile to socialism, the government had since the 1880s reluctantly coexisted with the working-class movement. By contrast in 1905 the Russian regime had unleashed both official and unofficial terror against socialists in Russia, shooting down peaceful protesters. Not only in Germany but throughout Europe a victory for the Tsar was perceived as a setback for the socialist future. The majority of German socialists therefore not only stopped actively opposing the war, but most of their Reichstag deputies voted for war credits in the Reichstag in August.

The claim that socialism was overwhelmed by nationalism in August 1914 is misleading. Socialists made their decisions on contingent grounds, motivated as much by their socialist ideals as by any patriotism. The danger of suppression by the forces of the state was at the back of many minds; civil liberties were suspended in the emergency and overt opposition could have been disastrous. Defending the rights won in a half century of struggle seemed more sensible than any grand internationalist gestures, and this defence included defending those rights against enemy-occupying forces. Indeed in France many of the 'subversives' who had been identified for arrest at the outbreak of war could not be found by the police because they had reported for military duty. Dealing with the hardship that war was causing absorbed the energy of many activists, as did solidarity with members who had been called up. Some socialists also believed that wartime conditions might ultimately strengthen the bargaining hand of the working class and force reform of the state in a socialist direction. This proved to be largely correct. Nevertheless, some socialists did continue their opposition to war. The British Independent Labour Party did not vote for war credits and although not acting against the war effort, they did argue from the outset for a negotiated peace and against many wartime measures. They may have done so in part because they were more influenced by Christian and humanitarian ethical ideas than by Marxism; indeed, the Marxist Social Democratic Federation backed the British war effort. Likewise the stance of the Bolshevik wing of the Russian socialists was driven more by its 'vanguardist' ideology than by any orthodox Marxist ideas of historical evolution. V. I. Lenin, the Bolshevik leader, welcomed a war that he sought not to end but to transform into a global class conflict.

The European women's movement was caught in similar dilemmas. Amongst the combatant nations only Australia and New Zealand had enfranchized women before 1914. But the campaign for full citizenship was widespread in Europe. Prior to 1914 the women's movement had been strongly internationalist and generally pacifist, seeing war as a manifestation of patriarchal violence. In Russia the Symbolist poet Zinaida Gippius initially supported the war as an Orthodox crusade, but her doubts were present from the start:

> In the hours of suffering undeserved,
> And of battles unresolved
> The purity of silence is gold
> And only quiet prayer should be heeded.

She soon came to reject the war entirely. Some felt that opposition to war would play into the hands of anti-suffragists who would use it to impugn the patriotic credentials of women, whilst others thought that the war might provide an opportunity for women to demonstrate their patriotism practically. The militant 'suffragette' Christabel Pankhurst, who in August 1914 was on the run in France for crimes of civil disobedience, had her own rationale for supporting the war, claiming that Germany represented the quintessence of male violence and that as such it needed to be opposed. By contrast her socialist sister, Sylvia, was opposed to the war, although she threw her formidable energies in the early months into relieving the economic distress of women in the East End of London.

The British declaration of war was made on behalf of the United Kingdom and the Empire. Ireland was in crisis in 1914, but the declaration of war saw a brief moment of unity, with both those who sought Home Rule and their Unionist opponents supporting the declaration. The Nationalists were particularly moved by the fate of Belgium as a 'small nation'. Only a small minority of convinced Republicans questioned Westminster's right to take Ireland to war. In 1914 this also caused little disquiet in the Dominions and the war witnessed manifestations of patriotic and imperial enthusiasm in most of them. Many Australians and Canadians were quick to volunteer; a significant number of them were recent immigrants from Britain. British emigrants outside the Empire, in Latin America and in the United States, also demonstrated and also volunteered.

These overseas volunteers provide some evidence of 'war enthusiasm'. But the popular mood in 1914 was complex and varied. The European aristocracies to a large extent did embrace war in 1914; the assertion of warrior values over those of commerce was congenial. The upper classes would generally pay a high human price for this enthusiasm. The enthusiasm of intellectuals and artists was perhaps more surprising, and is generally best understood as part of a rejection of a modernity perceived as materialistic and alienating. Most religious leaders similarly interpreted the war as punishment for materialism whilst supporting the war effort. The European churches were generally reflexively loyal to the ruling dynasties and in the French Republic the outbreak of war saw the suspension of hostilities between church and state.

Young men of the middle classes were the most likely to greet war with outright enthusiasm. In part this was because they were already the audience for much nationalist propaganda but also perhaps because the pre-war years had been frustrating for many. Growing competition for clerical and commercial employment from an increasingly educated female population had not only held down salaries and limited prospects, but had also brought into question the masculinity of such work. Military service provided a clear way of asserting a separate male sphere. In turn some young middle-class women would also look on the war as a potential form of liberation. Some were able to enlist as volunteer nurses. A cynical observer in Russia mocked these self-appointed sisters as 'parodies' of sisters of mercy, capable of doing little more than rearranging pillows. But the vast majority of these women in all nations would serve with dedication once they got past the initial shock of seeing great suffering at first hand. Before this reality sank in, students of both sexes and in all nations were prominent in the more boisterous celebrations of the outbreak of war. For example, even as early as 25 July, there had been rowdy demonstrations in the German university town of Freiburg demanding support for Austria.

Working-class attitudes were generally less visible. With the outbreak of war the protests organized by socialists and trade unions came to an end. Many working-class communities were most immediately concerned by the economic upheaval, and in parts of Poland, northern France, and Belgium, by invasion. Quiet despondency may have been widespread, but there was also a good deal of what might be called conditional patriotism. In the United Kingdom, which maintained voluntary recruitment, there was a significant amount of working-class volunteering in August, particularly once men were assured that their families would receive adequate separation allowances. Unemployment clearly played a role in this. More men enlisted from industries that had been heavily disrupted by the outbreak of war, but support for the national cause was also evident elsewhere and recruitment came to operate with rather than against working-class solidarity. Attitudes towards the state as a whole varied nonetheless: in France the levels of draft evasion and opposition were negligible, whereas in Russia there were dozens of mobilization riots against conscription.

Even more difficult to gauge was the attitude of the peasantry, who still made up the majority of the population of some combatants. One historian has characterized the mood in Bavaria at the outbreak of the war as despondent. Paintings by the Russian Jewish painter Marc Chagall show miserable faces reacting to the news of mobilization in the Jewish villages of western Russia. In France an elderly rural woman reacted to the ringing of the church bells announcing war with the comment, 'This is the death knell of our boys.' In most of Europe compulsory enlistment fell more heavily on those working in the countryside, with the result that the immediate impact of war was felt heavily. Men (and vast numbers of horses) were pulled away from the farms at just the moment when they were preparing to bring in the harvest. There was a great deal of resentment both from the men called away and the women left behind to bring the harvest in. In France the reality of invasion provided some sense that the defence of the land was meaningful, even if memories of 1870 brought with it a great deal of fear as well. The population of East Prussia similarly felt a degree of personal involvement. This may also have been true in Serbia, although there were signs after two years of war that it had already created weariness in the population. Comparative enlistment rates in the British Isles show that with the exception of the Highlands of Scotland, which had strong martial traditions and organization, rural areas lagged behind urban ones in terms of recruitment. In Ireland at the outbreak of war the divide between town and country proved more significant than that between Catholic and Protestant. In the British Empire it also seems that the urban centres took the lead in levels of war enthusiasm; indeed the high recruitment rates in Australia may have reflected a society that was, contrary to legend, unusually urbanized.

The 'spirit of August' was not straightforward. Assertions of national unity by the political elite served political purposes and propaganda was at work from the start, editing film and cropping photographs to provide images of universal patriotic fervour. A famous photograph of 'crowds' on the Unter den Linden in Berlin hides the fact that it was mostly empty. In Germany later in the war the idea of a 'community of August' would be used to criticize 'internal enemies' and remobilize the population. In post-war Britain and France war enthusiasm would become a stock image in the critique of patriotism by pacifist groups. The war was not, as is sometimes suggested, an inevitable consequence of the mass nationalism of the early twentieth century. But nationalism would underpin and sometimes undermine the willingness of populations to endure the terrible ordeal ahead.

Indeed it was the war itself that embedded nationalism in European societies both through the unrelenting propagandizing of wartime populations in the national cause and in the counter-reactions of nationalisms against multi-national empires. A war that had begun as a pre-emptive strike against Serbian nationalism would end up unleashing nationalism throughout Europe on an unprecedented scale.

The prospect of a *Volkskrieg*, a 'people's war', had potentially disturbing implications for the German military. Popular resistance in France and Belgium had the potential to disrupt the German advance, increasing the 'friction' in a plan that already faced many uncertainties. The German experience of 1870–71, when German armies had faced *franc-tireurs*, literally 'free shooters', irregular forces of local combatants, had convinced the German high command that popular resistance was to be expected. Although such civilian resistance in the course of an invasion was explicitly stated to be legal by the Hague Convention, the German military made it clear before the war that they intended to deal with any such activity in a draconian fashion, including using measures such as human shields and collective reprisals which were explicitly outlawed by the same convention. In fact there was no *Volkskrieg* in August 1914 in the west. There is no reliable evidence of any civilian resistance in northern France or Belgium. But German commanders imagined that it was occurring and draconian actions were taken. Ordinary military actions by French and Belgian troops and even some incidents of friendly fire between German units gave rise to atrocities.

A similar dynamic was at play in Serbia. The Hapsburg army was obsessed with the prospect of irregular warfare by *komita* bands, both in Serbia proper and in the Austrian territories of Bosnia and the Krajina. Hostage taking and executions were the immediate response. They increased as it became apparent that the invasion of Serbia was going badly. The Hapsburg offensive began on 12 August, but by 20 August the invading forces were in full flight. Serbia had won the first major victory of the war.

Lurid rumours of atrocities also inevitably accompanied the Russian advance into East Prussia. But ironically, despite the dreaded reputation of the 'cossack hordes' subsequent German investigations found that in August the Russian soldiers had generally behaved humanely, although petty pilfering was widespread and there was a certain amount of arson. Atrocities real and imagined were transmitted by excited press reporting and even more by rumour. Combined with the perfectly rational desire of civilians not to be caught on the battlefields, this unleashed the first great exoduses of the war. Tens of thousands of refugees were on the move by the middle of August, perhaps hundreds of thousands by September.

Conventional military resistance by the Belgians caused more initial problems to the German command than the actions of alleged *franc-tireurs*. The powerful frontier fortifications at Liège resisted the first German attacks on 6 August. An ambitious young staff officer, Erich Ludendorff, took charge of the attack and infiltrated German troops between the forts to seize the city on 7 August, winning the highest German medal, *Pour le Mérite*, as a consequence. But the Liège forts held on for another week and were only finally forced to surrender when the Germans brought up super-heavy 305mm howitzers to pound them into submission. Nicknamed 'Big Berthas', these formidable weapons were built at the Skoda works in Bohemia and were borrowed from the Austrians. Even as German troops invaded Belgium, French troops were advancing into Alsace. The city of Mulhouse was taken on 8 August but the French were thrown out by German counter-attacks three days later. The commander of the French army, Joseph Joffre, ordered further attacks into Lorraine and the Ardennes forest just as the Germans were starting their own advance.

The battles in the Ardennes were an almost perfect test case of the battlefield qualities of the French and German armies. Numbers were similar, both sides were advancing, and quantities of artillery were nearly identical. The result was a crushing German victory. This was not because French troops in bright coloured uniforms flung themselves heedlessly at German barbed wire and machine guns; this was a manoeuvre battle with both sides attacking. The actual reasons for German victory were primarily the superior training of ordinary German troops, a product of more generous provision of resources in the pre-war period, and a superior doctrine of command, which encouraged lower levels of leadership to take the initiative rather than await orders. Prior to the war German commanders developed a style of flexible 'alternative path tactics' developed by war-gaming exercises, in which officers learned to think about problems at a higher level of command than the one they exercised. The result was the dissemination of 'doctrine': common understandings of how battlefield problems ought to be tackled, which meant German commanders could anticipate the wishes of their superiors and the actions of their colleagues on either flank.

The Germans also had a more suitable provision of artillery for these battles. Arms procurement policies had meant that for reasons of economy the German army had not yet modernized its 77mm field guns but had instead concentrated on providing a large number of modern medium (105mm) and heavy (155mm) howitzers (*Mörser* in German). Their high-angle fire was designed to destroy enemy frontier fortifications, but it also provided an advantage in hilly terrain where indirect fire would be decisive. By contrast the French 75mm gun was a low-trajectory weapon which was supreme in open country. In the first clashes in the hilly Ardennes the German guns had a clear advantage. The brutal outcome was that by the end of August over 100,000 French soldiers were dead, perhaps five times as many as their German opponents. These opening battles took a terrible toll of the young French writers who had embraced the idea of action and faith. Ernest Psichari, whose anti-pacifist autobiographical novel *L'appel des armes* (1913) had caught the romantic nationalist mood of his generation, was killed at Rossignol; and Charles Péguy, who had sought to reconcile the revolutionary tradition with the spirit of Joan of Arc, was killed on the Marne.

Whilst the French advanced to defeat on the right, the British Expeditionary Force (BEF) found itself on the far left of the line in the path of the most powerful of the German armies. The British army was experienced in colonial warfare and had several real virtues: its troops had excellent rifle marksmanship skills and were uniformed in khaki, which helped camouflage them in action, its cavalry was trained to fight mounted and dismounted, and the artillery had excellent field guns. But it also had real flaws. Many of the soldiers were middle-aged reservists who proved to have limited fitness. The ordinary soldiers tended to be drawn from the poor and ill-educated; many of the officers were those who had shown little talent for other professions. One of the more talented generals, John Grierson, dropped dead of a heart attack before combat even started and was replaced as commander of 2nd Corps by Horace Smith-Dorrien, who had a bad relationship with the BEF commander Sir John French.

On 23–24 August the BEF fought the Germans at Mons, and on 26 August, 2nd Corps fought again alone at Le Cateau, 1st Corps under Sir Douglas Haig having failed to come up in support. The neighbouring French 5th Army under General Lanzerac had fought an uncoordinated battle at Charleroi to the British left on 23 August and had been badly beaten. The BEF narrowly avoided being routed but suffered heavy casualties, the worst that the British had suffered in battle since Waterloo a hundred years earlier. News of the battle stimulated mass recruiting as the press reported that the army was in desperate need of replacements.

There was a real fear at the end of August that France faced imminent defeat and Britain possible invasion and that the consequences of such an event for the civilian population would be horrific.

It was during this period that the worst German atrocities during the invasion of Belgium occurred. On 23 August the German III Army murdered 674 civilians in the industrial town of Dinant. The majority of these victims were young men shot in 'reprisals'. Between 25 and 28 August German soldiers went on a rampage through the university town of Louvain, destroying hundreds of buildings including the medieval University Library with its 300,000 volumes. The events at Louvain helped the British and French governments present the war as a defence of civilization itself. Academics rallied to the cause. German academics responded with a manifesto justifying German actions. Dissent at this point was rare. In Berlin, Albert Einstein courted unpopularity by refusing to sign the German manifesto. In Cambridge the philosopher Bertrand Russell opposed the war, beginning a course that would eventually see him imprisoned for propaganda against recruiting. But Russell's friend and colleague Ludwig Wittgenstein returned to Austria to serve in the army. The competing manifestoes prompted the French writer Romain Rolland, resident in Switzerland, to publish an appeal to reason entitled *Au-Dessus de la Melée* (*Above the Struggle*), published in the *Journal de Genève* on 22 September. But generally the cosmopolitan intellectual pre-war world had collapsed.

Even as the German army triumphed on the French frontiers it received a sharp shock in the east. The Russians had mobilized faster than anticipated and had moved with more energy than expected. On 20 August the German VIII Army commanded by the cautious General Prittwitz met the Russian 1st Army under General Rennenkampf at Gumbinnen. The resulting battle was chaotic like most initial encounters, but on this occasion the German commanders proved unable to transmute chaos into victory. Prittwitz was relieved of his command by Moltke on 21 August and replaced by Paul von Hindenburg. To assist Hindenburg, Erich Ludendorff was sent from the west to serve as Chief of Staff to VIII Army. Neither man was a favourite of the Kaiser; he regarded Hindenburg as slow-witted and Ludendorff as jumped up. Hindenburg was not immensely distinguished but, rather like Joffre, he was notable for his immense calm. In the crisis situation of a Russian invasion this was an asset.

The new command team, encouraged by the able staff officer Max Hoffmann, switched forces from facing Rennenkampf to deal with the emerging threat of the Russian 2nd Army which was advancing into East Prussia from Poland under the command of General Samsonov. Hoffmann would later claim he knew that a personal feud between Rennenkampf and Samsonov, dating back to the Russo-Japanese War, would prevent the former from coming to the assistance of the latter. This was a myth: in fact it was the former's instinctive caution and the latter's impetuousness that caused their armies to be uncoordinated.

The battle that followed was superficially a textbook triumph. Fighting on ground that was familiar to them from pre-war manoeuvres, German forces broke through on both flanks of Samsonov's army. The Russians found themselves surrounded in a classic double envelopment. Very few Russians escaped the trap and Samsonov committed suicide. Whilst the battle was being fought it was a much messier picture. At one point the highly strung Ludendorff broke down and it took Hindenburg's steadiness to calm him. The commander of 1st Corps, Hermann von François, clashed with Hoffmann who thought him initially overcautious and then on 27 August launched the daring move in defiance of orders that created the encirclement. Victory at Tannenberg in East Prussia was followed with a sharp strike at Rennenkampf's forces beginning on 7 September. Although the German General Mackensen was initially held in his frontal attack, François once again slipped around the Russian flank and only a precipitate retreat by Rennenkampf's army prevented a second encirclement.

Tannenberg was attractive to German commanders and public alike as a classic battle in the tradition of Frederick the Great. The invasion of German soil had been repelled and 90,000 Russian prisoners were taken. The Russian 2nd Army had been destroyed as an effective force. Various German commanders scrambled to take credit, and in the end Hindenburg was cast in the role of saviour, to the eternal annoyance of Max Hoffmann who claimed that the old man had slept through the battle. François, who had taken the crucial initiative, was initially promoted to command VIII Army but in November 1914 was relieved for his usual habit of disregarding orders. Even the German system of directive command couldn't tolerate constant insubordination.

The Tannenberg legend was also helping to divert attention from the fact that by mid-September the war was not going so well for Germany and Austria in the east. The Hapsburg Empire was in fact facing catastrophe. The invasion of Galicia saw the Austrian I Army win an initial victory on 24 August, but III Army was heavily defeated on 30 August and on 2 September its main opponent, the Russian 8th Army commanded by Alexei Brusilov, occupied the Polish city of Lemberg (Lvóv), which had been abandoned without a fight. Conrad von Hötzendorf now attempted his own ambitious encirclement battle, but instead I and IV Hapsburg Armies joined III Army in defeat. In total 350,000 men were lost. On 10 September Conrad was forced to appeal to the Germans for help. The Austrians were able to stabilize the line by late September, digging in around the city of Przemyśl, which the Russians began to besiege on 21 September.

In the west the French army fell back from the eastern frontier as Joffre realized the growing threat of the German advance through Belgium. The French government abandoned Paris for Bordeaux and many of the middle and upper classes, remembering the siege of 1870, left with it. The capital became a military zone under the control of the veteran colonial administrator General Gallieni. Joffre remained calm and transferred forces by railway from his right to his left flank. On 29 August the French 5th Army won a victory of sorts at Guise, buying some time, although not for its pessimistic commander General Lanzerac who was replaced by the fiery Louis Franchet d'Espèrey. In a move that would become legendary, the French 6th Army was transferred to the west of the capital by a fleet of taxis.

At the height of German military success in the west, Chancellor Bethmann-Hollweg commissioned a programme of war aims. Drafted by his assistant Kurt Riezler in consultation with several prominent political and business leaders, the 'September programme' called for the seizure of mineral-rich border districts from France along with a 10-billion Reichsmark fine on the French government, the annexation of Luxembourg and parts of Belgium, the establishment of a German protectorate over the rest of Belgium, the seizure of the Belgian Congo and parts of British and Portuguese colonies to create a giant German Central Africa, and the creation of 'Mitteleuropa', a German-dominated political and economic union in east-central Europe. Breathtaking as these plans were, they were actually the work of the 'moderates' and some of the German nationalists had even more ambitious ideas.

This programme, which was published on 9 September, has been taken as evidence that Germany began the war in order to create a massive new empire. This is far from clear and the programme is best understood as the opening move in a peace negotiation underpinned by a conclusive German military victory. Having apparently won the war, the programme intended to consolidate that victory into a permanent dominance. As it turned out the victory proved elusive in 1914, but the underlying ideas of the programme would remain privately the war aims of the German elite for most of the war.

Whilst German war aims were being formulated, victory slipped away on the river Marne to the north-east of Paris. In the centre of the line the French 9th Army under the pugnacious General Ferdinand Foch was badly beaten, but Foch, who liked to claim that the morale was ten times the strength of the material, simply refused to accept this. Somehow his men held and counter-attacked. This added to the worries of the German commander of II Army, who had Foch to his left, Franchet d'Espèrey in front of him, and who had lost touch with I Army to his right. Joffre, by appealing to the honour of the British army, was able to get Sir John French to end his retreat and move forward. The BEF cautiously advanced into the gap between the German I and II Armies. The battle of the Marne ended with Moltke ordering the German army to fall back to more defensible positions.

The advance to the Marne had stretched the German supply lines to breaking point; units had marched far beyond the railheads, and horse-drawn wagons consumed large quantities of hay, which limited their range. Germany had relatively few motorized vehicles. Combined with the massive expenditure of ammunition and the tiredness of troops who had marched at an extraordinary pace, this left the Germans in a poor position to fight a prolonged battle in early September. Overall the first months fighting in the west had favoured Germany and they had inflicted heavy losses on their opponents. Furthermore the German army was able to dig in and control many of the industrially developed areas of northern France and Belgium. In the event of a prolonged struggle these would be assets denied to the French and added to the German capacity to withstand a British blockade. Nevertheless the battle of the Marne was perceived as a French victory that had saved Paris, and Moltke took the blame. On 14 September he was replaced by Erich Falkenhayn, the Minister of War. Hard-working, ambitious, secretive, and intelligent, he was a favourite of the Kaiser.

The fighting in August and September was some of the bloodiest that had ever occurred. The initial campaigns were also exceptionally mobile; it was not unusual for soldiers to have marched 300 or 400 kilometres in their first month of operations, some of them much more. The tactical potential of defensive firepower did not lead directly to trench warfare. It was only in mid-September when the Germans made a deliberate strategic decision to dig in on parts of the front in France that the tactical problem posed by trenches really became apparent. The Germans had first done this to free up reserves for mobile offensive operations in Belgium and elsewhere, it was not yet a strategy in itself. But as the autumn wore on, all sides began to halt and dig. In part this was an inevitable reaction to the sheer pace and intensity of earlier operations. Men were exhausted and so was ammunition. Everyone had underestimated the duration of battles, and the speed of ammunition expenditure: ammunition stocks that had been planned to last for months were fired in days.

Before the lines solidified both sides in the west began what would be misnamed the race to the sea, but what was really an attempt to exploit an open flank. In fact, the Germans were initially making an effort on both flanks. In mid-September their forces made a significant advance around St-Mihiel south of the fortress city of Verdun and also pushed forward in the Argonne forest to the west of the city. But the main effort would be made towards the coast. The Belgian army and government had fallen back on the port of Antwerp and this represented a potential threat to the German flank. Falkenhayn moved quickly to eliminate it and then turn the Anglo-French line.

A hastily formed British force, consisting of surplus naval personnel, was sent to Antwerp by Winston Churchill. But by the start of October it was too little and too late. On 8 October the Germans began shelling the city itself, and to avoid massive civilian casualties the city was surrendered. Much of the Belgian garrison and most of the British troops ended up crossing into Holland where they were interned for the duration of the war.

The failure at Antwerp cast doubt on the reputation of Churchill. In his main role as First Lord of the Admiralty he had done well. He had mobilized the fleet before the British declaration of war. At its core were the new *Dreadnought*-type battleships. These ships, with a uniform armament of heavy guns, had rendered previous classes of heavy warship effectively obsolete. The first, *Dreadnought*, had been built in reaction to the German naval challenge and Germany had responded by building copies of it. This German naval challenge to Britain was central to the growth of Anglo–German antagonism before the war. The British had argued that their naval superiority was the vital guarantee of national defence against invasion or blockade whereas German naval building was constructing a 'luxury fleet'. Against this German naval enthusiasts, including the Kaiser himself, had argued with some justification that British naval superiority meant that Britain could at will isolate Germany from the world beyond Europe, stifling German trade and preventing German overseas imperial activity. Without a fleet sufficient to deter this, Germany would be at the mercy of the British. That was indeed the situation at the start of the war, although by a narrower margin than the British would have liked. Nevertheless from the very start of the conflict the British set out to dominate the North Sea and British light forces won several early clashes. In return German submarines and mines sank a number of British warships, a sign of things to come.

Traditionally cruiser warfare against commerce was the most effective tactic for the weaker naval power. The German Pacific fleet, based on the China coast, was the main force available for such raiding The German cruiser *Emden* broke away from the Pacific Fleet and entered the Indian Ocean to raid in this way, but most of the fleet, under Admiral Graf von Spee, chose instead to stay together as a unit. On 14 October a weak British squadron met the Germans at Coromandel off the coast of Chile and was badly defeated. When the news reached the Admiralty, Churchill despatched two fast battlecruisers to the South Atlantic. Off the

Falkland Islands on 8 December they met the German fleet and sank it along with its admiral. Only the cruiser *Dresden* escaped and remained at large until being sunk in March 1915.

The *Emden* had caused havoc for a month in the Indian Ocean, sinking a Russian cruiser at Penang in Malaya and bombarding Madras in India, capturing twenty-three vessels and disrupting trade, but in November she was tracked down and sunk by the Australian cruiser *Sydney*. The *Emden*'s Captain Müller survived and was honoured for his daring by friend and foe alike. At the other end of the Indian Ocean the cruiser *Königsberg* added to the chaos with a sudden raid on Zanzibar in September, before returning to hide in the Rufiji river delta of East Africa. Lacking coal, *Königsberg* was unable to cruise again, but it did manage to tie up significant British forces until sunk in July 1915. Her crew and guns reinforced the local German garrison.

The German Pacific fleet had been compelled to escape from the Far East by Japanese entry into the war in August. Japan had a treaty with the United Kingdom specifying that each would come to the other's aid if either found itself at war with two powers. When first signed this treaty had been directed at Russia and France, but Britain being at war with both Germany and Austro-Hungary meant that Japan declared war, even though Britain did not particularly feel the need for its support. The Japanese leadership could see the opportunity for seizing Germany's Asian colonies. Tsingtao, the German colony in China, was besieged at the end of August by the Japanese supported by a token British force. Despite being outnumbered six to one the German garrison held out until November. Japan also moved against German colonies in the Pacific.

In part due to the imperial ambitions of their own government and in part through fear of Japanese expansion, New Zealand and Australia also seized German Pacific colonies, most notably Western New Guinea.

A side effect of early naval operations was the entry into the war of the Ottoman Empire. Traditionally Turkey had looked to Britain as its guarantor against Russian ambitions, but as Britain increasingly settled its imperial differences with Russia, the new regime of the Young Turks began to look to Germany instead. In turn German support and investment, including the strategic railway from Berlin to Baghdad, increased

British suspicions of Turkey's intentions. The appointment of the German General Liman von Sanders to help retrain and rebuild the Turkish army after defeat in the First Balkan War added to these suspicions. But in reality at this point Turkish policy was far from settled.

Matters came to a head shortly after the outbreak of the war. The British requisitioned two dreadnoughts they were building for Turkey in order to guarantee superiority in the North Sea. At the same time the German battlecruiser *Goeben* managed to evade British and French forces in the Mediterranean and arrived in Constantinople, where, complete with a German crew, it was offered as a gift to replace the lost battleships. Its presence transformed the situation in the Black Sea; it was more powerful than the entire Russian Black Sea fleet.

During September there was a drift towards war. British attempts to negotiate neutrality foundered on an insistence that the *Goeben* be given up whilst at the same time Germany began to make offers both of support and reward if Turkey entered the war. On 20 October Enver Pasha, the leading figure in the government, gave the German commanders of the *Goeben* orders to begin hostilities against Russia in the Black Sea and on 29 October the Turkish fleet attacked Russian Black Sea ports. On 2 November Russia declared war against Turkey and on 3 November, before Britain had declared war against it, British naval units began firing at the outer forts of the Dardanelles which protected the sea approaches to the Ottoman capital.

On 14 November, with German encouragement, the Sheikh al-Islam in the presence of the Ottoman Sultan called for a holy war, a *jihad* against the British, French, and Russian Empires on the authority of the Sultan's claim to be the true Caliph (spiritual and political leader) of all Muslims. The Turkish government, which prior to the war had been embracing ethnic nationalism, had apparently found religion. The call for *jihad* found little immediate response. A partial exception occurred in Singapore. In February 1915 the 5th Native Light Infantry, an Indian Army regiment comprised of Muslim soldiers, mutinied at the instigation of pro-Ottoman civilian agitators. The mutineers tried to release prisoners from the *Emden* and thirty-two Europeans were killed. In the aftermath the British executed forty-seven of the mutineers. But generally British India proved remarkably loyal, and the Muslims who made up about 30 per cent of the population and more than 40 per cent of the army were no different from the Sikhs and Hindus in this respect. Two divisions of Indian troops were sent to France where they were in action by October; others were sent to Egypt and to seize the port of Basra in Mesopotamia. Less successful was an expedition to Tanga in German East Africa, which was defeated with heavy casualties in November.

Both British and German colonial administrators were nervous about the potential impact of a war in Africa. Nevertheless on 12 August 1914 Sergeant Major Grunshi of the West African frontier force fired the first shot for the British Empire in the war. The British invasion of the German colony of Togo was a local initiative, although London was happy to see the elimination of the Kamina wireless station supporting the German navy. The German governor of the colony surrendered almost immediately. The German West African colony of Cameroon was invaded by British and French forces. The British effort mounted from Nigeria went badly, and the German African troops, the Askari, defeated their Nigerian opponents in August. The French were more successful, but at the end of 1914 the Germans still controlled most of the colony. It was not until June 1915, when a British force captured the key town of Garua, that the German position deteriorated. The campaign in northern Cameroon dragged on into December 1916 when the German defenders, out of ammunition, crossed over into Spanish territory.

The campaign in the German colony of Namibia in South West Africa was closely tied to events in South Africa. In the aftermath of the Boer War the British had managed to reconcile the majority of their Afrikaaner former opponents, but a small minority were looking for an opportunity to rebel. The British appeal for South African assistance in the capture of Namibia gained a positive response from the Prime Minister of South Africa, Louis Botha, who had formerly led the army fighting the British. Botha hoped the prospect of territorial expansion would attract the dissidents; instead it triggered revolt. A small force under the command of 'Mannie' Maritz rebelled in October and he invited other Afrikaaner leaders to join him. But most Afrikaaners sided with the British and some 20,000 served under the command of another former enemy of the British, Jan Smuts, in repressing the revolt of less than 10,000 rebels. Maritz retreated into Namibia. Smuts went on to quickly conquer Namibia, which was lightly defended. At the start of July 1915 the Germans in Namibia surrendered to the South Africans.

The exception to beleaguered defence amongst the German colonies was German East Africa (modern Tanzania). Whereas in other German colonies the priority had been to keep society as intact as possible so that a victorious Germany could resume effective rule after the war, the German military commander in East Africa, Paul von Lettow-Vorbeck, subordinated local interest to the hope of diverting British resources away from Europe. At the very start of the war he invaded British East Africa (modern Uganda).

This prompted the Anglo-Indian expedition to Tanga which was repelled. For the next year the British refused to be drawn into sending strong forces to East Africa and instead concentrated on securing the other German colonies.

Falkenhayn was not too interested in the long game; he was trying instead to secure a fast victory in the west. The German advance through Flanders in October after the fall of Antwerp seemed to offer an opportunity to turn the allied flank and by the middle of the month had almost conquered the last corner of Belgium. The Belgian government authorized the desperate measure of opening the sluice gates and flooding the coastal areas. The Belgians, reinforced by French marines, stopped the Germans along the Yser river. To their immediate right the British and French armies, under the command of Foch, held a salient around the Belgian city of Ypres. This became the focal point of some desperate fighting. Scratch German forces were thrown into the fight in the hope of making a breakthrough before the winter set in. The 'battle of Langemarck' quickly became a nationalist myth of heroic student volunteers attacking regardless of casualties, arm in arm and singing 'Deutchsland über alles'. Most of this was nonsense; nevertheless one volunteer soldier, Adolf Hitler, would later make great propaganda capital out of his baptism of fire in this battle. One of the casualties of the October fighting was the son of the avant-garde artist and socialist Käthe Kollwitz. She would later create a moving memorial to him in the war cemetery at Langemarck, depicting his two mourning parents.

On 11 November the Prussian Guards almost broke through the British lines at Nonnebosschen and were stopped by the last reserve battalion, the Oxfordshire and Buckinghamshire Light Infantry. The Prussian 1st Regiment of Foot Guards had ten officers and 310 men killed in action that day. By this point the British defenders were so exhausted that one officer wrote that men had reached the point where they did not mind the idea of being killed, wounded, or captured as long as they could sleep. Other soldiers 'had a half mad look in their eyes'. The defence of the Ypres salient took on a particular significance as the epic last stand of the old British regular army. An unfortunate side effect was a developing obsession with this sector, particularly by the commander of the British defence, Sir Douglas Haig, which was out of proportion to its real strategic importance and would have baleful results later.

The battle petered out over the next few weeks as the weather deteriorated. One German volunteer wrote on 18 November, 'Well-being is here nothing else than not having to launch an attack across meadows that are completely flooded and poisoned by the odour of putrefaction, but rather to be able to sit peacefully and quietly in a trench with straw that is not completely soaked yet. Or sheer heaven, one or two days of rest.' The need to bail out flooded trenches, evacuate the wounded, and bury the dead combined with shortages of ammunition and sheer tiredness to encourage unofficial local truces. These developed into outright fraternization at Christmas 1914. The Christmas truce, primarily between British and German forces, was particularly striking, as the media of the two nations were busily demonizing each other. In October, Ernst Lissauer had composed the 'Hymn of Hate' with the line 'We have one foe and one alone, ENGLAND', which circulated widely in Germany and was then reprinted in many parts of Britain as an example of German 'kultur'. For the German propagandists the idea of *kultur* represented honesty, as opposed to the hypocrisy of the English and the French with their talk of civilization that was simply a mask for imperial power. For the British, 'kultur' represented a brutal lawlessness which seized any opportunity regardless of morality.

Lissauer had written of England cut off by 'waves thicker than blood' and the German navy was determined to bring the war to the British at home. The Germans had used their battlecruisers in December 1914 to bombard the towns of Scarborough and Hartlepool. The killing of British civilians in their homes enraged public opinion, and Winston

Churchill labelled the German navy 'babykillers'. Revenge came at the battle of Dogger Bank. The Admiralty codebreakers at room 40, commanded by Admiral 'Blinker' Hall, decoded a German plan to attack British fishing boats. British battlecruisers under Admiral Beatty intercepted the outnumbered Germans. In a brief action on 24 January 1915 the German battlecruiser *Blücher* was sunk and both the British and German flagships narrowly escaped destruction. Tactically the Germans had performed well, but it was still a British strategic victory. The British chose this moment to tighten the blockade.

With their surface fleet largely neutralized the Germans turned to the use of submarines. In some respects submarines were poor commerce raiders, as they were almost immobile when submerged and they lacked range. Crucially they were ill-suited for cruiser warfare, carrying few guns and having no space to accommodate prisoners. The German Admiralty argued that their principal advantages were surprise and terror, and that these would be best served by removing all restrictions on their use. Enemy merchant vessels should be torpedoed on sight without warning and even neutral vessels should be attacked within designated blockade zones. The possibility of sudden death would terrify enemy merchant crews and would drive up insurance costs, even though the number of U-boats was still small.

The British blockade of Germany did not have the quick impact originally anticipated. The large German merchant fleet was largely either captured or forced to hide in neutral ports and the cost of getting neutral shipping to run the blockade proved prohibitive. But the British were just as interested in preventing German exports as imports; the intention was for the British to capture German markets and deny income to Germany, whilst generating income for Britain which could be used to fund the war effort, including loans to the Allies. To some extent this worked, but the effects had been overestimated. Germany was able to borrow in order to fund the war and the needs of war industry created work for those who had lost jobs in the export trade.

The prevention of imports was also initially limited. Britain had declared a long list of 'contraband', items that could be used by the German military. This included food and animal fodder. The British blockade also used the concept of 'continuous voyage', which had been invented by the US government during the Civil War: this stated that if it could be demonstrated that a cargo bound for a neutral country was intended for re-export to a combatant, it could be seized. In practice in the first year of the war the British were quite cautious about using this concept and were forced to watch a suspicious boom in exports to Holland and Scandinavia. There was even a limited amount of British–German trade through the neutrals because both nations had a few industries which were crucially dependent on each other.

The British blockade nevertheless quickly exposed some crucial choke points in the German economy. The manufacture of high explosive required the import of nitrates, and natural nitrates were almost entirely imported from South America. In fact the German war effort would have collapsed completely by the end of 1914 had it not been for the invention shortly before the war, by the brilliant industrial chemist Fritz Haber, of a new process for capturing nitrogen from the air.

The winter of 1914–15 saw further disasters unfold for the Hapsburg Empire. In November the Russians almost reached Kraków and re-encircled Przemyśl. The Austrians were therefore unable to assist a German offensive aimed at Warsaw in December, which was checked with 100,000 casualties. On 3 December the Serbs mounted a counter-attack which routed the Austro-Hungarian army; one captured diary noted that a pontoon bridge over the river Sava swayed as the retreating troops elbowed each other aside in agitation and disorder. The Serbs took 40,000 prisoners and liberated Belgrade. It was a bitter victory. The American journalist John Reed noted that the returning refugees stood with all their belongings in sacks on their shoulders staring at the ruins of their homes. In late December a typhus epidemic began. In the town of Valjevo, Reed described victims of post-disease gangrene with flesh rotting away and bones crumbling. It is estimated that 100,000 Serb civilians died during the winter. Although Serbia was somewhat isolated, some international medical aid did arrive, most famously the Scottish Women's Hospital Unit which had been formed by the doctor and suffrage campaigner Elsie Inglis. Typhus is a disease spread by ticks; it is possible that better delousing procedures prevented its spread to the western theatre, but it ravaged eastern and central Europe in early 1915.

Widespread perception of the Ottoman Empire as the sick man of Europe was apparently confirmed in the early months of the war. Encouraged by the Germans, the Turks mounted ambitious offensives towards the Suez Canal and into the lost territories of the Caucasus. The former were repulsed by British imperial forces with contemptuous ease in early 1915. This was just embarrassing, but the campaign in the Caucasus was catastrophic. The Turkish army was short of overcoats and boots, literally fatal during winter in the high mountains. Advancing towards Sarakamish in December as much as 40 per cent of the Turkish 17th Division went missing as stragglers. At the end of the month the Russian General Yudenich counter-attacked. The Turkish III Army was broken by weather that fell to 36°C below freezing; the Russians found 30,000 frozen bodies around the town. Some 27,000 Turks were taken prisoner and 12,000 more deserted. It was a decisive battle. Turkish attempts to spread the war into central Asia were checked and the Russians were freed from having to commit massive forces to the south when they came under renewed pressure in the west in the spring of 1915.

But the Turkish offensives had already set off a chain of reactions in London. It seemed sensible to close down the Turkish threat before it became a major diversion of resources. The existence of a large number of 'pre-dreadnought' battleships in both the British and French navies, which would be hopelessly outdated for combat in the North Sea but which could feasibly intimidate Constantinople into surrender, provided the initial impetus. To approach the Ottoman capital they would need to force a way through the Dardanelles straits separating Europe from Asia. These narrows were blocked by a minefield covered by coastal artillery in forts on both sides. In a naval attack in March, the Turkish artillery prevented the minesweeping vessels from clearing the passage and when the battleships tried to push through regardless, several were sunk by mines. It was then resolved that a modest land force would be committed to capture the forts, clearing the way for the ships. British, Australian, New Zealand, and Indian troops, many of whom were already in Egypt defending the Suez Canal, would be joined by a small French contingent and by the Royal Naval Division, reconstituted after its disaster at Antwerp.

Churchill's later justifications for the Dardanelles campaign would be ever more extravagant, with visions of a grand Balkan alliance against

Germany and the freeing of the Russian war economy by access to the Mediterranean. This was nonsense. The real thinking was to use a modest investment of force to achieve an important strategic result in quickly knocking the Turks out of the war, which was a useful end in itself. In fact it is possible that Churchill initially pushed a modest campaign in the hope of ultimately saving more powerful naval forces that could be used for his real pet project of a landing on the Baltic coast of Germany.

The main attack mounted on 25 April 1915 was against Cape Helles on the tip of the Gallipoli peninsula on the European side of the Dardanelles. Lacking experience and equipment for an amphibious landing the British attackers suffered heavy casualties inflicted by a small Turkish defensive force. In the end a small beachhead was achieved by the courage of assaulting troops, the Lancashire Fusiliers famously winning six Victoria Crosses 'before breakfast'. At the same time a small French force landed on the Asian side of the straits and the Australian and New Zealand Army Corps (ANZAC) made a supporting landing further up on the west side of the European coast.

The landing at what became known as Anzac Cove achieved initial tactical surprise, in part because the troops landed in the wrong place, but the inexperienced Australian officers had trouble consolidating the bridgehead. A Turkish colonel, Mustafa Kemal, allegedly told his 57th Regiment that he did not order them to fight but to die and buy time by their deaths for reinforcements to arrive. Whatever the truth, the regiment did hold the Australians and in the process Kemal's exploits became legendary.

The English poet Rupert Brooke never made it to Gallipoli, dying of blood poisoning from an infected mosquito bite on a French hospital ship on 23 April. Throughout the war and afterwards his collected poems would be immensely popular, going through dozens of reprintings, and the lines 'If I should die, think only this of me:/That there's some corner of a foreign field/That is forever England' came to epitomize patriotic idealism. Brooke was a more complex character than the legend suggests, but the inscription on his grave on Skyros that he was an English soldier who died in the quest to free Constantinople from the Turk would become part of the romantic legend of the campaign.

The unromantic reality was a tough battle which quickly turned into a grinding fight for position with heavy casualties on both sides. Although the campaign would be most remembered for Anzac Cove, most of the fighting and most of the casualties occurred in the fighting between the British and the Turks at Cape Helles. A series of attacks on the village of Krithia were beaten back by determined Turkish counter-attacks which were as heroic as but less remembered than the sacrifice of the 57th Regiment.

Retrospectively the Gallipoli campaign was presented as a vital attempt to relieve the pressure on Russia. By the summer of 1915 that pressure was genuinely severe, but at the start of the campaign Russia was in fact winning the war against Austria in the Carpathians. On 23 March the city of Przemyśl surrendered along with its starving garrison of 150,000. The American journalist Stanley Washburn interviewed a Russian officer who claimed that when he had entered the city he saw bloody-faced Hungarian soldiers tearing at the raw carcasses of cavalry horses 'like famished wolves'. The victorious Russians immediately began to persecute the Jewish population of the city, joking that they would let them celebrate Passover before sending them all to Siberia. On 17 April a full-scale pogrom began: the Jewish population were assaulted, robbed, and many driven out of the city. Violence was not systematic but nevertheless commonplace and would intensify in the spring when the Austro-German armies counter-attacked. Russian brutality was driven both by the deep-seated anti-Semitism of army and society but also the widespread suspicion that the Jews were siding with Russia's enemies. A similar dynamic would lead to an even more terrible catastrophe inflicted by the Turks upon the Armenians.

Tensions between Turks and Armenians had been escalating since the 1880s, when the traditional view of the Armenians as a loyal minority began to fade. A massive Turkish massacre of Armenians had led to the creation of Armenian terrorist groups, and the Turkish government had well-founded fears that the Russians were sponsoring the Armenian independence movement. The outbreak of war with Russia turned suspicion into murderous paranoia. On 19 April 1915 an armed uprising began in the Armenian city of Van, triggered by the plausible suspicion that the governor's demand that the adult male population report for military duty was to be the excuse to massacre them. The presence of Armenian volunteers, who were after all Ottoman subjects, serving alongside the Russian forces in the area had led to widespread suspicion by the Turks of the loyalty of the Armenians. There had already been massacres with victims on both sides involving Kurds and ethnic Turks, some of the latter being resettled refugees from the Balkan Wars. The uprising and the approach of the Anglo-French invasion force towards the Dardanelles in turn provided the rationale for 'Red Sunday', 24 April 1915, the rounding up and deportation of the leadership of the Armenian people in Constantinople. Few of these men would survive the year. Through May and June this escalated into mass deportations, death marches, and massacres of Armenians regardless of age and sex throughout the Ottoman territories. Some of the Young Turk leadership would openly admit their intention to destroy the Armenian people once and for all, a crime that would later come to be known by the name 'genocide'. At least 600,000 and probably more than 1 million people would eventually perish by burning, drowning, shooting, and above all starvation and exhaustion. Some, mostly younger women, survived by conversion to Islam. At Van the Russian army ultimately raised the siege and rescued the survivors before both the Russians and Armenians were forced to retreat by a Turkish recovery in June. The massacres were not limited to the Armenians; by mid-summer there was also widespread killing of 'Assyrian' Christians who were equally regarded with suspicion by the Turks and their Kurdish allies. Perhaps another 250,000 died in this less remembered atrocity.

These events in Anatolia and beyond were overshadowed by a lesser atrocity with serious international implications. The sinking of the British cruise liner *Lusitania* on 7 May 1915 by a German U-boat was horrific in itself. The deaths of 1,198 people, including some hundred children and, crucially, 128 American citizens, shocked opinion outside Germany. It triggered days of rioting against German civilians resident in several British cities. President Woodrow Wilson initially tried to calm American opinion by stating that there was such a thing as a man 'too proud to fight', being conscious that whatever the initial emotional reaction, American opinion was still divided on the war. Wilson's Secretary of State, William Jennings Bryan, preferred restricting American dealings with the alliance of the Triple Entente, which he saw as the underlying problem, to taking firm action against Germany.

British propagandists stirred the pot; in Germany a private firm had struck a medal celebrating the sinking, and the British made thousands of copies which they circulated in the United States, implying that it was an official government production. The British also used the moment to release the findings of the distinguished jurist Lord Bryce on the behaviour of the German army in Belgium. Although this did not involve any deliberate invention, it did reproduce without sceptical scrutiny some extremely lurid 'eyewitness accounts' of German sadism which were at the very least exaggerated. Despite these efforts, still largely conducted by volunteers with government support, rather than directly by the government itself, British propaganda had little real impact on American opinion, which was more conditioned by pre-existing sympathies at this stage.

Everywhere the war was beginning to break pre-war ideas of civilized behaviour. On the Western Front the Germans had used poison gas in a tactical offensive aimed at capturing the city of Ypres on 22 April 1915. This was in clear violation of pre-war treaties, although the Germans would claim that certain forms of artillery shell used by the French had already violated the conventions. The instigator of this chemical warfare was Fritz Haber, who argued that chlorine gas was more humane than high explosive and high-velocity bullets. This was disingenuous because chlorine had not replaced these weapons but simply added a new and insidious horror to the battlefield. The French North African troops who were the first exposed broke and ran, perfectly understandably. The inexperienced Canadian forces who were rushed into the breach suffered horrendously from the gas and from intense shelling by concentrated German artillery. But the gas cloud proved to be an unreliable weapon and it held up the German advance as much as it assisted it. The British commander, Horace Smith-Dorrien, fell back to a more defensible line closer to the city and was sacked for his decision. But the front stabilized in May.

Both sides in the west fought other battles in the spring of 1915 believing that the resumption of mobile warfare would not be long delayed. Once again the Germans had the best of it. The French 10th

Army attacked the German positions on Vimy Ridge on 9 May. The 33rd Corps under General Pétain managed to advance through the first German lines, but was then driven back by German counter-attacks. Even so Pétain's painstaking offensive, well supported by artillery, was noticed and his rise through the ranks continued. The other French attacks were quickly stopped as was the British supporting attack at Aubers Ridge. A further French attack in June made no gains and resulted in heavy casualties. Prolonged fighting in the St-Mihiel salient further to the east went equally badly. In May and June the French suffered 140,000 casualties.

Falkenhayn was convinced that the war would ultimately have to be won in the west, but first he needed to rescue his beleagured Hapsburg allies. He also hoped that if the Russians could be hit hard they could be tempted into a compromise peace that would free his hands in the west. At the start of May the Germans launched their offensive to relieve the pressure on the Hapsburgs. To the annoyance of Hindenburg and Ludendorff, the attack was mounted south of Warsaw under the command of Mackensen. Between Gorlice and Tarnów 1,500 artillery pieces were concentrated on a 45-kilometre front. On 2 May 1915 a four-hour bombardment crushed the Russian front line. Von François, commanding a reserve corps, described how 'trees break like matches, huge trunks are hurled through the air, the stone walls of houses cave in'. Advancing at more than 15 kilometres a day during early May, the Germans took 150,000 prisoners in a week. On 3 June Bavarian troops recaptured Przemyśl from the Russians, and General Mackensen rather maliciously 'laid the town at the Austrian emperor's feet'. By this point the Russian army had already lost 412,000 men. On 22 June the Germans allowed the Austrians to recapture Lemberg. Gorlice-Tarnów, as it became known, was the greatest victory of the war and was genuinely decisive. Without it the Hapsburg Empire could not possibly have withstood the new blow that was delivered from the south.

The Italian decision to enter the war was genuinely cynical. Under the pretext that Austrian activity in the Balkans had negated the Triple Alliance, Italy finally abandoned its pre-war allies in February 1915. Through the spring Italy had negotiated with both the Triple Entente and the Central powers. Under German pressure a resentful Vienna offered the Trentino and a border at the Isonzo, but the Italian Prime Minister Salandra and Foreign Minister Sonnino were convinced that a better deal could be had from the Entente. Russia initially resisted Italian claims on Dalmatia, which had been reserved for Serbia. Meanwhile by March, Austria was offering more than Italy had wanted in January, but by this point the Italian government's greed had increased. Giovanni Giolitti, the Italian Liberal leader, became a rallying point for anti-war sentiment in Parliament, but Salandra called his bluff on 13 May by getting the whole cabinet to offer their resignation. This brought noisy pro-intervention mobs onto the streets and pushed King Victor Emmanuel III into backing his Prime Minister and the Treaty of London, which promised Italy the Austrian province of Tyrol and much of the coastline of the Hapsburg Empire.

The Austrian border defences were feeble, less than 20,000 men holding a front of 400 kilometres. An Austrian officer wrote on 23 May that the Italians could be inside Austria proper in a day if they advanced. But the Italian army, 400,000 strong on that date, did not advance significantly for three weeks. There was no proper plan for a war against Austria. By mid-June the Austro-Hungarians had rushed 200,000 men to the front, blown up bridges in front of the Italians, and begun constructing proper defences.

The last veteran of the first battle of the Isonzo, Carlo Orelli, was interviewed in 2004 by Mark Thompson. He had been called up on 25 May 1915. A socialist who had become pro-interventionist, he claimed that the troops had not been 'enthusiastic' but had been determined to 'recapture' the Trentino and Trieste, 'our own lands'. The desperately unprepared Italians were simply shot down by their dug-in enemies. Of the 330 men who had gone into the line with him at the start of July, only twenty-five would be unwounded by September. They were mostly illiterate peasants from Calabria: 'They could not read or write, but they never complained, they died in silence.' Orelli was wounded in September and never returned to the front.[1]

[1] Mark Thompson, *The White War* (London, 2008), pp. 92–3.

Peasants and workers, clerks and students, in Flanders and Poland, in the Carpathian mountains and the Caucasus, in the forests of East Prussia and the Argonne, at the Dardanelles and on the Danube, and the Isonzo: killed and wounded, missing and captured. Germany and Austria-Hungary had gambled on war. The former had come very close to winning the decisive victory over France and Russia it had sought, but with British support they had proved willing to fight on in the face of hard blows and were now starting fully to mobilize their resources. The British Empire was also mobilizing and the British grip on global trade had intensified. The Hapsburg Empire had been rocked by its defeats and was now increasingly dependent on German support. Germany needed to either make peace or find a quick route to victory.

CHAPTER 2
THE SECOND YEAR 1915–1916: ATTRITION

On 5 August 1915 German troops entered Warsaw and within a fortnight they had also captured the major city of Kovno (Kaunas) and massive stores of munitions. The Tsarist army and administration were everywhere in panicked retreat; they burnt crops and houses, and executed Lutherans and Jews as suspected spies. They ordered mass evacuations of the civilian population, who in any case had been deprived of the means to support themselves. In Vilna they even attempted to steal away the church bells, only to be prevented by indignant Lithuanian parishioners. Hundreds of thousands trekked east. General Gurko wrote that 'no horrors on the field of battle can be compared to this awful spectacle of the ceaseless exodus of a population knowing neither the object of movement nor the place they might find rest, food and housing'. Konstantin Pautovski, a medical orderly, wrote of men tearing basins of food from each other's hands and women trampling children underfoot in the scramble for sustenance. It was in the midst of this disaster that Tsar Nicholas II arrived on 5 September at the army headquarters at Mogilev to take personal command of his army. He wrote to the Tsarina that the headquarters had a delightful view. He did not dwell on the derivation of the place name from the Russian word *mogila*, meaning 'grave'. He had certainly had doubts about his prospects before taking on the task, musing that a sacrificial lamb might be needed to save Russia, but his wife had comforted him that it would be a 'glorious page in your reign and Russian history' and assured him that Grigori Rasputin's prayers on their behalf would be heard in heaven. Reassured, the Tsar announced that his sole aim was to drive the enemy from the borders.

The Tsar's stance would prove fateful for three empires and ultimately fatal to himself and his family. General Falkenhayn had hoped that Russia would be willing to contemplate a separate peace after a summer of defeat, but ironically the Tsar did not feel strong enough to respond to the tentative German peace feelers. To open serious negotiations would have exacerbated internal tensions and fuelled the anger of 'progressive' elements frustrated with a government that they saw as being at best incompetent and at worst treacherous. The issue of a separate peace in the east was divisive on the side of the Central Powers as well and Bethmann-Hollweg obstructed Falkenhayn's desire to make an open approach to the Russians. The Chancellor was playing a devious game of appeasing the Pan-German advocates of an eastern empire and encouraging the personal ambitions of Hindenburg and Ludendorff. Hindenburg's popularity had benefited from a burgeoning cult of personality created by the proliferation of memorabilia, which was both propagandistic and commercially opportunistic. A 12-metre wooden statue in Berlin was the most striking manifestation of this; the public was asked to subscribe to war charities in return for the privilege of striking an iron nail into the statue which would eventually be transformed into an iron colossus (it was never completely covered). Hindenburg and Ludendorff also made no secret of their contempt for the Hapsburg Empire and actively plotted to exclude Vienna's influence in the newly conquered regions.

Whilst others dreamed of empire, Falkenhayn was all too aware of the dangers of diminishing returns. Russian underdevelopment was a formidable defence. Supporting large armies moving east was rendered difficult at the best of times by low agricultural productivity, which limited the available surpluses, and by poorly developed road and rail networks, which made moving supplies difficult. The movements of refugees and the poor sanitary conditions had encouraged the spread of both waterborne diseases like typhoid and tick-based typhus, which had become epidemic. Disease losses for the German army were much higher in the east and even in defeat the Russian army was still capable of inflicting severe losses on the battlefield as well. The real centres of Russian power were unattainably distant and soon the campaigning season in the east would be closed down first by mud and then snow.

Better to leave the table whilst ahead and transfer forces to where they might do more good. Falkenhayn turned his attention first to Serbia where a relatively modest investment could provide decent dividends.

Serbia's disaster unfolded in part due to the broader failure of the Entente's eastern strategy. At the start of August General Hamilton had made a final bid for victory in the Dardanelles, with a new surprise landing on the peninsula at Suvla Bay on 6 August by 9th Corps, under the command of General Stopford. This was supported by other attacks from Helles and Anzac Cove. The assault failed, with Stopford blamed for his lethargy and dismissed. The Australian Light Horse suffered 372 casualties whilst mounting a futile diversionary attack at the Nek, an event which would give rise to a great deal of Australian legend. The New Zealanders suffered equally at Chunuk Bair where they were halted by forces led by Mustafa Kemal. The Gurkhas at one point managed to seize the high point of Sari Bair only to be struck by Royal Navy gunfire. At Suvla, the Sandringham company of the Norfolk Regiment, raised from the staff of George V's country home, disappeared completely. Decades later it was established that they had mostly been captured and summarily executed by the Turks. Both sides suffered heavily in this fighting. The losses of the 10th Division brought the war home to Ireland, both north and south, in that autumn, and the Turks named the battlefield at Suvla 'the field of bones' because it was so littered with unburied bodies.

It was all futile. There was by this time little real chance of dislodging the Turkish defences. An ambitious Australian journalist, Keith Murdoch, acted as a conduit for bitter criticisms of Hamilton's leadership that he was given by an official British journalist. Murdoch, after being arrested by the French on his way back to Britain, eventually managed to communicate his criticisms to the Australian Prime Minister and was credited with hastening Hamilton's dismissal. All of this made for a dramatic story, but the campaign was already winding down.

British failure at the Dardanelles and the Russian retreat made it apparent to many of the Bulgarian leadership that the time was ripe to take the opportunity for revenge against Serbia by siding with the Central powers. In 1913 Serbia had defeated Bulgaria in the Second Balkan War and Bulgaria's traditional protector, Russia, had sided with the Serbs. Macedonia, recently conquered from Turkey, was lost. Many 'Bulgar' refugees from Macedonia fled to the Bulgarian capital Sofia and educated opinion wanted the restoration of Bulgarian rule over the area. By mid-summer the government thought a deal might be possible with the Entente, indeed the American ambassador in Constantinople later claimed that the population of the city was expecting an imminent Bulgarian attack. But British failure at Gallipoli changed the calculation.

King Ferdinand of Bulgaria got a better deal from the Central powers; it would secure Macedonia and part of Serbia and included a secret promise of further gains from Romania and Greece if these were to join the war on the Entente side. He also gained financial support, heavy artillery, and some excellent German officers. By September a 'Macedonian Legion' was parading on the streets of Sofia, with some 60,000 'Macedonians' enlisted, joined by Albanians and even Armenians who had fled from Turkey. On 18 September the opposition, with the King's support, mounted a coup against the pro-Entente government and by 22 September mobilization was announced.

With Bulgaria committed to act, Falkenhayn transferred General Mackensen south to command the combined offensive. On 6 October German and Austrian artillery unleashed a massive bombardment on Belgrade. Troops crossed the Danube and a ferocious street battle broke out in which Serbian civilians participated. Fighting was fierce all along the line with the Serbian army making one last desperate effort to hold. In the first fortnight Mackensen's troops advanced some 30 kilometres and they were joined on 14 October by a Bulgarian force. Although the Bulgarian I Army was halted, the Bulgarian II Army broke through on the Vardar river and further German reinforcements bolstered the offensive. The French had in the meantime landed forces at Salonika (Thessaloniki) in far northern Greece, an action intended to support Serbia by establishing a firm communications link to the Aegean and the outside world. The expedition had been mounted in large part in order to find a role for General Sarrail, a general favoured by Republican politicians, and had been strongly supported by David Lloyd George. But it was a dubious action in a state that was officially neutral. The Greek Prime Minister, Eleftherios Venizelos, had welcomed the French forces, but the pro-German King Constantine was deeply opposed. The French forces were unable to link up with the Serbs who tried to break through to meet them at Skopje, and by November the French were retreating back to the original beachhead, pursued by the Bulgarians. By this point, both the Serbian army and a significant proportion of the population were already being forced to retreat towards Albania under terrible conditions. On 25 November a formal decision was taken to head for the Adriatic coast. This turned into a terrible ordeal for the Serbs and their Montenegrin allies, who had bravely covered the retreat. By 1 December the army had come close to disintegration, starving, freezing, and preyed upon by Albanian bandits. Typhus swept through the ranks. Thousands died and thousands more deserted. The civilians accompanying the army suffered even more hardship. Even when they had cleared the mountains they found little relief on the Albanian coast, despite the efforts of some local Albanian authorities to assist. The Entente proved unable to provide all the food and shelter initially promised. The head of the French military mission described old people and children without shelter, in rags, hungry, and crying for help. King Peter, who had stayed with his people, wrote, 'Even if Serbia survives I fear there will be no more Serbs.' King Nicholas of Montenegro by contrast fled into exile after surrendering in January 1916, although many of his people continued a guerrilla resistance in the mountains. The collapse of Montenegro meant that the Serbian foothold around Durazzo (Durrës) was no longer tenable and it became imperative to organize a naval evacuation. By the end of February 135,000 Serbs, 90,000 of them soldiers, had been evacuated to Corfu. But the dying continued, nearly 5,000 by the end of March. A French nurse recalled corpses piled up like planks of wood. The Serbian poet Vladislav Petković Dis wrote:

> We were wonderful, glory's favourites
> Instilling fear in our foes
> We had the blood and soul of a healthy race
> And now? Who are we now? And where is our home?

The poet would be killed when the ship taking him from Corfu was torpedoed.

Gradually a semblance of order was restored. An old score was settled when the head of the Black Hand who had planned the assassination of

Franz Ferdinand in Sarajevo was arrested as a traitor and executed, probably as punishment for the disaster he had visited on the nation. The army was resupplied and re-equipped with a view to redeployment. Some 3,000 primary and secondary school children and 1,164 university students were evacuated to France, and some of the former went on to Britain and Switzerland.

The defeat of Serbia had bolstered the Hapsburgs and released troops for other fronts; it had also diverted British and French forces into a secondary campaign against Bulgaria at relatively little cost to the Germans. This would contribute to Falkenhayn's overall strategic vision for 1916, a return in force to the Western Front.

On one score Falkenhayn was frustrated. He had wanted the vigorous pursuit of U-boat warfare to maintain the pressure on Britain. But the sinking by U-boat of the liner SS *Arabic*, leading to more American deaths on 19 August, threatened a new crisis in German relations with America and Bethmann-Hollweg acted quickly with an assurance that Germany would cease attacks on passenger vessels if the USA would pressure London to lift its blockade. Admiral Tirpitz was deeply unhappy about restricting operations and offered his resignation, which the Kaiser refused, whereupon Tirpitz responded by withdrawing the U-boats completely from the Atlantic. This allowed the flow of supplies to continue uninterrupted to Britain and France on the eve of their planned great offensives.

The crisis of Entente fortunes in the east had meant that pressure needed to be applied on the western and southern fronts to pin down German and Austrian forces. By the summer of 1915 some French commanders had started to recognize that trench warfare was not the temporary interruption of a mobile campaign, but they differed significantly about what ought to be done. General Joffre saw the fundamental problem as one of reserves. Only by putting Germany under simultaneous pressure at a number of points and in a sustained fashion would it be possible to break the line somewhere. In a broad strategic sense Joffre was right: the difficulty on the Western Front was that the ratio of troops and guns to space was so high as to mean that any break-in could be quickly countered by the defender moving reserve forces to counterattack and seal the gap. Despite the German casualties of the first year of fighting and despite the transfer of forces to the east, it was still perfectly feasible to maintain the strong positions that had been established in 1914. Indeed the precise point of digging in was to reduce casualties and in absolute terms the problem was that trench warfare was now nowhere near deadly enough. In past wars a large army that stayed in one place too long would run out of local food supplies and would eventually be forced to move or face starvation; railroads and food preservation meant that armies now had the capacity to stay put. Improvements in medical knowledge since the middle of the nineteenth century had also played an important role: sanitation was given proper priority, water supplies were disinfected, delousing was used to control skin parasites, and medical screening and vaccination were used to control other diseases. The result was that the armies in the west were the healthiest that had ever undertaken a prolonged campaign and suffered unusually low levels of death from disease. Armies of a size that simply would not previously have been able to hold their positions were now able to stay in the field.

It is important not to mistake this for a suggestion that trench warfare was really not too bad. There were attempts to present this idea to civilians; in the latter half of 1915 model trenches were built in Berlin with all the comforts of home, and indeed the German soldiers in the west had made an effort to make trenches as comfortable as possible. Yet even if casualties were infrequent, the sense that individuals had no ability to control their own fate was disturbing, particularly perhaps for the articulate middle class who wrote of the experience. Otto Heinebach, a student of philosophy from Berlin, wrote in September 1915 of his best friend on sentry duty being killed by a shell which tore his abdomen open. He died crying out for his 'poor parents'. Heinebach recalled a conversation in which this friend had expressed disgust about the endless crawling underground, the perpetual intimidation, the everlasting inaction, and how he had longed for open battle where he would have welcomed death.

Of course many men had broken down in open battle as well, but the ever present threat for soldiers in constant contact with the enemy created a situation which was a challenge to traditional visions of active masculinity. Some of the more sophisticated psychologists spotted significant similarities between the nervous collapse of soldiers, 'shell shock' as it came to be known, and the symptoms of 'hysteria', a psychological condition that had been particularly associated with house-bound middle-class women.

There were two methods for mitigating the strain. One was to rotate troops so that they spent a significant amount of time out of the line and away from the threat. This was most practical for the British army as it was holding a relatively short length of line and was gradually introducing new units to the trenches during 1915. The other was something that the soldiers did for themselves often against the wishes of the high command. This was cooperation with the enemy. Local truces reduced the intensity of the threat, but were particularly deplored by the French and British commanders who feared that they would allow the Germans to transfer even more forces to the east and that they would undermine the 'offensive spirit'. Commanders tried to disrupt these informal truces by ordering raiding and bombardments. The men responded with the 'ritualization of aggression'. This involved mounting attacks and bombardments in a predictable fashion that allowed the opposing troops to put themselves out of the way. This was a collusion by the opposing front-line troops to fool their own commanders. By its nature this was a covert activity and as such leaves only subtle traces in the historical record, but it seems likely that it was widespread in all theatres whenever the same units faced each other for long enough for understandings to develop. Of course the deep irony was that these spontaneous measures to make trench warfare more bearable in turn made it less deadly and therefore more sustainable, prolonging the static war. But it should always be remembered that these arrangements were pragmatic and local and despite the fears of some commanders did not yet lead to a general abandonment of the cause. Soldiers were still ready and perhaps sometimes even eager to participate in the big offensives when ordered to do so.

The debate amongst the French commanders as to how to conduct such offensives produced three distinct visions. The most pessimistic rejected the idea of decisive battle altogether. General Pétain argued that the tactical conditions in the west meant that only carefully prepared minor offensives were possible and that they should be halted quickly when they had achieved their limited aims. The only practical aim of operations was attrition, fighting in such a way as to minimize French casualties and maximize German ones. Joffre rejected this vision as having no obvious strategic purpose; it was apparently a recipe for an unending war. General Foch was more positive about the possibilities of the offensive; his vision was a well- prepared 'step by step' methodical offensive on a limited front sustained over time. General Castelnau disagreed completely; simultaneous attacks over a broad front utilizing surprise would stand a better chance of gaining momentum before the German reserves could come up and seal the breach. Commanders had to be encouraged to seize any fleeting opportunity. German losses and transfers meant that the opportunity for breakthrough still existed for the time being. With the resources available in 1915 and in the tactical conditions prevailing, Pétain, who had the best grasp of the situation on the ground, was right. But he was also still relatively junior, as was the British general Henry Rawlinson who had similar views. Although Foch had a coherent view, in some ways it was a dangerous and potentially bloody compromise. Joffre sided with Castelnau and ordered a massive offensive for September 1915 with the French attacking in Champagne and an Anglo-French attack in Artois. The hope was that by assaulting both sides of the German salient simultaneously German reserves would be overstretched and at best a grand encirclement could be achieved. At worst the Germans could be forced to abandon their forward positions, which remained a potential threat to Paris. Sir John French was unenthusiastic about the British role in the offensive, but was told by Kitchener that the British had to be seen to be willing to shed blood in the Allied cause and the attack at Loos would provide a first real test for the volunteers of 1914.

On 25 September 1915 the French attacked with eighteen divisions under Castelnau in Champagne and with a smaller force under Foch in Artois. Castelnau relied primarily on surprise and a sudden bombardment, whereas Foch had mounted a week of preliminary bombardments. To the left of Foch, the British attacked at Loos.

In Champagne the 2nd Army commanded by Pétain, with substantial artillery support, won some initial successes, breaking through three trench lines. The 2nd Colonial Corps also made progress. But by the end of 27 September Pétain was warning that his forces were worn out and that the next line of enemy defences could only be breached by meticulous preparatory bombardment. Poor information convinced Castelnau that a breakthrough was imminent and the attack was pressed for three more days; the result was high casualties for little result. Foch made some limited gains in Artois, capturing Souchez. The French assault on Vimy Ridge came close to success but was halted by the arrival of the Guards Corps newly returned from Poland. The British attack at Loos was accompanied by the first British use of poison gas, which in many sectors ended up blowing back into the British lines. The 15th Scottish Division, a 'Kitchener' unit, managed an initially spectacular advance whish would be celebrated in one of the most popular novels of the war, *The First Hundred Thousand* by Ian Hay (John Hay Beith). But the attack faltered and by early October the German army was able to counter-attack with some success.

By the second week of October the fighting died down. The offensive had cost the French 191,000 casualties and the British some 60,000. German losses were about 150,000. Amongst the dead was John Kipling, serving in the Irish Guards. His heartbroken father, the poet Rudyard Kipling, would dedicate most of the rest of his life to commemorating his son and all the British war dead. His son's body was not found in the poet's lifetime and was only identified ninety years later.

Amidst this hecatomb one death stood out in particular. On 12 October 1915 Edith Cavell was shot by a German firing squad for her role in aiding the escape of Entente soldiers from Belgium. Under military law her guilt was not in question and she accepted that her sentence was not unreasonable, but the French and British press seized on the case as highlighting German brutality and lack of mercy and chivalry. The execution of male Belgian civilians for the same offence had caused little comment.

The heavy French casualties of the first year of the war intensified a pre-existing fear of population decline. Postcards explicitly represented motherhood as patriotic duty. The government allowed soldiers to marry the mothers of illegitimate children by proxy, eventually even retrospectively legitimizing the children of dead soldiers. The children of mothers raped by German soldiers caused intense debate, but the general view was that these 'children of the barbarian' could be redeemed for France.

The tempo of killing was rising everywhere. The assaults on Russia and Serbia had provided both opportunity and need for offensives on the Italian front. From 7 to 23 July the second battle of the Isonzo was mounted to increase the pressure on Austria whilst it was heavily engaged in Poland. The result of fierce fighting on the Carso was heavy losses on both sides as the Austrians inflexibly defended incomplete forward positions. Through August a series of fierce local actions was fought at the northern end of the Isonzo. Field Marshal Cadorna became frustrated at the lack of progress and, like his counterparts in other armies, blamed the shortage of shells and artillery, as in other cases this was partially true. In October another offensive was mounted on the Carso, attempting to capture the strong points over a 50-kilometre front, this time in the hope of exploiting the transfer of Austrian troops to Serbia. But by now the Austrian positions were formidably developed and the barbed wire generally prevented the Italians from advancing. A month of fighting in the mud cost 67,000 Italian casualties to add to the 40,000 of the July offensive. In late November the attacks were resumed, concentrating on Mt. Mrzli. The Italians nearly reached the ridgeline and at one point the front lines were only 8 metres apart. In the end the exhausted Italians were pushed back as deep snow brought the fighting to an end, by which time another 49,000 casualties had been added. The first six months of fighting had cost Italy more than half of its pre-war army and was already taking the lives of wartime volunteers. Scipio Slataper was one of the small number of recruits from 'Italia irredenta' who were much celebrated by Italian propaganda. Born in Trieste, before the war he had written extensively about the complex cosmopolitanism of his home region and with some sympathy towards the local Slovenes. But finding himself in Italy in August 1914 he became increasingly strident in his calls for Italian intervention and at the outbreak of war he volunteered to join the Sardinian grenadiers. On 3 December he was killed in action not very far from his birthplace. Such volunteers were treated with contempt by many of the reluctant conscripts of the Italian army. One soldier's song berated them:

Cursed be those young students
Full of learning
They put Italy in widow's weeds
She'll be grieving a century or more.

A different sort of disillusionment could be found in the writings of another volunteer. Benito Mussolini complained that the static warfare that had come to dominate the Italian front like all others was unsuitable to the temperament of Italians. The patience and tenacity required were the antithesis of the bold aggression that he claimed came naturally to them. In fact Mussolini was completely wrong: the peasant conscripts grumbled and hated a war they did not understand, but in many respects their tough civilian lives and the stoicism that this inculcated made them capable of impressive endurance in some of the worst conditions of the war. Meanwhile their commanders prepared to give them the chance to demonstrate their natural aggression in the spring.

The Chantilly conference of 6 December organized by the French to plan an Allied strategy called for a coordinated offensive on all fronts to be mounted 'as soon as possible', with it being highly desirable that the operation should begin in March. The realignment of resources saw the final end of the Gallipoli campaign. Most of the troops on the peninsula were destined for redeployment to France, with a few going to Egypt and Salonika. The ANZAC/Suvla beachhead was evacuated in December and Cape Helles in January 1916. The evacuation was brilliantly handled, surprise was achieved, and the land forces got away without further loss. Nevertheless the campaign as a whole had been a real victory for the Turkish defenders. From the Entente point of view there were a few compensations: it had drawn Ottoman troops away from the Caucasus and the Suez Canal and it had contributed to the serious attrition of the Ottoman army in 1915. One result of this was the successful Russian offensive in January 1916 that led to the capture of the massive fortress complex at Erzerum. The success at Erzerum became the subject of a very popular film in Russia in 1916. Gallipoli had also allowed a British/Indian force under General Townshend to advance almost to the gates of Baghdad, and the withdrawal from Gallipoli put that force in a very dangerous position. The campaign had already become a source of pride for Australia and New Zealand. But the defeat had also shaken British prestige throughout the Muslim world.

The details for the combined offensive of 1916 were initially vague and there was one significant command change before they were finalized. The casualties at Loos and the lack of a result led to the British government and the King finally and completely losing faith in John French. Douglas Haig conspired against his chief and on 19 December 1915 was rewarded with command of the British Expeditionary Force. Haig had hardly covered himself in glory at Loos; he had made some serious mistakes and indeed his record in the first year of the war was largely undistinguished. But he was the most experienced and senior officer available to take over from John French.

On Christmas Day 1915 Joffre wrote to Haig asking him to ready the BEF for an offensive north of the river Somme which would occur in conjunction with an attack south of the river that was already being planned by Army Group North commanded by Foch. Foch was never particularly enthusiastic about the Somme as a battlefield, arguing that it was full of fortified villages, and Haig consistently favoured offensive operations in Flanders in the hope of turning the German flank. But the two men had worked successfully together in the past and were prepared to make an effort. The hope was that a massive Franco-British offensive in the spring could make good use of the newly arrived 'Kitchener Armies' and the massively increased French artillery resources, and that this could be coordinated with a massive offensive on the northern part of the Russian front. Supporting offensives on the Italian front, at Salonika, and on the Russian south-west front would tie down enemy reserves and the great breakthrough would be achieved, probably in the east. There would then be a real prospect of victory in 1916.

The possibility of this massive combined attack rested on the very real achievements of the arms industries of the Entente powers during 1915. Capacity had increased massively. Russian armaments production had undergone a remarkable transformation. Between 1914 and 1916 the production of rifles had increased more than fourfold: field artillery had increased by a factor of ten, machine guns and small arms ammunition by a factor of fourteen, and artillery shells by a factor of thirty. Some of the increases came through efficiency gains in state arms factories: the Sestroryetsk arsenal producing rifles managed to increase its output per worker by a factor of fifteen. But there was also a massive increase in production by private industry. The thirty-nine largest engineering firms invested 130 million roubles in the first eighteen months of the war, much of it lent to them by government. The two sectors eyed each other with suspicion, and in February 1916 engineering firms created a permanent body to represent their interests to government. Corporations opposed proposals to levy an excess profits tax, although this was finally approved in May 1916. The expansion of Russian military capacity came at a tremendous cost. The daily expenditure on the war in December 1915 was double what it had been in December 1914 and 75 per cent of this was being financed by borrowing, spread quite evenly between long-term domestic borrowing, short-term borrowing, and overseas borrowing. Such was the scale of Russian domestic borrowing that the relative significance of overseas debts actually diminished quite sharply. More immediately significant was inflation: Russia experienced a fairly modest initial increase in prices, but by 1916 retail prices rose rapidly. This was partly a product of the increased money supply, but even more a result of the shortages of civilian consumer goods. For example, a quarter of all cotton manufacturing firms had gone out of business by the end of 1914 and by 1916 some 60 per cent of all cotton goods were being produced for the army. The Russian government delivered what the army needed, but in the process created the conditions that would lead to societal collapse.

In France, the socialist Albert Thomas was appointed Secretary of State for Armaments on 18 May 1915; *The Times* commented, 'Pacifist becomes producer of guns'. Thomas hadn't abandoned his socialism. In speeches to munitions workers he stated that they would take up the class struggle again after the war, but he claimed that if the workers were seen as having patriotically contributed to national defence, they would have an unarguable moral right to reshape post-war France in their favour. In the meantime industrial work would be reshaped by a new spirit of cooperation between capital and labour overseen by the state. In August 1915 Thomas declared, 'The government for its part will have the duty to regulate and organize production.' But in France's hour of need the reality was that capitalists were perfectly prepared to exploit every opportunity. Profiteering was epic in scale. The machine gun makers

Hotchkiss, which had begun the war with 6 million Francs in *capital*, had generated *profits* of at least 37 million francs by 1916.

By the end of 1915, 500,000 former soldiers had been returned to the munitions industry in France, bringing the total workforce for the first time back to pre-war levels in metallurgy and chemicals. But the army then vetoed the release of any further troops. The French turned to workers from their colonial Empire and women entered the factories in numbers, usually working-class women who were transferring from other employment. The total workforce in arms production rose from 313,000 in May 1915 to 880,000 in June 1916.

French shell production in August 1914 had been 6,000 per day; by March 1915 it had already reached 62,000 per day and by July 1915 had reached 80,000 per day. The result was that the central reserve of shell stocks for the army by August 1915 was 2,681,486. By this time the real shortage was less one of shells than of guns to fire them. A year of fighting had led to the destruction and wearing out of a lot of French artillery and many disruptions had held up the delivery of replacements. Only in October 1915 did artillery production begin to exceed pre-war levels.

The achievements of the French armaments industry were extraordinary, but they could not have been achieved without the massive support of the United Kingdom, through loans for capital investment and the facilitation of massive imports of raw materials both from Britain and from the USA. This support was being delivered at a time when Britain was itself engaged in a huge expansion of armaments production.

Britain already had the largest expenditure on weapons per capita in the world in August 1914, but this was hugely misleading in terms of the development of its armaments industry, because that expenditure was geared towards the maintenance of the largest and most technologically advanced navy in the world.

Most of the expansion in British arms production was a result of decisions taken by the War Office before May 1915, but Lloyd George undoubtedly drove a further expansion by allowing demand to dictate supply rather than vice versa. His basic approach was to ask what the army needed and then add more of everything. His critics would claim that this primarily served to drive up costs and increase waste, which it probably did, although the creation of an enormous Ministry of Munitions gave the government, as purchaser, impressive negotiating power. What Lloyd George had in abundance were the political skills needed to tackle bottlenecks in arms production. In July 1915 Emmeline Pankhurst organized a rally in London demanding 'women's right to serve' under Suffragette banners. Unknown to most at the time, she had done so in cooperation with Lloyd George who was looking to pressurize the Trade Unions to relax their opposition to 'dilution'. In the course of 1915 and 1916 women flooded into the armaments factories. Most of these women were married working-class women re-entering the workforce or younger women who were moving from textiles and domestic service. Conditions were tough and hours were long; in 1915 many worked seventy hours per week. Over time excessive hours which exhausted workers were found to be counterproductive and shift working made better use of machinery. Factory welfare was also improved with the introduction of proper canteens and nurseries. Better-educated women also entered the workforce, mostly in shops and offices, replacing men drawn into the army. The total increase in the number of women working outside the home was modest, from 3 million before the war to 4 million by the middle of 1916, but the proportion of women in a shrinking civilian workforce rose to 46 per cent by 1916.

Alongside the massive commitment of armaments, the British had bowed to the need to utilize conscription to maintain the strength of the army in the field. From January 1916 single men began to be called up and from April married men. The hope was that by providing the resources to allow the BEF to be used in a sustained offensive operation, the war could be brought to a more rapid end than by holding back. Conscription was controversial and in the end was only able to be passed into law by the provision of a series of grounds for exemption. One of these was conscientious objection and some 16,000 men would go before tribunals to express their opposition to combatant service. Hundreds of thousands appealed on grounds of domestic hardship and many of these received temporary exemptions to put their affairs in order. In any case enlisting and training conscripts took time and the British army in 1916 would remain an almost entirely volunteer force.

The Entente plan was in essence to use the mass of new soldiers and weaponry to crush the Central powers in a huge simultaneous attack. There was nothing particularly subtle about this strategic vision. Falkenhayn could easily anticipate that his enemies would use their resources in this fashion. He had every reason to want to seize the initiative first and similarly every reason to try to produce a decisive result in 1916. The British blockade was working only slowly, but it was biting, and agricultural and industrial productivity were being damaged by the double pressures of blockade and mass mobilization. The inability to import from outside Europe meant that Germany was forced to divert resources into import substitution to circumvent bottlenecks, never an efficient process. Civilian living standards were falling: small indicators were the banning of Christmas *Stollen* cake and New Year fireworks, whilst more ominously the black market was growing in importance. Up until this point civilian health had held up well, but the long-term prospects were poor. Austria-Hungary was already in a precarious position and Germany's ability to prop up her allies was limited. Falkenhayn therefore sought a fast victory in the one place where that could be achieved: France.

Historians are divided on his precise intentions, but certain things are clear. Falkenhayn had confidence in the tactical advantage of the German army and the experience of successful limited offensives on the Western Front in 1915 gave him confidence that it could mount a larger attack and win. Germany still had a potential advantage in heavy artillery, particularly howitzers, which could be exploited. The best place to mount an attack would be Verdun. The Germans already dominated three sides of the town and could bring up large forces in secret in the hilly and forested terrain. They could position artillery that could cut the main railway supply line to the city whilst they could easily access their own railway system. For reasons of prestige and because it was the hinge of the French defensive line, the French would fight to defend Verdun, but the experience of 1914–15 suggested that the fixed fortifications would not help the defenders much and would be vulnerable to super-heavy howitzers.

It is difficult to be sure whether Falkenhayn thought that the city would be taken. It is clear that he thought a large part of the French army could be destroyed there, perhaps encircled and forced to surrender. He also seems to have assumed that the pressure on Verdun would force premature counter-attacks on other parts of the front. In particular a premature British/French relief attack on the Somme would seal the destruction of the French army and largely destroy the inexperienced British, of whom he had a low opinion. The German army had recognized that the Somme was likely to be the arena of a major attack and had begun a programme of intensive fortification in depth. Once these victories had unfolded at Verdun and on the Somme, Falkenhayn would then strike in a third major battle, attacking in Artois and Flanders to drive the British into the sea and resume the hook around the French flank. For this purpose he would hold a large section of the German army in reserve on the right of the Western Front for the first half of 1916. Once the Western Powers were forced to acknowledge defeat, the Italians and Russians would quickly follow suit.

In January 1916 the army commanded by the Kaiser's son, the Crown Prince, took up positions around Verdun. Some of the defenders in the region began to voice warnings about the vulnerability of the position, the Verdun fortresses having been largely stripped of their artillery to support offensive operations elsewhere. In particular Colonel Driant of the *Chasseurs*, a popular writer on military tactics and technology, took his complaints to members of the National Assembly. The high command continued oblivious.

Some 1,400 artillery pieces and mortars opened fire on the French positions along the right bank of the Meuse on 21 February 1916. German infantry began their attack the next morning, using infiltration tactics and supported by flame-throwers. Colonel Driant died of wounds sustained in this initial attack. By 24 February the French position looked desperate. Joffre ordered Pétain to take his 2nd Army headquarters to Verdun and reorganize the defences, whilst Premier Briand travelled to Joffre's headquarters to plead with him not to abandon Verdun. Briand believed that if Verdun fell, the blow to French civilian morale would be fatal. Pétain arrived at Verdun on 25 February only to discover that the strongest fort defending the city, Douaumont, had been surrendered to the Germans almost without a fight. But even as Pétain was arriving there were signs that the French resistance was stiffening and he calmly reorganized the French defences, massing artillery for effective counter-battery fire and instituting the relief of shattered units using the reinforcements rushing to the battlefield. Crucial to the French ability to hold their ground was a reorganization of the supply lines. German artillery had cut the railway into Verdun, but road transport remained possible, largely by the deployment of significant numbers of African and Indo-Chinese labourers in road-repair units. This allowed the creation of a road for motor vehicles only, bringing in ammunition, food, and replacements. For the first time an army was kept supplied entirely by means of trucks, a reflection of the strength of the automotive industry in France and its allies and their ready access to petroleum and rubber (for tyres). The German commanders probably did not anticipate this possibility.

The domination of the battle by artillery and the attempt to interdict supplies gave an enormous significance to the use of aerial observation at Verdun. This in turn produced a new emphasis on two important innovations: camouflage and air combat. In 1915 under the leadership of the academic painter Lucien-Victor Guirand de Scévola, the French army had formed a *Section de camouflage* to conceal military equipment on the battlefield. The commander had been an admirer of Picasso and it was soon established that the cubist fascination with depth perception and abstract form could be utilized to conceal as much as to reveal. Modernist painters were recruited to design camouflage schemes, although the suggestion by Jean Cocteau that the new French infantry uniform should be a harlequin costume was rejected as a bit much.

A very different modern method of thwarting aerial observation was the use of fighter aircraft. Aerial combat had begun in August 1914 when the Russian pilot Pyotr Nesterov rammed an Austrian aircraft with his French-built monoplane. As this led to the death of both crews it was not a method that caught on widely. By early 1915 experiments with various forms of weapons had led to some pilots establishing a reputation as effective air fighters. The term 'ace' was used in France to denote a pilot who had downed five enemies, adapted from a term celebrating successful cyclists prior to the war. The first ace was the pre-war test pilot Adolphe Pégoud. But it was the Germans who really established the fighter aircraft as a weapons system. In June 1915 the *Eindecker* monoplane, designed by the Dutchman Anthony Fokker, entered German service. It was equipped with a forward-firing machine gun which was synchronized with the action of the propeller. This allowed German pilots to point their aircraft at the target, a vastly more effective method of combat. The German pilots and rivals Oswald Boelcke and Max Immelmann became celebrities, 'knights of the air'. Immelmann was credited with inventing many of the individual manoeuvres of air combat, whilst Boelcke was the pioneer in the creation of squadron tactics.

It was Boelcke, a friend of the Crown Prince, who organized the attempt to create a zone of impenetrable air superiority over the German forces in the first days of the Verdun battle. The French response was vigorous and effective. By April 1916 they had formed a *group de chasse* (fighter wing) in the vicinity of Verdun, concentrating a formidable number of the new Nieuport biplanes which were more effective than their German opponents and massing a great deal of individual fighting talent. Georges Guynemer serving with the Escadrille N3, 'The Storks', became a national hero, as did Charles Nungesser who flew with the Lafayette Escadrille. The latter was mostly composed of volunteer American pilots.

Pétain on 10 April sent a message congratulating his troops on holding back the Germans, including the phrase *courage, on les aura*. The phrase does not translate easily—colloquial English would be 'Be brave, we'll have 'em'. The message would soon be seen on the iconic posters for the 2nd French war loan, accompanying an advancing *poilu* (a French soldier in the First World War). The soldiers needed all the encouragement they could get. The artilleryman Paul Pireaud wrote to his pregnant wife Marie on 23 May that the landscape was nothing but shell holes and dead horses. The cannon were mouth to mouth; for both sides attacks were no longer possible. He wrote with shells falling 15 metres from his position. It seems clear that he did not expect to survive. After a month under intense fire he was able to leave the battle unscathed on 20 June. Pireaud had refused to give way to despair; he had genuinely responded to Pétain's message.

Verdun was not the bloodiest battle of the war nor the most destructive. Yet it came to take on particular mythic qualities for both sides. For the French it was a defensive epic, a microcosm of the greater struggle to defend France. It was also a vindication of French manhood. The self-doubt and the fear of degeneracy that had accompanied the defeat of 1870–71 were laid to rest at least in the short term by the tenacious resistance. The system of troop rotation took most of the French army through the battlefield at some point; Verdun was a common reference for the whole army whereas other battles were more exclusive. But it was also a purely French battle, fought by the French and their imperial subjects without allies. It came to lend itself to religious imagery as a national Calvary and the road to the battlefield was labelled the 'sacred way'. The surgeon Georges Duhamel wrote a memoir of the battle, an unsparing account of the suffering of the wounded entitled *The Lives of the Martyrs*.

He described the procedure of 'triage': the hospital treated only those who might live and who were too injured to be transported out. 'Ten times a day we thought we had emptied this reservoir of misery', only to find more wounded arriving. The suffering of the wounded was intensified by the intolerable uproar of never-ending bombardment. New weapons added to the suffering. One man was brought in having been subjected to gas shelling: 'his eyes had disappeared under his swollen lids' and his clothes were so impregnated with gas that the fumes caused the medical staff to cough and weep. Duhamel also treated the German wounded. One of them had been lying alone for six days in the open before he was brought in to have his leg amputated.

The extremities of the battle were perhaps best encapsulated in the fighting at Fort Vaux at the start of June. The French garrison fought the German attackers at point-blank range in its underground galleries until its commander, Colonel Reynal, finally capitulated on 7 June. He had his sword returned to him by the German Crown Prince, an anachronistic gesture in a battle of flame-throwers and phosgene gas.

For at least some of the Germans, Verdun was instead the first battle of the 'new man'. The German soldier was no longer portrayed as the youthful enthusiast of 1914, but instead was now the steel-helmeted machine warrior. This was no longer a war of the Romantic era; it was something harder, more relentless, a storm of steel. As the battle turned against the German army it became less about the ground gained and more about transcendence, about demonstrating an indomitable will.

The first attempt to relieve Verdun was the Russian offensive conducted at Lake Naroch towards the north of their front on 18 March, supported by attacks at Riga and Dvinsk and diversions in the south. These attacks were a disastrous failure, conducted in awful weather and over appalling terrain in the face of well-organized German artillery; they resulted in 100,000 Russian losses by April compared to 25,000 German. Russian commanders blamed the lack of artillery, falsely, because by this stage they actually had more than their German opponents. The Russian soldiers rightly blamed their commanders. General Evert, the commander of the Russian Western Front, voiced doubts that offensive operations could ever succeed.

Conrad von Hötzendorf was encouraged by evident Russian weakness to transfer troops to the Italian front in order to mount a punishment expedition through the Alps. Victory would boost Hapsburg prestige and assert independence from his German allies. The war on this front had largely been a matter of specialist units of *Alpini* and *Jäger* fighting for control of the peaks and spectacular engineering feats to assist them in doing so. The terrain did not seem propitious for a major offensive. As a result the attack launched on 15 May initially achieved surprise, as Cadorna had refused to heed the numerous warnings he had received. Amongst those who had warned of the attack was Cesare Battisti, a prominent volunteer from Trent. Battisti was captured in the Austrian attack and was taken back to Trent where he was hung in public as a traitor to the Empire. He would be Italy's most famous martyr of the war. The Austrian advance broke through as far as Asiago, and Salandra considered sacking Cadorna, but in the end reinforcements from the Carso contained the Austrian advance. In the meantime Conrad's action had come close to destroying the Hapsburg Empire. He had withdrawn forces from the Russian front without fully informing Falkenhayn, who was relying on the Austrians to contain the Russians. In June 1916 the Russians struck.

The new commander of the Russian South West Front was a man of intelligence and activity. Aleksei Brusilov was appointed in April 1916 and immediately began preparing for a large attack. At first his front was seen as subordinate to the main effort that would be mounted further north, but it soon became clear that other Russian commanders were seeking excuses to delay. Brusilov proceeded regardless. He had paid close attention to some of the developments in attacking technique that the French had used in Champagne in 1915 and he began to make preparations which were unusually painstaking for the Russian army. The enemy lines were extensively photographed, mapped and modelled, and Russian reserves were brought forward to be hidden in deep shell-proof shelters. Brusilov planned to attack on a very wide front and without a huge superiority of numbers. As a result his enemies, seeing that there had been no transfer of forces to his sector, doubted that he was seriously intending a breakthrough. Four full divisions, numerous other troops, and nearly all the heavy artillery on the southern part of the Hapsburg front had been transferred to the Tirol in March and April, but the Hapsburg commanders remained confident. The troops spent their time digging in deeper rather than training for active defence. As a result they developed something of a shelter mentality which would prove very costly.

A last-minute panic by General Alexeyev failed to persuade Brusilov to postpone his attack, and at dawn on 4 June a bombardment began along a wide front. After three hours it stopped and Hapsburg forces rushed out only to be hit by a renewed precision bombardment. The cat-and-mouse game carried on for most of the day until Russian infantry began to advance at 6 p.m. Initially the Russian attack was held in most places, but limited breakthroughs also occurred. Then on 5 June the Russian 9th Army rolled over Hungarian and Croatian troops facing them and broke through the enemy lines. Over the next two days the Russian 7th Army turned the retreat into a rout, smashing the Austrian VII Army and taking 16,000 prisoners. The Russian 8th Army had also attacked on 5 June; two Hapsburg regiments were captured almost without loss when the Russian assault troops trapped them in their deep shelters. Over the next four days the Austrian IV Army was routed and some 44,000 prisoners were taken, although the Russian 8th Army had suffered 35,000 casualties.

The offensive came close to finishing the Hapsburg Empire. The VII Army alone lost 133,000 men in June and in two months the total losses would mount to almost half a million. Austrian commanders claimed that Czech forces in particular had surrendered en masse without a fight, but in fact Hapsburg units of all nationalities, including Germans and Magyars, had acted similarly. This did not stop an intensification of denunciations of Czechs living in Vienna as subversives. Conrad was forced to go to Berlin to plead for help from the 'Prussians'. An angry Falkenhayn sent four divisions from his reserves in France and substantial quantities of artillery. He also demanded that a German general, Hans von Seeckt, be given control of the remnants of VII Army.

Brusilov's success is sometimes taken as a reproach for commanders on the Western Front, but it needs to be pointed out that the operational method used would have been unlikely to succeed in the west and could have led to a terrible disaster. Indeed much of the thinking was based on Castelnau's 1915 attack in Champagne which had not been a great success. The relative lightness of the artillery bombardment and the attack over a wide front could only succeed against an enemy that was relatively weak and seriously complacent; the Germans in the west were neither of these things. Brusilov's offensive also benefited from its opportunism, as it was launched purely to inflict a battlefield defeat on the enemy rather than to capture any obvious strategic point. Indeed the intention was that it would be followed up by a genuinely strategic offensive further north. This was not to be. General Evert continued to stall and in the event the South West Front was ready for a new offensive to be mounted before the supposed main assault was ready.

At the start of July, Brusilov's forces attacked along the line of the Stokhod river and once again broke through. By contrast Evert's attack, which he mounted on 4 July, turned into another terrible failure. Russian artillery once again failed to suppress the German defences, and the Russians took a limited amount of ground only to be driven back by a German counter-attack on 14 July. The Russian forces had suffered 75,000 casualties in just over a fortnight, whilst the Germans had lost only 15,000 men. The Russian high command decided to give up attempting to force a decision in this area and began to transfer forces south to reinforce Brusilov.

By this time Brusilov was approaching the key strategic junction of Kovel. This was the lynchpin of the German/Austrian rail network in the east and was the obvious strategic target. So obvious that German forces were rushed to defend it. Kovel was surrounded by the Pripet marshes, terrible terrain on which to advance. Brusilov's operations were further hampered by mass desertion. It has been estimated that 57,000 soldiers from the South West Front absented themselves during the first phase of the offensive. This was one in ten of Brusilov's force, but it was not a new phenomenon: hundreds of thousands of Russian soldiers had disappeared during the first year of the war. In many cases soldiers in transit behind the lines were simply 'lost'—indeed it is possible that large numbers genuinely lost touch with their units during train movements. Many peasant conscripts were unused to the rigid timetables of railways, but many others were probably acting in the manner which would later be made famous by the fictional Czech 'good soldier Švejk', and pretending incompetence in order to escape. Contrary to reputation it seems that the formal disciplinary procedures of the Tsarist Army were actually quite liberal by contemporary standards. For example, soldiers under the age of twenty-one were exempt from the death penalty and very few ethnic Russian soldiers were officially executed for desertion before 1916. (Court martials during the great retreat were more harsh towards non-Russians, particularly Poles and Jews.) Procedures do seem to have tightened in 1916, and indeed the high figures for desertion in Brusilov's army may reflect a greater ability to detect and capture deserters through better policing of the railway stations. But it is undoubtedly also a sign that war weariness was setting in and that the high casualties amongst the officer corps and the best of the pre-war soldiers were undermining the morale of the most active of the Russian forces. Despite later mythology there is little evidence that at this stage the activities of anti-war Bolsheviks were playing any noteworthy role in undermining the morale of the Russian soldiers. But opposition to the war was starting to re-emerge more broadly as the carnage continued without let-up.

The first organized international opposition to the war came from the feminists. At The Hague in April 1915, an international conference of suffragists founded the Women's International League for Peace and Freedom. One of these feminists, the Jewish Hungarian Rosika Schwimmer, managed to persuade the industrialist Henry Ford (America was still neutral) to sponsor a peace ship on a voyage through the war zone to Norway in December 1915. Although the effort was much ridiculed,

H. G. Wells was sufficiently inspired to claim that the ship would one day be seen as the truly important historic event of the war. International coordination of feminist opposition proved difficult in wartime, but individual feminists were often effective opponents of the war on a national level. This was most particularly true of feminists with socialist sympathies including Sylvia Pankhurst in Britain, Clara Zetkin in Germany, and Hélène Brion and Marie Mayoux in France. Indeed it was Zetkin's International Socialist Women's conference at Berne in March 1915 which paved the way for a revival of socialist opposition more generally.

On 5 September 1915 at Zimmerwald in Switzerland an attempt was made to reconstitute socialist internationalist opposition to the war. Delegates representing socialists from France, Germany, Italy, Bulgaria, and most of the European neutrals were present. They agreed to condemn the leadership of the Second International for failure to oppose the war (Lenin had mocked Zetkin's failure to do this) and sent a message of solidarity to persecuted socialists in Germany and Russia. But opinion was divided as to the proper course of action. Lenin, his Bolshevik Party, and a handful of sympathizers formed the 'Zimmerwald left' and took a more militant stance than the 'Zimmerwald centre' led by the Swiss Robert Grimm. At a further conference at Kienthal in April 1916, Lenin condemned any attempts to rebuild the unity of the Second International, stating that the 'patriotic' socialist leadership was hopelessly compromised; instead all socialists should work for the immediate defeat of their bourgeois governments and seek to transform defeat into a revolutionary overthrow of capitalism. Lenin would go on to argue that for tactical purposes socialists should align with other oppositional groups, particularly nationalists, to attain this end; he praised James Connolly for having joined the national revolt in Ireland for precisely this reason. Lenin had no time for mere pacifism. Opposition to the war on humanitarian grounds was purely sentimental: the war was not to be ended, it was to be transformed.

A different transformative vision was emerging nearby, one that did take a firm moral stance against the war. In February 1916 Hugo Ball, a German theatre director living in exile in Zurich, founded the Cabaret Voltaire. Its purpose was to protest at the absurdity of the war; the name was both a tribute to Voltaire's humanitarian iconoclasm and an ironic attack on the cult of rationality. As the battle of Verdun raged the Cabaret staged the events that gave rise to a celebration of the anti-rational in modern art and life and climaxed, as the battle of the Somme got underway, with the publication of the Dada manifesto.

Elsewhere a group of poets and intellectuals took a more direct hand in the war. Since the start of the conflict there had been tentative cooperation between the German high command and Irish republicans. But the attempts of Roger Casement to enlist Irish prisoners of war to fight for the German cause had failed miserably and by 1916 some of the republican leadership in Dublin had decided that they would act regardless of German support. Padraig Pearse in particular seems to have regarded the act of rebellion as a mystic end in itself and the inevitable martyrdom of a failed rebellion as a blood sacrifice for the resurrection of Ireland. He was able to persuade the more pragmatic James Connolly, leader of the tiny socialist 'Citizens Army', to cooperate in planning an uprising. When the German ship *Aud* carrying arms for the rebels was intercepted by the British, it became apparent to the leader of the Irish volunteers, Eoin MacNeill, that the rebellion stood no chance of success. This was also the opinion of Casement who had sailed to Ireland in the secret hope of postponing action, only to be captured by the British. Most of the volunteers stood down, but Pearse and Connolly ignored the cancellation order and roughly 1,000 rebels seized positions in Dublin on Easter Sunday. One of the rebels in arms was Constance Markiewicz, the daughter of a wealthy Anglo-Irish family who had joined Connolly's band of socialist revolutionaries. The uprising resulted in bitter street fighting and great suffering for the population of Dublin, many of whom jeered the rebels after their surrender. By contemporary legal standards the British had the right to execute as traitors all of those who had taken up arms in Dublin. In the event they court martialled and shot fourteen of the prominent rebels, mostly signatories of the Declaration of the Republic. Eamon De Valera, who had successfully commanded one strong point, was spared as a goodwill gesture to the Americans. Markiewicz was spared despite her boast of having shot British soldiers, perhaps in part due to her family connections and in part because the British government did not want to be seen executing a woman. Yet the leniency of response did no good. Pearse had correctly calculated that British executions would produce visceral nationalist responses in both Ireland and Irish America, and in particular the shooting of the wounded James Connolly, executed sitting in a chair, coupled with his last-minute readmission into the Roman Catholic Church, unleashed a wave of anger at the British. The constitutional nationalists felt that their position had been undermined. The British government belatedly tried to counter this mood by leaking extracts from Casement's diaries that detailed his pre-war homosexual activities before hanging him on 3 August, but the damage had been done. Although Sinn Féin, led by the pacifist Arthur Griffiths, had not been the instigator of the rebellion, it quickly became the beneficiary, acting as the vehicle for anti-British protest votes.

More successful from the point of view of the Central powers was a German-Turkish joint effort to encourage the Senussi rebels in Libya. In November 1915 military advisers were landed by submarine who galvanized the revolt, partly tribal and partly religious, against the Italians in Libya and the British in Egypt and Sudan. The success of the rebels in seizing oases in the western desert helped prevent the British from mounting any immediate operations against the Turks in Sinai.

Up until this point the Germans had been the main proponents of subversion as a weapon, but in June 1916 the British were for the first time able to manipulate a rebellion for their own ends. Early in the war the British had backed Ibn Saud as their man in the Arabian peninsula, but the defeat of Saud's forces and the death of his British liaison officer caused the British to look elsewhere. In late 1915 an Arab officer, Mohammed al-Faruqi, had deserted to the British at Gallipoli. He was a member of a secret group of Arab nationalist army officers in Damascus and he informed the British that his group was in negotiations with the hereditary Sherif of Mecca, Hussain bin Ali. The Sherif was out of sympathy with the Young Turk regime in Constantinople and feared that they planned to depose him. The British government in Egypt, represented by Henry McMahon, made contact with the Hashemites and promised them support in creating a great dynastic Arab empire across much of the Middle East. What they did not at this time reveal is that the British government had also been conducting negotiations with the French, which had led in May 1916 to the Sykes-Picot agreement to partition the same area between the British and French empires. Encouraged by British support, in early June 1916 the Sherif raised the flag of revolt and on 16 June 1916, supported by the Royal Navy, captured the coastal city of Jeddah. This was a small event in military terms, but one of tremendous propaganda significance. On 29 April General Townshend had surrendered to the Turks at Kut during the Mesopotamian campaign and 10,000 mostly Indian troops had been taken into a brutal and humiliating captivity. British prestige in the region was low and the willingness of any Arab leader to bet on a British victory was of considerable value.

Too late to assist the Irish rebels, the German High Seas Fleet commanded by Admiral Scheer mounted a sortie into the North Sea at the end of May 1916. German intentions were known to the British Admiralty due to the work of the code-breakers of Room 40 and as a result the Grand Fleet commanded by Admiral Jellicoe was despatched to meet the German force long before it could mount a raid on the English coast. The battle that resulted saw the British battlecruiser squadron under Admiral Beatty clash with his German equivalents under Admiral Hipper. Hipper then lured Beatty onto the guns of the main German fleet, resulting in severe losses to the British when three battlecruisers exploded. The surviving British battlecruisers were then chased by the German main fleet, until it came into contact with the British main fleet which proceeded to inflict some serious damage in turn. At which point the German fleet turned tail and fled for home and the British fleet failed to pursue due to the risk of losses from mines and U-boats. The Germans had sunk more ships and killed more men, and the battle was proclaimed by German propaganda as a great victory. The British by contrast were shocked that Jellicoe had not won a decisive victory in the tradition of Horatio Nelson. In fact nothing had really changed. The British still dominated the sea, the German fleet remained largely confined to port. Strategically the Royal Navy was winning its war in an unglamorous but efficient manner, whilst the German fleet was proving a waste of resources. But a further shock to British opinion shortly followed when the ship carrying Lord Kitchener to Russia sank in early June, drowning the emblematic leader. The loss of Kitchener soon became the subject of a great deal of speculation and legend.

By now the armies that Kitchener had raised were gathered for their greatest test. The spring months had seen continued German pressure at Verdun. The result of this constant pressure was a significant reduction in the French contribution to the Somme offensive. The attack would now be a mostly British effort. Haig placed the main attack on the Somme under the command of Henry Rawlinson. Rawlinson had commanded the first successful British assault on a trench line at Neuve Chapelle in 1915 and he had come to believe that the only sensible approach to trench warfare was to use a fast and heavy bombardment to neutralize the defences, and then a short deliberate advance to seize ground and resist counter-attack. His views were almost identical to those of Pétain. Haig by contrast favoured a much broader and deeper model of battle, aiming for a strategic breakthrough. Rawlinson bowed to Haig's vision and the resulting plan of attack was a peculiarly dangerous compromise between the two views. The British preliminary bombardment was spread over a much greater breadth and depth than Rawlinson had originally wanted, and to have any chance of effectiveness it had to be prolonged in time as the British simply did not possess enough heavy artillery to mount such a large-scale bombardment in one quick effort, particularly as a large amount of the British ammunition turned out to be faulty. This of course meant that all hope of surprise was sacrificed. The infantry were instructed to go into battle carrying a large amount of equipment and ammunition. This made sense in a set-piece battle, but made it difficult to attack in a sudden rush to capture the German trenches when the barrage lifted. Indeed most attacking units eschewed sophisticated plans of attack as British generals did not believe that the 'Kitchener men', drawn to a large extent from urban backgrounds, were skilful or well-trained enough to implement sophisticated fire and movement tactics. In this they were terribly mistaken; the wartime volunteers were in fact physically and mentally superior to peacetime British soldiers, but many would never get the chance to prove it.

The first day of the Somme was terrible for the BEF. The bombardment had been spread too thinly to suppress the defending machine guns and artillery, and in many places the attacking infantry advanced too slowly. Along much of the front heavy casualties were sustained for no progress: the Newfoundland Regiment was almost wiped out attacking Beaumont Hamel; the Tyneside Irish were devastated before they even made it to the British front line. The Ulster Division made a partially successful attack near Thiepval, but the leading units found themselves cut off and were effectively counter-attacked by the Bavarian defenders. The Ulster unionists would nevertheless celebrate the Somme as a moral victory and as a sacrifice that would justify their permanent exclusion from any united Ireland, particularly one including the 'traitors' of the Easter Uprising. By nightfall the British had suffered 60,000 casualties, including more than 20,000 dead. Almost half of the British attacking force, including two divisions that had mounted a diversion at Gommecourt, had been put out of action. The scale of the casualties swamped the British medical services and even some of the German defenders became sickened by the number of bodies piled up in front of their positions.

Only the far right of the British attack gained any real success, in part due to French support. The French by contrast had a very successful day. The Germans had not expected the French to be able to mount a major assault and the attackers gained real surprise. French infantry tactics benefited from the experience of Verdun and heavy supporting artillery was plentiful. General Fayolle's army made good progress north of the river and even better progress to the south. In the first two weeks of July the French army took 12,000 prisoners on the Somme, although German resistance stiffened and losses mounted. Amongst those killed in the advance was the American poet Alan Seeger, serving in the French Foreign Legion. Even after a year at the front, Seeger's poetry still extolled the redemptive value of war and comradeship and proved very popular when posthumously published in the United States.

Haig and Rawlinson do not appear to have realized at first the scale of the losses that the BEF had suffered. Haig nevertheless prevented Rawlinson from renewing the frontal assault on 2 July and ordered him instead to reinforce the southern sector. There was no discussion of halting the offensive. French success and British resilience now combined to turn the battle into a crisis for the German command. Despite the staggering scale of losses they had inflicted on the British, the Germans had not stopped the Somme offensive in its tracks as their plan demanded. German losses had not been negligible and quickly mounted further. The British attack was realigned towards a grinding advance through the woods and villages to the south. Smaller-scale attacks were mounted day after day and each small battlefield became a bloodbath for the units involved. Mametz Wood would become forever associated with the Welsh Division and Delville Wood with the South African Brigade. From a force of less than 1,000, the first battalion of the German Lehr Infantry Regiment lost 10 officers and 685 men at Pozières in four days, many of them torn to pieces by heavy artillery fire. The Australians facing them suffered equally or worse. The intensity of fighting on the Somme exceeded even Verdun. More men became casualties in a smaller area than ever before. Mutilated dead bodies lay everywhere.

On 14 July Rawlinson mounted a new full-scale attack. Preceded by an effective and heavy bombardment which suppressed the defences, British forces attacked just before dawn. For a brief moment the Indian Cavalry Division were able to mount an attack, but as usual the defenders quickly sealed the gap. One Muslim Indian trooper wrote home that the 'leaders did not consider that the occasion was suitable for a cavalry charge and stopped the pursuit' but that 'in the future when opportunity occurs we shall wreak vengeance on the Germans for the blood of our brothers', and he hoped that God would bring an end to the war before he had to face another European winter.

Prince Rupprecht commanding the Bavarian Army on the Somme wrote bitterly in his diary on 17 July that the Somme defenders had not been adequately reinforced and that Falkenhayn was to blame. On 30 July the new army group commander General von Gallwitz issued an order of the day stating that 'the decisive battle of the war will be fought out on the battlefield of the Somme' and that 'sacrificial action' would be needed to prevent the enemy from taking any more ground. In the meantime the German offensive at Verdun had failed to capture Souville on 12 July, effectively ending the last hope of a breakthrough. In order to hold ground on both battlefields and provide reinforcements to the east, Falkenhayn was forced to break up his strategic reserve in the west and abandon the hope of a victory offensive.

Falkenhayn's strategy had failed and his credit was exhausted. He was physically and mentally drained. He had in the short term disrupted the Entente offensive plans, but only at the cost of fighting an expanding war of attrition on all fronts, one that Germany had little hope of winning. Even before the war, the German nightmare had been to fight against the fully mobilized resources of France and Russia simultaneously. Now they were fighting exactly that battle and the British Empire as well. The Dual Monarchy was at the end of its resources, and although Turkey had proved robust, the Ottomans were still in need of support rather than being a resource to support Germany. The same was true of Bulgaria. By the start of August it looked deeply improbable that the Central powers could survive another year.

CHAPTER 3
THE THIRD YEAR 1916–1917: EXHAUSTION

On 30 July 1916 the munitions depot at Black Tom, New Jersey, was destroyed by an explosion; the blast was measured at 5.5 on the Richter scale. Seven people, including a baby, were killed and shrapnel was embedded in the arm of the nearby Statue of Liberty. The investigation indicated that the blast had been caused by deliberate sabotage by German agents. Later Indian and Irish nationalists would also be linked. This reckless move is an indicator both of the increasing desperation in German policy and the sense that the United States, through its vital supply of the Entente powers in the battle of materiel, had already become in effect an enemy.

August 1916 saw the German army continuing to be put under pressure on the Somme and at Kovel, but managing to contain these assaults. On the Somme organized trenches were ceasing to exist and the battle was becoming one of clinging on to shell craters. The young German officer and later novelist Ernst Jünger claimed that it was the fighting on the Somme around Guillemont that first made him aware of the 'war of materiel' and that in a zone of one kilometre behind the front line 'explosives held absolute sway'. The fighting in late August and early September saw terrible losses on both sides. British efforts degenerated into small localized assaults which lacked the force to make any real gains. They were met by vigorous counter-attacks which, although frequently successful, wore down the defenders.

On 20 August Prince Rupprecht, now commanding the German forces on the Somme, wrote to the head of the military cabinet formally expressing his loss of confidence in Falkenhayn. The Chief of Staff was now surrounded by enemies. The field commanders in the west had joined those in the east in demanding his removal; Chancellor Bethmann-Hollweg had wanted him gone for some time, as had prominent figures in the Reichstag. Leading industrialists were also convinced that they could take advantage of his dismissal. The Kaiser alone had remained loyal, sensing that many of Falkenhayn's enemies were less respectful of his own person. Whilst the elites were plotting for an intensification of the war effort, mass opinion was simply fed up. An indication of working-class opinion was a letter from 'several war wives' to the Senate of Hamburg on 11 August which stated, 'We want our men and sons back and we don't want to be hungry any longer—Peace has to be made.' A Catholic trade unionist noted that soldiers' letters home were full of 'moans for peace'.

The Romanian declaration of war on 27 August was the final cause of Falkenhayn's fall. It provided an excuse to transfer him to coordinate the response. He had already anticipated the Romanian offensive into Transylvania and on 1 September General Mackensen led a mostly Bulgarian force against southern Romania into the Dobrudja, surrounding the fortress of Turucai which was captured on 6 September. For the second time in a year the forces at Salonika failed to break through and rescue an ally in trouble. General Sarrail's forces were significantly stronger in 1916, but a Bulgarian spoiler offensive disrupted and delayed plans to mount an offensive in support of Romania.

Ironically, Falkenhayn now quickly demonstrated a renewed vigour as a field commander. At the end of August, General Groener had described him as seeming to be an old man, but he proved far from decrepit in the field. His forces counter-attacked though the Carpathian mountains, defeating the Romanians at Hermannstadt (Sibiu) in late September and at Kronstadt (Braşov) in early October. Breaking through into the lowlands, Falkenhayn's armies were able to link up with Mackensen's force advancing from the south. In little over a month the Romanian army lost over 300,000 men, of which half had been taken prisoner and 90,000 were missing.

The dismissal of Falkenhayn meant the appointment of Paul von Hindenburg as Chief of the General Staff supported by Erich Ludendorff in the post of 'First Quartermaster General'. One of their first acts was to cancel offensive operations at Verdun permanently and review all strategic options. On the last day of August 1916 there was a high-level meeting in Pless Castle which gathered together Bethmann-Hollweg, Hindenburg, Ludendorff, Gottlieb von Jagow of the Foreign Office, Karl Helfferich, head of the Ministry of the Interior, and representatives of the navy led by Admiral von Holtzendorff, the Admiralty Chief of Staff. Holtzendorff argued that by this stage Germany's enemies were completely dependent on Britain, that therefore all possible means must be used to prevent Britain from continuing the war and that failure to use the most potent weapon, unrestricted submarine warfare, would mean the end of Germany. He was met by a hostile response from the civilians. Jagow stated that Germany would be seen by all neutrals as a 'wild dog' and Helfferich argued that there was no certainty the U-boats could effectively blockade Britain and that the entry of the United States into the war would be disastrous. For the moment the civilians prevailed, but it was clear that the issue would not go away.

In the meantime Ludendorff sought to implement his ideas about vigorous mobilization of German industry in support of the war effort. Massive targets for increased production were set which were to be pursued regardless of cost. Hindenburg demanded that Germany should double its output of shells and triple its output of machine guns and artillery by the spring. Leaders of German heavy industry had been lobbying for some time to be allowed to command a greater share of national resources, but they had been partially restrained by the War Ministry. Now they were given their head in what became known as the 'Hindenburg programme for industry' that sought to match the Western powers and the increasing firepower of the Russians as well. But as the French and Russians had discovered in 1915, writing blank cheques to industrialists led to massive profiteering. The industrialists had also hoped to benefit from a more militarized approach to labour relations. They were taking their lead from the British who had introduced some quite draconian methods of controlling the labour market, including forcing workers to obtain 'leaving certificates' from their employers if they tried to change jobs (which along with 'no strike' agreements in war industries had seriously undermined the ability of the working class to utilize a situation of labour shortage to push up wages).

War-related expenditure as a proportion of German GNP increased between 1916 and 1917 from about 36 per cent to well over 50 per cent. The Hindenburg programme caused real wages to fall sharply in occupations that were not associated with war industry, declining by almost 50 per cent compared to 1916 levels by the end of the war. The fall was largely a result of inflation. This was because the production of consumer goods including foodstuffs suffered from the shift in priorities. Reduced supply inevitably pushed up prices and encouraged the black market. Those working in war industries saw a much lesser decline in their living standards, because wages increased more. The attempt to control these workers through an 'Auxiliary Labour Law' in the end failed in part because of collusion between trade unionists and industrialists.

The drive for increased production had impacts outside of Germany. In October and November 1916 the German occupation authorities undertook widespread deportations of Belgian labourers to Germany. This was announced as an attempt to deal with the possible social problems resulting from mass unemployment in Belgium, but was clearly designed to appropriate additional labour for German war industry. The result was a further propaganda debacle: Cardinal Mercier of Brussels, already a rallying point for Belgian resistance, made public his protest. Entente propagandists made particular use of the deportation of young Belgian women to imply sexual depravity on the part of the Germans.

It is easy to be critical of the Hindenburg programme as ill-considered, wasteful, and excessive, but it is worth noting that even after its implementation the Germans were still committing a slightly lower proportion of their GNP to military production than the British were using of their *significantly larger* GNP. So although the turn in German war policy would indeed lead to a significant civilian hardship, it is not really the case that the British made a more clear-cut choice to protect civilian living standards. Being significantly richer to start with, the British were able to expand military production and protect vulnerable civilians. More obviously the German high command had to respond to the fact that by September 1916 the battle of materiel was clearly being lost.

Even as the Somme battle raged in August the British public were being reassured by an extraordinary piece of propaganda. The film *The*

Battle of the Somme had been rushed out to cinemas. Most of the footage was concentrated on showing the scale of British preparations for the battle, lines of marching soldiers, heavy artillery firing. The film does contain some remarkable combat footage showing distant soldiers going into action on 1 July, but its most famous scene, of British soldiers going 'over the top', was a re-enactment staged with participants some days later. The apparent death of one of these soldiers had a profound impact on the public and indeed at least one cinema owner refused to show what he believed was a distasteful and ghoulish film. Some neutral viewers felt that the film was a powerful piece of anti-war propaganda, with its scenes of battlefield burials and fields of wounded. But most viewers seemed to adopt the intended message, that the fighting was serious and bloody, but that British might was overwhelming. It was the omissions in the film that covered up the scale of the disaster of 1 July; there was no footage of unburied bodies or untreated wounded. Remarkably the film was shown to British troops in France in August and September, within earshot of the actual battle.

On 12 September the French 6th Army broke though the German lines and reached open country. The gap was quickly sealed but on 15 September a massive British assault followed just to the north. The results of the day's fighting were mixed; the British did make significant gains, finally clearing High Wood. But although the bombardment was twice as heavy as on 1 July, it was only half the weight of that on 14 July. This battle of Flers-Courcelette is best remembered for the first deployment of a new weapon: the tank. The British had been developing an armoured vehicle which moved on tracks over rough terrain for over a year. Amongst those supporting its development was Winston Churchill, who encouraged use of a 'land battleship'. The idea of a vehicle that could break through barbed wire and destroy strongpoints with its own weapons whilst protecting its crew from bullets was in some ways an obvious one. But the practical difficulties were substantial, in particular the building of an engine sufficiently powerful and reliable to propel an armoured vehicle. The first vehicles were in fact terribly slow, incapable of moving at more than walking pace. They were successfully concealed from German intelligence; the rhomboid steel vehicles were described as 'water tanks' before their first use, and the name stuck.

The first combat use of tanks had had mixed results. Many broke down before they even reached the start line. The image of a tank driving down the main street of the devastated village of Flers was memorable, but it is arguable that the tanks may have worked against the British by disrupting the artillery bombardment where they were deployed. The Guards Division suffered particularly heavily from this, but pressed on nevertheless and stormed Bavarian positions at Lesboeufs. As was so often the case, they were met by a vigorous counter-attack and pushed back. Psychologically tanks symbolized an increasing British mastery of the industrial battlefield. They quickly became a familiar image on the British home front, illustrated in the press and reproduced as toys. For the German soldiers at the front line they represented a new source of terror in a battle that had developed a singularly grim reputation. The Somme was their hardest test to date. Most of the army in the west was drawn into the battle at some point and all of the units involved suffered terribly. More men were killed and maimed in a much smaller area and in a much shorter time than at Verdun.

Pressure continued through October and November. The British finally gained some of the higher ground at the end of November, the 51st Highland Division managing to capture Beaumont Hamel where the Newfoundland Regiment had been massacred on the first day. The latter stages of the battle were fought in ever-deteriorating conditions as the battlefield became a muddy wilderness and then a frozen wasteland. The battle cost the British Empire 420,000 casualties, the French 200,000, and the Germans at least 480,000. At least 300,000 of those who had fought were dead, many with no known grave. But in the end the German army held the line and the British and French did not fully attain even their first objectives. The extraordinary determination of the ordinary German soldiers and the tactical skill of the lower-level leadership earned this bloody victory.

Strategically the price had become too high. At the end of 1916 the German military leadership shuddered at the prospect of fighting again in the same positions and at the same tempo in the spring. The British army had not been broken on the Somme, despite their high casualties, and the French had not merely held Verdun, but were counter-attacking. On 24 October troops commanded by General Mangin, predominantly Moroccan and Senegalese, recaptured Fort Douaumont which was evacuated by the Germans after it had been the target for more than 100,000 155mm howitzer shells and fire from massive 400mm railway guns. On 15 December Mangin attacked again taking more than 11,000 German prisoners. He apologized to the German officers for the cramped conditions, gloating that 'we did not expect there to be so many of you'. Although 1916 had not cost Germany as many casualties as 1915 because of a reduced effort in the east, it was nevertheless imperative to reduce the burden. Whilst the autumn fighting continued, a new fall-back line of defence was being built behind the Somme battlefield.

On the furthest flung battlefield, the last remnant of the German overseas empire was being slowly ground down. Jan Smuts had been sent to East Africa in early 1916 to take command of the reduction of the German outpost, bringing with him South African veterans of the Namibian campaign. Smuts began his advance during the rainy season. The result was a terrible rate of loss amongst the horses of his mounted southern Africans and a serious toll amongst the men as well; the 1,000-strong 2nd Rhodesian Regiment, recruited from white settlers, would suffer only 36 combat deaths between 1915 and 1917 but would see 10,000 cases of illness. By the time he captured Dar es Salaam in September, Smuts had reluctantly conceded he would need to draw more heavily on black African manpower. The Africanization of the campaign by the British proceeded through the year; in July the Gold Coast Regiment arrived in East Africa and in November they were joined by the Nigerians. Smuts reluctantly agreed to a doubling in size of the King's African Rifles recruited in British East Africa. But black troops were at least as vulnerable to disease as white: 715 out of 980 members of the Gold Coast Regiment were invalided in November 1916.

As Smuts manoeuvred south, Belgian forces advanced from the west out of the Congo. In Burundi and Rwanda, German civil officials rejected resistance, ordering that the colonies should be kept functioning for when they were returned after the imminent German victory. Belgian forces captured Kigali and then pushed on further into German East Africa until ordered to stop by Smuts, who did not want to allow the Belgians to establish more territorial claims. Portuguese forces who had been clashing with the Germans since 1914 had also now become involved in the wider campaign.

General von Lettow-Vorbeck's aim of diverting British troops from Europe had not been achieved. One British battalion of sportsmen-adventurers had been sent, but the forces which had fought in East Africa were overwhelmingly African and for political reasons the British (unlike the French) were unwilling to deploy combatant black Africans in Europe, and many South Africans refused to serve outside the continent. The one resource diverted was shipping to supply the forces in East Africa.

Their absence as combat troops did not spare British African subjects from contributing to the death toll in Europe. Members of the South African Native Labour Corps were shipped to France to provide vital support for the front line. This resulted in a tragedy on 21 February 1917 when the SS *Mendi* was involved in a collision in the English Channel and sank with the loss of 616 lives. As the ship went down the Zulu pastor, Reverend Isaac Dyoba, supposedly addressed the men of various tribes as fellow 'sons of Africa' and called on them to die as brothers.

Having been almost fatally weakened in the spring by the Brusilov offensive, the Hapsburg Empire now faced a series of hard blows from the south. On 6 August the Italians, with odds in their favour of 2 to 1 in troops and in artillery of more than 3 to 1, attacked Mt. Sabatino, key to the defences of Gorizia. With their King watching them, they swept aside the Dalmatian defenders. The fighting at Mt. San Michele was harder and the Catanzaro, Brescia, and Ferrara Brigades took heavy losses in securing the summit. But the conquest of that mountain was highly symbolic: some 20,000 Italians had died in the struggle for this near impregnable position. The Hapsburg defences were smashed open and there were no reserves to prevent a major Italian advance. On 8 August the Pavia Brigade entered Gorizia, but by this time the defenders were conducting a skilful withdrawal to positions behind the town. Hapsburg reserves came up and hurried and poorly-planned Italian attacks, conducted without the artillery, which had lagged behind, were stopped in their tracks.

This sixth battle of the Isonzo had seen the first clear Italian victory. The Hapsburg forces had been driven back 6 kilometres, but at the cost of another 100,000 casualties. Furthermore the new line behind Gorizia showed signs of being just as tough as the old. Colonel Douhet, Chief of Staff of the Carnia Corps, wrote an anonymous memorandum to some senior politicians arguing that the capture of Gorizia was irrelevant and that General Cadorna was an incompetent. The high command got wind of this and Douhet was court martialled and imprisoned. Cadorna also transferred Capello, whose troops had captured Gorizia, to a secondary front in order to deny him the limelight.

In the meantime the Hapsburg lines were rapidly being strengthened, in part by the labour of 20,000 Russian prisoners, and reinforcements had been brought up. By the launch of the seventh battle of the Isonzo on 13 September it was business as usual: one Austrian artillery officer commented that the close-packed Italians looked like an attempted mass suicide. On 3 November the Italians came close to a complete breakthrough at Fajti on the Carso, stopped by an ethnically mixed group of Hapsburg soldiers of the 61st Infantry from the Banat on the Hungarian frontier, who bought time for a Galician division to come up. Even so it was the failure of Cadorna to commit his reserves that meant that the 39,000 Italian casualties did not buy a complete victory. Cadorna responded with a circular on 19 November banning off-duty soldiers from theatres and bars in the war zone. In December he reduced the rations. Mussolini noted in his diary on 21 January 1917, 'What great weather for dreadful *morale*, murmuring'. He blamed women for undermining the troops on leave. Certainly Italian women were protesting against the war: some 500 demonstrations occurred in the winter of 1916–17, usually on a Monday, allowance day, with thousands of women demanding the return of their menfolk. Mussolini believed that the women were being influenced by their priests, who in turn were in league with the enemy. But his outburst of misogyny might have another explanation. In February 1917 Mussolini was invalided from the front; traditionally this is ascribed to an accident with a grenade. But his medical file suggests that the underlying medical reason was neuro-syphilis. If so he was hardly alone: venereal disease infection was a major problem in all the armies, leading to increased efforts to regulate prostitution.

Civilian morale on the Austrian side of the line was even worse. By September 1916 the police in Vienna reported that there were now daily lines for bread, potatoes, milk, oil, coffee, sugar, eggs, soap, beer, tobacco, plums, and cabbage. To stand a chance women started queuing started at 3 a.m. Women were also at the forefront of the protests in Vienna; in March 1917 they hijacked a potato wagon shouting, 'We want bread, we are hungry, our men are bleeding to death on the battlefields and we are starving.' Postal censorship reported that soldiers were receiving letters from their families stating, 'When you return home you won't find us alive.' Bread consumption in the Empire as a whole was 40 per cent below pre-war levels because agricultural output had fallen significantly, but there were huge differences between localities. The Austrian half of the Empire believed that the more agrarian Hungarian half was deliberately withholding supplies. In peacetime Austria had 'imported' 1.4 million tons of grain, but this had fallen to less than 30,000. The Hungarians not unreasonably responded that they had taken on the responsibility of feeding the combined army in the field.

As the Hapsburg Empire bled away in 1916, its aged Emperor went into terminal decline. Franz Josef died on 21 November and was succeeded by his great-nephew Karl.

The new Emperor was a devout Catholic with a similarly devout Italian wife (who would suffer from a slander similar in kind to that of the Tsarina: accusations that she was in league with the enemy). Although Karl had served as a general and authorized the use of poison gas by his troops, he seems to have developed an abhorrence for the war, reinforced by a shrewd sense that the continuation of the conflict would destroy the dynasty, and by a desire to maintain an alignment with the papacy which was increasingly signalling a desire to broker a peace.

The German leadership were not immune to the temptation to call a halt. The harvest of 1916, with agriculture suffering from shortages of horses, labour, and fertilizer, was poor. Food riots began to break out as Germany headed into what would become known, due to the lack of potatoes, as the 'turnip winter'. Prior to the war Germany had imported 40 per cent of its food and fodder. Initially it had managed to maintain a level of imports from the neutral countries on its borders; one estimate is that exports from Holland alone were providing the minimum food ration for 4 million Germans in early 1916. The German Army tried as much as possible to support itself by local food requisitioning and some further supplies were sent from occupied territories back to Germany. The bigger problem was a decline in the productivity of German agriculture and difficulties with equitable distribution. In 1915 the government had recognized that the feeding of grain to livestock was an inefficient way of providing calories to the population and had ordered a mass slaughter of pigs. The result had been a short-lived glut of meat followed by a severe shortage that had incentivized farmers to produce meat illegally for the black market. Generally by the end of 1916 rationing and price control efforts had begun to push a greater share of food into the barter economy and the black market, and the poor harvest of the year, which also reduced imports from the neighbouring countries, was the final straw. Germans were not starving in the winter of 1916, but they were hungry. There was a shift from a high protein and high fat diet to one that was possibly technically healthier but which was far less psychologically satisfying. Hundreds of substitute (*ersatz*) products were in use, most of them deeply disliked. Just as bad was the increasing need for the middle classes to resort to illegality in order to meet their needs. For a society deeply imbued with a sense of itself as law-abiding this was damaging to people's self-image and the prestige of the state. A particularly cold winter combined with a growing shortage of coal for domestic use added to the misery.

The bright spot for Germany was ironically the place that had finally precipitated the summer crisis. By October the Romanian Army had been reduced to a remnant of 90,000 defeated men. The Russian forces sent to help had also suffered heavily. Bucharest was captured on 6 December. The prospect of the next year's wheat harvest and the capture of the oilfields (despite widespread sabotage of equipment and destruction of oil stocks conducted by British agents led by the British MP and colonel of engineers John Norton Griffiths) were welcome to the hard-pressed Central powers. The Romanian collapse helped precipitate a general crisis in the political leadership of the Entente, already shaken by the failure of the combined summer offensive to bring about a fast result.

War weariness was in part a reflection of casualties. The Russian poet Zinaida Gippius wrote in the autumn of 1916:

> Today on earth,
> There is something hard
> Something so shameful
> Something almost impossible
> Something so difficult:
> It is to lift up the eyes,
> And look into the face of a mother
> Whose son has been killed.
> Let us not talk about it.

But to a large extent the death toll strengthened the argument that the war had to be fought better and brought to a victorious conclusion. Speaking to the Duma in Russia, the Liberal leader Miliukov was blunt: 'With this government we cannot legislate, any more than we can, with this government, lead Russia to victory . . . Is it stupidity or is it treason? Choose either one, the consequence is the same.' Prime Minister Sturmer, supported by the Tsarina Alexandra and Rasputin, wished to close the Duma and prosecute Miliukov. But Tsar Nicholas, warned by other family members that the monarchy was in crisis, decided to dismiss him instead. Alexandra nevertheless was able to insist on the retaining of the equally unpopular minister of the interior, Protopov, a favourite of Rasputin's. Her insistence that 'in Russia the Tsar rules and not the Duma' goes some way to explaining the depth of hatred that had developed towards her and the 'special friend' by the end of 1916. But it should also be remembered that it was by now widely believed that she was both a German in loyalty and an adulteress. As such she became a lightning rod for the intensity of both moral panic and xenophobia just as many other queens had done in the past. One of her leading accusers, Duma deputy Vladimir Purishkevich, joined the louche aristocrat Felix Yusopov and the Tsar's cousin Grand Duke Pavlovich in a conspiracy to murder Rasputin. Lured by the prospect of a liaison with Yuropov's wife to his house, Rasputin was poisoned, shot, beaten with a dumb-bell, and thrown into the icy river Neva where it appears he finally drowned. This murder, brutal and semi-farcical, was a clear signal of how deep the crisis of the regime had become.

In the United Kingdom the sense that Asquith was insufficiently energetic in the conduct of the war saw a growing clamour in the press for more decisive leadership. Lloyd George had grown close to senior figures in the Conservative Party and had won the support of the great press proprietors Lord Northcliffe and Lord Beaverbrook. The death of Asquith's son Raymond on the Somme may have reduced his determination to hold on to office when the plot against him came into the open. A new Conservative-dominated coalition was formed, understood as signalling a greater commitment towards a fight to a finish. Behind closed doors it was not quite that simple; one prominent Conservative, Lord Lansdowne, had already made it known that he thought a decisive victory would cost too much in blood and that the weakening of the social elites would open the door to revolution. Lloyd George was horrified by the losses on the Somme and although he acceded to the promotion of Douglas Haig to Field Marshal, he had already lost confidence in British military leadership. Similar sentiments were emerging in France.

On 28 November the French Chamber of Deputies met in closed session and decided to abolish the post of Commander in Chief. Joffre threatened to resign at this downgrading of his role. Briand, also under pressure, organized an apparent promotion for Joffre, in fact a move to sideline him. Command of the armies in France was given to Robert Nivelle on 13 December. He was the man of the hour, the recapture of the forts at Verdun being fresh in the public mind. He was promoted over the heads of his more senior colleagues: Castelnau, Foch, and Pétain. This was partly because as a Protestant he did not alienate anti-clerical politicians, and Joffre had given his backing, impressed by Nivelle's confidence. Nivelle made great play of the idea that his attacks at Verdun showed he had the 'formula' for victory. It seems that he placed confidence in rapid bombardments in depth, methods similar to those that had been used by the Germans, rather than the step-by-step methods used by Foch and Fayolle on the Somme. Improved provision of heavy artillery and better training of French infantry convinced him that a battle of fire and manoeuvre was now possible.

Nivelle immediately ran into difficulties with Haig. Nivelle's plans for the future offensive operations in France ran up against Haig's incompatible desire to mount an offensive in Flanders. By February, in a meeting at Calais, Lloyd George had decisively intervened in support of Nivelle and placed Haig effectively under Nivelle's command. This was to a large extent a product of Lloyd George's dislike and distrust of Haig. The ill-feeling generated came close to a crisis both in Anglo-French relations and between the military and civilian leaderships in Britain.

The original plan for 1917 was for a renewed Franco-British offensive on the Somme. But German withdrawal to the new *Siegfried stellung* from mid-February (known to the Allies as the Hindenburg line) pre-empted this. The British and French were caught by surprise and were unable to exploit in pursuit, particularly because of skilful German use of sabotage, booby traps, and delaying forces. The withdrawal was an acknowledgement that the old defences were no longer tenable, and giving up ground which had cost so much blood was painful for the Germans and cheering for the Allies. But at the same time the skill of the withdrawal and the revelation of the new stronger defences were a reminder that offensives in the west were difficult to bring to a decisive conclusion. The German army also gained benefits in shortening its line, freeing reserves that could be deployed to block the inevitable spring offensive.

The withdrawal clearly marked a strategic shift in the west. The loss of the great Noyon salient meant that the immediate threat to Paris had been lifted and raised the question of how the Germans could bring the war to a victorious conclusion. In response to enquiries from President Wilson, Bethmann-Hollweg had indicated that Germany was willing to negotiate peace. This public response was disingenuous; privately the German military leadership had set minimum terms for a peace in early November 1916 that included substantial territorial expansion in the east, a client Kingdom of Poland, a continued occupation of and economic union with Belgium, and the annexation of the Belgian Congo. Belgian 'independence' would be restored only with the payment of a substantial financial indemnity by Britain. As these terms were clearly unattainable without a clear victory, the war would need to be continued to that end. German strategy was being driven towards a single all-or-nothing point. Only unrestricted submarine warfare would force Britain to concede defeat. The German Admiralty produced a memorandum on 22 December

1916 identifying Britain's wheat supply as its key vulnerability. In October and November submarine 'cruiser' warfare had succeeded in sinking 400,000 tons of shipping per month. The Admiralty argued that this figure could be increased by at least 50 per cent if restrictions were removed: sinkings of 600,000 tons per month would have a cumulative impact on British import capacity such that its people would be facing starvation by August 1917, before the domestic harvest was ready.

Almost every part of the Admiralty paper was based on circular reasoning: it was imperative that the U-boats defeat Britain before August and therefore the calculations were designed to demonstrate that this would happen. Assumptions about the current state of British food supply, the tonnage required to transport grain, ship-building capability, the impact of convoying, and British organizational capabilities and morale were all based on justifying the policy. Helfferich's cogent objections to unrestricted submarine warfare were not so much refuted as evaded. Above all the policy required that victory be attained before the inevitable intervention of the United States proved decisive.

On 8 January 1917, as the German forces prepared to withdraw on the Somme, a high command conference formally endorsed the policy of all-out U-boat warfare. With this Germany embarked on a policy leading to certain defeat. The repeated American warnings that such a course must lead to war with the USA were fully understood by those who took the decisions, although the consequences were not. It is tempting to see this decision as irrational, driven by a 'cultural' tendency to pursue the total destruction of the enemy which had become rooted in the thinking of the German military, a maximization of brutality and violence for its own sake. But it is perhaps more convincing to see this decision in terms of 'bounded rationality', a willingness to be convinced that there was a simple unconventional solution to winning a war that had come to appear almost unwinnable by conventional means, and a solution which allowed an exaggerated assessment of a genuinely effective military weapon to take root. (The British infatuation with strategic bombing of Germany from 1940 onwards is a strikingly parallel case.)

At the moment the German high command prepared to unleash hunger as a decisive weapon against the British, hunger demonstrated its capacity to bring a mighty empire to its knees when combined with the right political circumstances. The food supply for Russian cities had become ever more precarious. This was not because of a disastrous fall in agricultural output: there was a fall in output which might have been in the order of 10 million tons of grain in 1916 compared with pre-war, but the end of grain exports meant that a similar amount of food remained in Russia. To a large extent this was an extraordinary achievement of the peasant women who kept up production despite the loss of horses to the military, and developed new skills in farm management. The problem was that food wasn't consistently reaching the cities. The requirements of military transportation meant that there was little or no spare capacity to shift civilian goods. The rail network was further handicapped by a general shortage of coal: although coal production had actually increased, much of it had been absorbed by the expansion of war industry. Perhaps most fatally of all, the production of rolling stock fell during 1916 as more and more resources were shifted to armaments. Peasant households also concluded that the difficulties of bringing food to market and the lack of consumer goods to buy made it more sensible to keep food at home and to use cereals to boost the consumption of meat and illegal vodka. In Petrograd the special council for food supply had concluded in 1915 that the city required 12,150 wagonloads of food per month. By January 1917 the arrivals were 6,556. Rumours of increased rationing meant that even the food that arrived was being hoarded by speculators.

With prophetic precision a Russian secret police report in January 1917 stated that the women lining up for food on the streets of Russian cities, worn out by the suffering of seeing their children hungry and sick, had become more dangerous to the Tsarist regime than the opposition in the Duma, and that the slightest spark could ignite a conflagration of protests. The spark was a strike at the Putilov munitions works on 7 March 1917 and the decision of the management to fire the strikers. The next day was International Women's Day. Tens of thousands of protestors, predominantly women, took to the streets. Amongst the slogans shouted were 'Down with the German Woman, down with Protopov, down with the war'. By 10 March every industrial enterprise in Petrograd had been closed down and the government was losing control. Mikhail Rodzianko, Chairman of the Duma, sent a telegram to the Tsar begging him to reassert control, but the order to the garrison to impose martial law on 11 March backfired as 60,000 troops refused to obey orders, including the elite Preobrazhensky Regiment. In large part the garrison troops of Petrograd had lost sympathy with the regime and they were unwilling to use violence against the women of the city, many of whom had relationships with the soldiers.

Following a model from the events of 1905, the Petrograd strikers had formed a 'soviet', a council of workers to advance their demands. Other cities quickly followed suit. When the Tsar abdicated on 15 March 1917, power apparently fell into the hands of the Duma, which proclaimed itself a Provisional Government. But in practice from the start there was a situation of 'dual power', with the soviets claiming greater legitimacy as representatives of the people.

The fall of the Tsar helped Wilson come to a decision about American policy. The new Provisional Government in Russia could be presented as a suitable democratic ally for the American Republic and did not carry the baggage of hostility the old regime had suffered from with immigrant groups in the USA, particularly Jews who had fled its anti-Semitic discrimination. Nevertheless there was still a substantial component of public opinion hostile to involvement in a European war. Then the German government unwittingly assisted Wilson in expanding support for war. Once the decision to launch unrestricted submarine warfare had been taken, with the resulting American hostility, the new German Foreign Secretary, Arthur Zimmermann, undertook a bold move to try to distract the USA from intervention in Europe. On 16 January 1917 he sent a cable to the German ambassador in Mexico, offering an alliance to the Mexican government which would return Texas, New Mexico, and Arizona to Mexico, and suggested a wider alliance against the United States to incorporate Japan (which was currently at war with Germany!). This bizarre geopolitics seemed plausible to German diplomats given that tensions between the USA and Mexico were high as a result of an American cross-border incursion hunting the revolutionary leader Pancho Villa, whose forces had attacked the US frontier in 1916. It was also guaranteed to infuriate public opinion in the south-west and west of the USA, areas that had been generally indifferent to the European conflict. The telegram was intercepted and decoded by Room 40 of the British Admiralty. The message was then handed over to the US government.

The British faked a cover story that the telegram had been stolen by a spy in Mexico City in order to prevent the Germans from knowing that their codes had been broken (although trusted figures in Washington were allowed to know the truth). The US government in turn released the story to the press at the start of March. Determined isolationists claimed that the story had been faked by British propagandists, but Zimmermann, already convinced that American belligerency was inevitable, openly admitted that he had sent the message on 3 March and confirmed that the transcript was accurate on 27 March. The message was a clear and cold-blooded act of war, sent to a neighbour of the United States whilst Wilson was still actively working for a 'peace without victory'.

Wilson spent March 1917 in despair. He stated in an interview that war would inevitably lead to a triumph of illiberalism at home, that once the people were led into war they would forget there had ever been such a thing as tolerance and that freedom would be sacrificed. American involvement would end the hope of a war without victors and it would end with a dictated peace imposed on Germany. But he felt there was no choice. On 2 April he delivered a message to Congress calling for war against Germany. Both Houses voted for war by substantial majorities, the opponents coming exclusively from the west and midwest.

The United States had been drawn into the war in defence of its rights as a neutral. In practical terms this primarily meant the right to do business with the Entente powers, a trade making a lot of money for a lot of American citizens. The decision has often been presented as either idealistic or cynically materialistic. It is a false dichotomy. The populist and isolationist argument that the USA had been manipulated into a war that was none of its business by an unholy combination of 'east coast elites' and British propaganda was to a large extent a propaganda construct reflecting long-standing ethnic and sectional hostilities. Anglophilia and anti-Germanism did exist at the highest level of American politics and business and there was a fairly widespread sentiment that believed there was a community of ideals and interests between the great 'English-speaking' powers. There was also some sentimental attachment to the 'sister Republic' of France. But there was also no shortage of Anglophobia in American public life. There was abundant German business influence in the country, particularly in the newly prosperous midwest, and plenty of reflexive isolationism in the press. With anti-war figures as varied and prominent as the populist politician William Jennings Bryan, the automobile manufacturer Henry Ford, the social reformer Jane Addams, and the newspaper proprietor William Randolph Hearst, the case against American involvement got a fair hearing. German actions spoke much louder than British propaganda; the *Lusitania* sinking and the acts of terrorism on American soil, such as the bombing of Black Tom, needed little exaggerating (although exaggerated they were).

Americans banks had bet heavily on the victory of Britain and its Allies but these investments in loans and bonds represented a decision taken on sound economic grounds of good returns at manageable risk much more than on sentiment. British credit-worthiness remained strong at the end of 1916. The decision of the US Federal Reserve to warn against Allied loans has been generally misinterpreted as an economic judgement of Entente bankruptcy. In fact it was a *political* measure designed to put pressure on the Entente powers to accept Wilson's proposed mediation because it was felt that they were a bit too confident of the inevitability of their victory to be willing to compromise. If the USA had not entered the war it is likely that the position would have been abandoned because it was in danger of throwing the USA into recession. Indeed the Federal Reserve's action had already caused a serious run on Wall Street.

America did experience something resembling war enthusiasm in the spring of 1917, but it was also subject to intense domestic propaganda and ferocious censorship. The Committee of Public Information was created under the chairmanship of George Creel on 13 April. It used both the techniques of commercial advertising and mass mobilization to build support for the war. Thousands of 'four-minute men' gave millions of short addresses at public meetings and hundreds of propaganda films were distributed. Opposing views were suppressed. A film by the German-American Robert Goldstein entitled the *Spirit of '76* was released in May 1917. It depicted British atrocities during the American Revolution (some of them quite imaginative: there was a scene where George III punches Benjamin Franklin) in a deliberate attempt to counter anti-German atrocity propaganda. The film was quickly banned and Goldstein sentenced to ten years' imprisonment under the new Espionage Act. Despite this effort many Americans remained detached from the war. Conscription, introduced immediately, was widely unpopular. Many poor southerners, both black and white, evaded the draft.

As the USA entered the war, Nivelle's plans for a decisive battle in the west were coming under increasing attack from his subordinates. Pétain in particular stated bluntly that the bombardment in depth which had succeeded at Verdun would fail if attempted on a broad front, telling the new French Premier Painlevé that it would be like pouring the waters of Lake Geneva on to the Sahara. On 3 April a high-level meeting of the military and civilian leadership saw Painlevé arguing that the events in Russia and the American declaration of war had removed the need for an offensive. Nivelle in response claimed that he could attain victory within forty-eight hours, that American help was months if not years away, and that it was imperative to attack before Russia and perhaps Italy were forced out of the war. His final argument was that having gained control of the British forces in France, delaying the offensive would see this arrangement collapse. A second meeting at Compiègne on 6 April saw a wider participation of politicians including deputies and the President as well as the army group commanders. Faced with an evident lack of confidence, Nivelle offered to resign. Pétain, his bluff called, urged Nivelle to stay on for the sake of the country. Poincaré summarized the meeting by concluding that if the attack did not attain decisive results quickly it would be called off. There would be no repeat of the Somme.

The weather and minor changes in plan as well as these strategic debates led to delays in the French offensive, which was pushed back about a week. The result was that the British attack at Arras would become a preliminary diversion to draw away German reserves. The principal attack would be conducted by the 3rd Army of Edmund Allenby, known without much affection as 'the Bull'. In addition, the Canadian Corps, part of 1st Army, would assault the German positions at Vimy Ridge that provided excellent observation for miles around. The ridge had a bad reputation, having been the scene of fierce fighting and huge casualties in 1915. The Canadians, who had been positioned near Arras since November, prepared meticulously for the assault.

This attack was an example of how offensive tactics had evolved since 1915 and also of the wealth of new resources made available by full industrial mobilization. Vimy was an artillery battle. A detailed counter-battery plan was developed using aerial reconnaissance, radio interception, and sound ranging (the use of timed triangulated notes of the sound of enemy guns firing to identify the location) to identify and destroy German artillery. German front-line positions were subject to a week of intensive fire. On the day of the attack a creeping barrage by field guns covered the infantry advance. One particularly useful new weapon was the 106 instantaneous fuse which allowed high-explosive shells to destroy barbed wire much more effectively than shrapnel. Guns and howitzers were supplemented by mortars and by machine guns concentrated to provide 'indirect' barrage fire which would prevent movement behind the German front-line trenches.

The infantry, who were deployed safely in cellars and tunnels prior to the attack, had extensively practised on replicas of their targets prior to the battle. The key weapons for attacking infantry were now hand grenades, rifle grenades, and the Lewis light machine gun. Small groups moved forward in rushes whilst providing each other with covering suppressive fire. 'Mopping-up' units were detailed to seek out forces that had hidden and allowed the advance to roll over them, a German tactic used on the Somme.

Vimy Ridge became a national legend. The claim was that the Canadians had succeeded where the French and British had failed. This has tended to overshadow the fact that the first day of the battle of Arras saw quite widespread British success. The Canadians were not the only units to have learned lessons on the Somme, and Arras demonstrated what would become increasingly clear in 1917, that a properly prepared attack was now capable of breaking into the front lines of an enemy position if sufficiently well supported. But as Arras would also demonstrate, if the defensive lines were sufficiently deep and if the enemy was able to bring up reserves, this did not translate into the prospect of a breakthrough, and casualties would quickly mount in a process of diminishing returns.

Furthermore not every battle was well planned or well supported. An attack by the British and Australians commanded by Hubert Gough at

Bullecourt on 11 April, which was launched without proper artillery support (Gough relied on surprise and tanks that broke down), produced huge casualties for no result. One thousand Australians were taken prisoner and 78 per cent of the 4th Infantry Brigade became casualties. A second attack in May took the village but again at huge cost. Australian suspicions of the British as a whole, Gough in particular, became intense.

The British needed air superiority in order to make effective use of their artillery, but the Germans made the Royal Flying Corps pay a heavy price. The German Albatros fighter aircraft were superior to their opponents and German organization for air fighting was better during 'Bloody April'. British casualties were severe and the flying ace Manfred von Richthofen, 'the Red Baron', became a German national hero. For the British, April was the cruellest month to date, and May no better. The ground fighting at Arras was on a daily basis even more bloody than the Somme. Allenby, who had earlier clashed openly with Haig on several occasions, was transferred from the Western Front in June to take command of the Egyptian Expeditionary Force.

The British war against Turkey had achieved mixed results in the winter and spring. In Mesopotamia a largely Indian army under the command of Frederick Maude advanced up the Tigris river beginning in December, reaching Kut in February where the Turks were pushed from their defensive positions. It was a systematic operation with great stress on secure river lines of logistic support. On 9 March, Baghdad was captured leading to conflict between the authorities in India, who wanted to assert control over Mesopotamia, and the Colonial Office in London. London prevailed and on 19 March, Maude released a proclamation to the Arab inhabitants stating that the British had come 'not as conquerors or enemies but as liberators'.

The courting of Arab opinion reflected the growing impact of the Hashemite rebellion. The capture of Al Wajh on the Red Sea by a joint Royal Navy-Arab force had allowed the build-up of supplies to the Arab forces, and T. E. Lawrence, an Oxford archaeologist turned guerrilla fighter, succeeded in directing the rebellion towards attacking targets in support of British operations. From March 1917 the main focus was on destroying the Hejaz railroad tying up Turkish forces in a futile attempt to defend it, and this was followed up by a bold strike in July 1917 which captured the port of Aqaba at the top of the Sinai peninsula.

But these operations behind Turkish lines had not prevented a frustrating and bloody stalemate from developing on the Egyptian frontier at Gaza. In December the forces commanded by Archibald Murray had won a victory beyond the Egyptian border at Magdabha, but in two battles in March and April the Egyptian Expeditionary Force suffered bloody repulses. When after the first the British claimed a victory, the Turks responded by dropping pamphlets from an aeroplane stating, 'You beat us in communiques, but we beat you at Gaza'. On 17 April the second battle of Gaza was launched using both tanks and poison gas against the Turks. It was an even greater disaster—the attackers suffering nearly 6,000 casualties, half of them from the 54th East Anglian Division, which sustained losses comparable to units on the Western Front. In these circumstances it seemed logical to replace Murray with a Western Front general who might be able to make the losses count for something. After touring the front, Allenby requested reinforcements before resuming the attack in the autumn, and three divisions would be transferred to Sinai from Salonika in the course of the late summer.

One bright spot for the British was the end of the campaign against the Senussi, which had diverted forces away from the struggle against the Turks. In 1916 the campaign had spilled over from Libya into Sudan and Egypt west of the Nile Delta, but gradually through the use of armoured cars, the Camel Corps, and imperial forces including South Africans and New Zealanders, the British regained control, recapturing the key oasis of Siwa in February 1917. The Senussi leader Sayiid Ahmed stepped down and went into exile, to be replaced by his cousin Sayiid Muhammed Idris who negotiated a peace with first the British and then the Italians. By early 1917 German and Turkish hopes of inspiring global *jihad* were fading.

On 11 July 1916 protests over the extension of conscription in the central Asian city of Tashkent were brutally suppressed by Russian forces. This triggered a massive uprising across most of central Asia by what the Russians called the *Basmachi* (bandit) movement. Although the Germans and the Turks had encouraged uprisings in this area with Pan-Turanian and jihadist propaganda, the main cause was the economic upheaval caused by the Russian government's encouragement of cotton farming and the tension between the indigenous population and Russian settlers. The latter, armed and encouraged by the authorities, took the lead in a savage counter-insurgency campaign, particularly brutal around the area of Khiva, and which it is claimed may have led to a million deaths in the region.

The French faced an uprising of the Touareg on the borders of southern Algeria and Niger, an uprising which got support from the Turks and Germans as well as the Senussi. The town of Agades was besieged and the French appealed to the British for help. On 3 March a detachment of the Nigerian regiment broke the siege and in effect this rebellion. Simultaneously another rebellion broke out in the north-east of the country around Constantine. This area had been particularly unenthusiastic about the war and when in September 1916 the French intensified conscription for both military and labour service, elements of the population rebelled. The French response was savage and disproportionate: 14,000 troops, many of them Senegalese, were used to collect a few thousand conscripts, women were raped and villages burnt, resulting in a famine in 1917. But overall French North Africa proved a crucial pool of manpower. Algeria, Morocco, and Tunisia recruited 273,000 soldiers and 142,000 labourers during the war. These forces along with large numbers from sub-Saharan Africa would be utilized in full during the offensives of 1917.

At dawn on 16 April the French army attacked the German positions on the Chemin des Dames. The initial attack broke through the German front line but then ran into the German defences in depth based on machine gun posts on the reverse slopes. The first French deployment of tanks went catastrophically wrong because a design flaw meant that many caught fire when their fuel tanks were penetrated by bullets. The 'Nivelle offensive' was not a disaster by the standards of some earlier operations. The 6th Army had made one of the largest advances that the French Army had made to date and nearly 30,000 German prisoners had been taken. The German high command suffered some nervous moments. But the results had come at too high a price. In little over a week the French had lost nearly 140,000 casualties including 30,000 dead. These were losses not dissimilar to the British during the first week on the Somme and this was the worst rate of loss for the French in such a short time since 1914. For an army and nation that had been convinced that Nivelle held the key to imminent victory it was too much. On 15 May Nivelle was replaced by Pétain, who had earlier been promoted to Chief of the General Staff (he was in turn replaced in that role by Foch). Pétain inherited a crisis in French morale.

Isolated incidents of disobedience had occurred before 15 May amongst regiments involved in the attacks, but from 16 May until the end of the month this increased to forty-six incidents, some involving whole divisions. Not all of these divisions had been directly involved in the offensive and the protests became more severe, including calls for an end to the war. By the start of June there were widespread threats and even incidences of violence towards officers.

Remarkably the Germans do not appear to have been aware of the parlous state of the French army. Even French prisoners seem to have withheld the news from their captors. Everywhere the lines were held. The fundamental willingness to hold on was largely maintained. The demands of men in the 36th Infantry Regiment in June were:

1. Peace and the right to leave, which is in arrears.
2. No more butchery, we want liberty.
3. On food, which is shameful.
4. No more injustice.
5. We don't want blacks in Paris and other regions mistreating our wives.
6. We need peace to feed our wives and to be able to give bread to the women and orphans.
   We demand peace, peace.[1]

French soldiers were asserting their rights as citizens but also as male heads of household. A central tension was emerging in all combatant nations: the war was being justified in all cases as a defence of the family, but the men at the front were unable to directly guarantee the well-being of their dependents. Peasant families were particularly aware that another harvest season was approaching in which the young men would be

[1] Cited in Leonard Smith, *Between Mutiny and Obedience* (Princeton, NJ, 1994), p. 188.

absent, and that once again their women and children were going to face backbreaking labour in the fields.

France in the spring of 1917 had seen a massive bout of inflation. In Paris in April and May coal had nearly doubled in price, fresh vegetables had more than doubled, and the price of meat increased by more than 50 per cent. The result was a spate of strikes, largely involving women workers in non-war-related industries. In June there was a walkout by 5,000 female munition workers in Toulouse. Postal censorship indicates a real fear of revolution on the part of the middle classes and intense complaints about profiteering from almost everyone. In Bordeaux the postal inspectors noted a significant increase in references to peace. Some 47 per cent of these were vague, 35 per cent specified peace through victory, 13 per cent favoured compromise peace, and 5 per cent 'peace at any price'. But the crisis was short lived and by July a much higher proportion (47 per cent) were specifying peace through victory.

In 1916 Henri Barbusse had published his novel *Le Feu* (usually translated into English as *Under Fire*, it was in fact a slang term for 'the front'). Subtitled 'The Story of a Squad' and based on the author's experiences at the front in 1915, it was a work in the realist tradition of Émile Zola intended primarily to make civilians aware of the sufferings of the men facing the enemy. In this it was more than successful with both the critics and the public, becoming a bestseller and winning the Prix Goncourt. Some of the women readers who wrote to the author felt that they had vicariously lived in the trenches through his prose. Barbusse at this point was very much a socialist of the Second International. In the book he praised the German socialist Karl Liebknecht as a hero who had protested against the war and been imprisoned for it, but he also seems to have believed at this point that the French were fighting a legitimate war of defence. Barbusse condemned the profiteers and the shirkers who were betraying those at the front, and the novel ends with an apocalyptic vision of peace, but nevertheless the book could not be described as in any way defeatist.

The German high command had realized the uses of defeatism. Making contact with Lenin in Zurich, they arranged a 'sealed train' to carry him across Germany so that he would be able to agitate for Russian withdrawal from the war. On arriving in Petrograd in April 1917, Lenin would once again reiterate his call for an immediate uprising against his own government, but revolutionary defeatism was not particularly popular even amongst Russian socialists, and some Bolsheviks also had doubts at this point.

If defeatism was beyond the pale, calls for a negotiated peace did become more common in the spring. Amongst those who read Barbusse was the English officer and poet Siegfried Sassoon. In July 1917 Sassoon wrote a letter to *The Times* formally protesting that the war was being prolonged for no good purpose. Faced with a court martial, Sassoon was persuaded by his friend and fellow poet Robert Graves to accept treatment for 'shell shock' at Craiglockhart hospital in Scotland. From there Sassoon would pen some of his bitter poetic satires on the war, as a form of therapy. He also met and encouraged a genuinely shell-shocked officer, Wilfred Owen, to work on his own poetry.

Sassoon and Owen were formally very much in the tradition of pre-war British poetry; real artistic innovation was more pronounced in France. On 18 May 1917 in Paris the modernist pioneers *Ballets Russes* premiered a co-production by the musician Éric Satie and the dramatist Jean Cocteau entitled *Parade*. The set designs were by Pablo Picasso and the programme note by the poet Guillaume Apollinaire, who was on leave from the front having been wounded. For the production Apollinaire coined the term 'Surrealist'. The parade was not a military parade but a circus parade, yet the involvement of a Russian company dancing to American ragtime music had obvious resonance in the spring of 1917 as a commentary on revolutionary times. As had been anticipated the production aroused critical hostility, and when Satie replied to one critic with a public obscenity he was hauled in front of the courts for slander. His opponents launched a withering attack on the avant-garde in general as 'Boche' and Satie found himself fined and imprisoned. The early summer of 1917 was not a good time to be accused of lack of patriotism in France.

The fall of Nivelle freed Haig to do what he had long wanted: make an attempt to break the German flank and win through to the open country of Flanders, capturing the railway junction at Douai where the British cavalry could roll up the German line. Initially this would require the capture of Messines Ridge, a feature that dominated the British position at Ypres. The commander of the British 2nd Army, Herbert Plummer, had been preparing to attack this position for almost two years. Tunnelling units, drawn from miners recruited all across the British Empire, had planted nineteen mines containing almost a million pounds of explosive under the ridge. Plummer's army conducted a systematic week-long barrage on the German positions and then at 3 a.m. on 7 June detonated the mines. The British, Australian, and New Zealand infantry then advanced on the devastated German positions, supported by a massive and effective creeping barrage and well-planned counter-battery fire. The attackers took 10,000 stunned prisoners and perhaps as many German soldiers were killed by the mine explosions. The BEF made a limited gain but there was then a pause before the offensive could be resumed. Haig wanted the main attack to be spearheaded not by the methodical Plummer, but by the 'thrusting' Gough.

One interesting feature of the battle was the deployment alongside each other of the 16th (Nationalist) Irish Division and the 36th (Ulster) Division. When the brother of the Irish Nationalist leader John Redmond was killed, his burial was attended by men from both communities. The unity this symbolized gave some hope that the forthcoming Irish Constitutional Convention might succeed in overcoming the bitter legacy of the Easter Uprising in 1916.

The other Irish Division, the 10th, was serving at Salonika with the British forces which had attacked near Lake Doiran in May and had been stopped dead by a ferocious Bulgarian resistance. An offensive by French colonial, Italian, and Russian troops in the Cerna bend had also been repulsed by Bulgarian troops supported by a few German regiments, and the French forces which had managed to gain a toehold on the mountain at Monastir were wiped out by a counter-attack on 18 May. The combined force was forced back on to the defensive for the summer and found that its main enemy was now the mosquito. The armies on this front owed the majority of their losses to malaria. One Irish medical orderly wrote in his diary, 'What a useless sacrifice of poor men's lives'. Similar sentiments were emerging in all the armies.

In London, Lloyd George was sceptical about the prospects for operations in Flanders and sought to transfer artillery to support the Italians. At the time it was hard to comprehend why exactly the Italian front was any more promising than the western one. The 10th battle of the Isonzo fought in May showed the usual butcher's bill: 150,000 Italian casualties including 36,000 dead. The Italian general the Duca D'Aosta privately told Colonel Gatti that the war at this rate could not be won for ten years and that the people would rebel before this happened. In the last week of June the Italian parliament debated the conduct of the war in closed session. Fortunato Marazzi, a Liberal supporter of the war and a divisional commander, mounted a blistering attack on Cadorna's command, but the government survived a confidence vote.

The continued pressure on the Austrians from the south served to assist the Russians, at least in theory, by tying down the best Hapsburg troops. The hope was that the Russian people, freed of their unpopular and incompetent leaders, would return reinvigorated to the battle. On 16 June the Russians attacked in what became known as the 'Kerensky offensive' after the new Minister of War. Commanded by Brusilov and with ample supplies of weapons and ammunition for the first time, facing the weakened forces of the Central powers, the Russian offensive in 1917 appeared to have every chance of success. For the first few days it made good progress. Then with startling speed the Russian army fell apart. The generals blamed Bolshevik agitators and the loss of the deterrent of the death penalty which had been abolished by Provisional Government. Trotsky would claim that the army 'voted with its feet' against the continuation of the war. Some would suggest that peasant soldiers returned home to participate in the illegal land seizures that marked the summer of 1917. A large part of the explanation may be that the heavy casualties of 1915 and 1916 had stripped the Army of its more respected junior leadership and that the effectiveness of the procedures to round up deserters and return them to the front in 1916 may have increased the proportion of those in the ranks who were vehemently hostile to the army and the war, as may the presence of men who had been radicalized as civilians before their call-up. One initiative of the Provisional Government backfired badly. The Women's Battalions of Death had been raised as a revolutionary initiative at the behest of Kerensky by Maria Bochkareva, who had initially enlisted in the Russian army in 1914 with the permission of the Tsar in order to escape from an abusive husband. Although other nations had discussed enlisting women and several had formed non-combatant corps, Russia was the only one to form a female combat unit. The hope was that these patriotic women would inspire the men who served with them. Unfortunately the peasant soldiers tended to see the women's battalions as a mark of disgrace and desperation on the part of the regime, and their presence was dispiriting and unpopular. One of the few units to avoid demoralization was the Czechoslovak Infantry Brigade, which attacked on 2 July at Zborov and for few casualties took 3,000 prisoners; but by this point the offensive had collapsed.

As with the French, dashed expectations when enemy defences hardened may have acted as the trigger, but the Russian mutiny was far more serious and complete. Failure at the front helped trigger an uprising in Petrograd known as the July Days. This rebellion was largely spontaneous; the Bolsheviks who under Lenin's leadership had called for such an uprising were caught by surprise, and their leadership was forced to flee to Finland when loyalist troops put down the uprising on 19 July. For the moment the Provisional Government had precariously retained some degree of control.

In Germany, July saw a political crisis reach its climax. Matthias Erzberger was an eloquent and ambitious leader of the centre left who had made his name as a critic of colonial policy. In these respects he was remarkably similar to Lloyd George, whom he also resembled in his patriotism, deviousness, and lust for life. Erzberger had played an important role in drawing up the annexationist September Programme and had been involved in intrigues against Falkenhayn. But Erzberger was not only a political leader of German Catholics. He was genuinely influenced by his religious belief, and the increasingly open call from the Vatican for a negotiated peace, transmitted via the papal nuncio in Bavaria and echoing the Hapsburg initiatives, helped persuade him to withdraw support from Bethmann-Hollweg. Ludendorff had also decided the Chancellor had to go, although for completely the opposite reasons, and this loss of support in the Reichstag allowed the high command to pressure the Kaiser into accepting Bethmann-Hollweg's resignation. Erzberger used the opportunity to engineer a Reichstag majority, consisting of the Catholic *Zentrum*, the Progressives, and the majority Social Democrats, to pass a resolution calling for peace without annexations or indemnities.

The Reichstag peace resolution reflected the fact that the majority of the German people felt the cause that had taken them to war in 1914, self-defence against the threat of Tsarist aggression, had now been achieved by the overthrow of the Russian regime. What most Germans did not realize was that the annexationist ambitions of some of their political and military elite had actually been fuelled by the developing Russian collapse. A rift was opening up within Germany which would have terrible long-term consequences.

Preceded by a week of massive artillery bombardment, the British attacked out of their positions in the Ypres salient on 31 July. Success would allow the possibility of linking up with an amphibious landing on the Belgian coast. There were two significant problems with this plan. The first was that it would involve attacking out of a salient which was commanded on three sides by German artillery observers on the low ridges; and the second was that the advance would need to be conducted through country with poor drainage. The former made movement to the front exceptionally difficult, particularly when the Germans unleashed a new weapon, 'mustard gas', a corrosive semi-liquid which blistered exposed skin and could linger for days in shell holes. The latter meant that when the heavy bombardment destroyed the drainage system, heavy rain could turn the battlefield into a huge swamp. This was precisely what happened at the start of the attack, entirely predictably for anyone who knew the average summer rainfall for Belgian Flanders.

The Germans had adjusted their defences to the terrain. Unable to build deep dugouts in this swampy area, they relied instead on massive numbers of concrete 'pill-boxes' which created a web of interlocking machine gun posts. These were supported by powerful forces intended to counter-attack when the enemy had advanced beyond their supporting artillery and were exhausted. As a result on 31 July the attacking Allied forces suffered some 30,000 casualties for a gain of 3 kilometres at most. Amongst those killed were two great poets at the height of their powers. Francis Ledwidge was an Irish nationalist volunteer who had already served at Gallipoli and Salonika. He was blown to pieces by a shell. The Welsh poet Hedd Wyn (Ellis Evans) had by contrast only been conscripted into the army in March 1917; he died of wounds a few hours after being struck by a shell cap in the abdomen, never knowing that he had triumphed at the 1917 Eisteddfod. Ledwidge had provided an epitaph:

> Where are the faces laughing in the glow
> Of morning years, the lost ones, scattered wide.
> Give me your hand, O brother let us go
> Crying about the dark for those who died.

The defenders also paid a high price; it was during this battle that Erich Maria Remarque was wounded by shrapnel after a month at the front. He would spend much of the rest of the war in hospital.

As the third year of the war came to an end the Russian army was disintegrating and the French army was paralysed. The Hapsburg Empire was tottering and German public opinion had turned from the hope of victory. The British government was alarmed by huge losses of merchant shipping and rising industrial militancy. Ordinary Italians, never enthusiastic about the war, were becoming openly mutinous, and Turkey was nearing the end of its resources. The various European combatants had strained every sinew to destroy their enemies and it was starting to look as if they had all succeeded. The United States had entered the war, with Wilson fearful for the domestic consequences yet hopeful for the international ones. But American power would take time to exercise and by the time it gathered strength the world might be beyond saving.

CHAPTER 4
THE FOURTH YEAR 1917–1918: REVOLUTIONARY WAR

On 1 August 1917, in the name of the 'common father who looks upon all of his children with equal affection', Pope Benedict XV issued his seven-point plan for peace, in which the 'material force' of war would be replaced by the 'moral force' of law. The Pope's appeal to the combatants could be dismissed as a desperate attempt to rescue the Vatican's traditional protectors in Vienna and to pre-empt Europe's descent into revolution. But this would be unfair to Benedict who was genuinely appalled at the loss of life and the disgrace of Christians slaughtering each other. The Pope's appeal largely fell on deaf ears. Where his plan was heeded this was usually due to it coinciding with other imperatives; for example, the opposition of the Catholic clergy to conscription in Canada and Australia was driven as much by ethnic resistance, *Québécois* and Irish, as by universal religion.

The strongest instance of popular religious resistance to war was in Portugal, which had entered the conflict in 1916 due to German interference in its African colonies. After Lúcia Santos and her two young cousins began seeing visions of the Virgin Mary in Fátima in May 1917, the mayor of the town, disturbed by what he perceived as the anti-government tone of the growing crowds, imprisoned the children in August and tried to get them to admit that they were lying. They were soon released but the visions continued. In October a crowd estimated at 70,000 allegedly witnessed the final miracle of the sun dancing. Certainly in the wake of Benedict's call for peace it is easy to suggest that this crowd was gathered in opposition to an anti-clerical government pursuing an unpopular war.

The visions were in all likelihood prompted by Papal actions. Benedict had added an invocation to the Virgin as 'queen of peace' to the litany of Loreto and a week before the first vision had made a direct appeal to Mary to help end the war. It has also been suggested that the imminent call-up of Lucia's brother might have helped to crystallize her desire for peace. At a later date Lúcia would claim that Mary had specifically alluded to events in Russia as part of her prophetic message; it is certainly possible that rumours of the revolution helped provide an apocalyptic framework for the miracle.

At much the same time as the visions at Fátima another teenage girl, Claire Ferchaud, was attempting to enlist the 'sacred heart of Jesus' to the cause of France. The attempt to add this symbol of Catholic devotion to the tricolour flag of the French Republic climaxed in the summer of 1917, only to founder on opposition from anti-clerical politicians and from the Vatican, which was aghast at the idea that any nation could appropriate the image.

Like the events at Fátima, socialist opposition to war had also been galvanized by the Russian revolution. Over the course of the spring Scandinavian socialists tried to organize a new conference in response to the Petrograd Soviet resolution, a task that gained further urgency with the Reichstag resolution. Initially the British government had been willing to allow socialist representatives, including the Labour cabinet minister Arthur Henderson, to travel to this conference in Stockholm in accordance with an overwhelming vote at the Labour conference in August. But at an Entente conference the French and particularly the Italian governments had proved fiercely opposed to such a gathering, with both nations worried about opening any crack for the call for a compromise peace on their fragile home fronts. The crucial intervention was from the Americans who also opposed the issuing of passports to socialist delegates. In response to this travel ban the socialist parties of the Entente nations issued a statement on 9 September condemning their governments and particularly Wilson, who had disappointed them.

Through the summer of 1917 Britain had experienced a wave of industrial action, worse in fact than in any combatant nation except Russia. But although occasionally those involved endorsed the call for a negotiated peace, most of the discontent was due to falling living standards for the skilled and semi-skilled working class and increasing frustration with the constraints on both individual and collective wage bargaining. In some areas government restrictions on alcohol consumption were blamed. The Lloyd George administration tended to encourage employers to settle in a generous fashion even if this was pushing up the wage bill for the war. It is significant that by the autumn, subscriptions to the government war loans tended to be high in working-class areas with a few exceptions. This was less true in France, where subscriptions to the third war loan in November 1917 showed a distinct decline in the armaments centre of Le Creusot. Nervousness about popular morale led to the arrest in October and November of several prominent women members of the teachers' union who had supported peace negotiations.

In Germany the socialists had split in April between moderates and radicals. The mainstream party had backed the call for a negotiated peace but still were prepared to support national defence whereas the radicals, led by Karl Liebknecht and Rosa Luxemburg, were calling for immediate action to stop the war. German conservatives responded to what they saw as the threat of socialist subversion with a new propaganda campaign. Admiral Tirpitz sponsored the creation of the *Vaterlandspartei* in September 1917. Backed by secret funding from the army high command, it rapidly drew together a vast amount of support from the nationalist-minded middle class for a 'victorious peace'. The military counterpoint to this was a campaign of patriotic instruction designed to foil the potential threat of subversion amongst the soldiers themselves. In part this was a response to fears that as the war wound down in the east, fraternization between German soldiers and Russians 'infected' with revolutionary ideas would become more common. But it was also a reaction to increasing signs of strain on the veterans of the Western Front.

The British decision to push on in Flanders, in what was becoming known as the battle of Passchendaele, was justified by the need to allow the French to recover from the summer mutinies and by Admiralty pressure to capture the Belgian coastal ports to relieve the U-boat threat. Neither excuse is convincing. The French had recovered sufficiently by August to mount a successful limited attack to recapture Mort Homme at Verdun and a French army was participating in Flanders. The Belgian ports were of minor importance in the U-boat war and never came close to being taken.

Increasingly the main justification of Allied operations was that they were wearing out the Germans. The incessant bombardments did put a tremendous strain on the defenders. But the fighting damaged morale on both sides: intelligence reports informed the German commander Prince Rupprecht that British soldiers were not holding against German counter-attacks and that when they surrendered they complained bitterly about their commanders. This was the context in which occurred the one wartime 'mutiny' in the BEF. The riots at the Étaples military base began on 9 September and lasted for three days. To a large extent they were directed against the military police and training staff: exhausted front-line troops resented the lack of real rest and leisure time whilst out of the line.

The Salonika front remained stalled. Clemenceau, the radical politician and journalist, had mocked the forces there as the 'gardeners of Salonika' and German generals referred to it as their largest POW camp, a view that seriously underestimated the efforts of the 'guards', predominantly Bulgarian but now including forces from all the Central powers, in keeping their enemies caged. The presence of these massive military camps on the outskirts of the city of Thessaloniki would have a disastrous consequence when on 18 August a fire broke out in the city. Because most of the city's water had been diverted to supply the camps, fire-fighting was badly hampered and the old city was devastated, leaving more than a third of the population homeless.

In August and September 1917 the Romanians, supported by some Russian forces and extensively reorganized by French military advisors, fought an epic struggle to maintain a hold on part of their country. Fighting against the Austro-Hungarian armies at the battles of the Oituz valley and then at the battle of Mărăşeşti, which became a 'Romanian Verdun', they managed to inflict heavy losses on their opponents, although at a cost of more than 50,000 casualties. Amongst the dead was Ecaterina Teodoroiu, who was killed in action on 3 September whilst serving as a 2nd Lieutenant and who became a national heroine. She had enlisted to avenge her brother killed in action in 1916.

At the start of September the Germans mounted an offensive at the other end of the Eastern Front, attacking the Latvian city of Riga. The assault was noteworthy for the coordination of artillery by Colonel Bruchmüller in such a way that map-registered fire without ranging shots was unleashed on the Russian positions, and for the use of stormtroop tactics of infiltration. The Russian 12th Army defending the city disintegrated under the attack, although only 9,000 prisoners were taken, in part because most Russian units simply ran away. This collapse of discipline helped to precipitate a wider crisis in the Russian state.

The Kornilov affair was a murky episode. General Kornilov had replaced Brusilov after the summer offensive and immediately demanded that he be given a free hand to restore discipline. A procurator of the Orthodox Church, Vladimir Lvov, visited Kornilov's headquarters in early August offering the general a series of options including a dictatorship led by Kerensky and a military dictatorship headed by Kornilov himself. Lvov claimed to be acting on Kerensky's behalf—a claim Kerensky would deny. Kornilov indicated his preference for a military dictatorship with himself at the head. Kerensky got wind of this decision and panicked. Kornilov was dismissed. In response Kornilov ordered his troops to march on the capital. Kerensky called on the soviets for support, providing them with arms and releasing Bolshevik prisoners from the July uprising. Faced by resistance from the soviets that paralysed movement on the railways, Kornilov surrendered and was imprisoned with other generals. It was a farce with serious consequences: the incapacity of the Provisional Government was starkly revealed and dual power began to transmute into 'soviet power'.

By contrast on the Italian front the summer offensive had come tantalizingly close to complete success. On 24 August the Italians had finally captured Mt. Santo. The conductor Arturo Toscanini improvised a concert on the summit to celebrate the victory. The British ambassador in Rome telegraphed the Prime Minister, Lloyd George, that the complete destruction of the Hapsburg Army seemed imminent. Lloyd George, increasingly concerned about Passchendaele, renewed pressure to transfer artillery in support of the Italians. But by early September the attack had been halted at San Gabriele, which turned into another bloodbath for both sides. The Italians suffered 166,000 losses in this 11th battle of the Isonzo; their opponents lost 140,000 in a daily casualty rate higher than Passchendaele. The defenders were now on their last legs. If the attack had been sustained there was nothing preventing a breakthrough to Trieste. But the Italians were also suffering from cumulative strain on the home front. Italian industrial development during the war had been impressive but had created the same kind of imbalance between the civilian and military economy that had produced the Russian revolution. Women protesting at food shortages in Turin on 22 August triggered a week of strikes that saw barricades on the streets. Rural Italy was equally alienated. The poor provision of separation allowances led to letters to the Prime Minister. One 'Maria Rosa' wrote after her allowance was stopped, 'I hope that you will assert my rights as my husband is asserting the rights of the nation.'

The British Prime Minister has been derided for his obsession with Italy in the summer of 1917, but a relatively small amount of Anglo-French support *might* have enabled a breakthrough in September. The Emperor Karl would never have given Trieste away to the hated Italians, but faced with an Italian capture of the city he might have accepted its loss. Vienna's withdrawal from the war might in turn have made Berlin's position untenable. None of this is certain; it may indeed have been little more than an evasion of the hard truths of the main battlefront in the west. In the event it was Germany that would make a small investment on the southern front and reap massive dividends.

The aftermath of the French military mutinies had led to upheaval in the French political establishment. The widespread conviction that the loyal army had been corrupted by agitators led to a search for defeatist elements. Paul Bolo was identified as a German agent charged with corrupting the press, and the Dutch exotic dancer Margaretha Zelle, better known by her stage name Mata Hari, was executed for espionage. Louis Malvy, a leading socialist proponent of peace by negotiation, was accused by Clemenceau of treason and forced to resign as a minister in August. He was arrested in November and Clemenceau's old enemy Joseph Callaux was arrested in turn in January 1918. The appointment of Clemenceau as Premier was the embodiment of a new and ferocious resolve. A supporter of Alfred Dreyfus in the affair which had split

France, a friend of Claude Monet and a hater of Germany, the 'Tiger' had criticized each wartime ministry in the name of patriotism. Now he had a chance to show his leadership.

Whilst the French political establishment was being purged, Pétain was working to restore the morale of the French army by military methods. At the end of August he ordered a limited objective attack at Mort Homme near Verdun, which was preceded by a bombardment of nearly 3 million artillery shells. The attack made a limited breakthrough and was then halted. On 24 October the French mounted another limited attack at Malmaison on the Chemin des Dames. This managed to seize most of the positions which had been disastrously attacked in April and did so for a fraction of the casualties.

Operations in Flanders were taking on a similar style. The main effort was taken away from Hubert Gough and entrusted instead to the methodical Plummer and his 2nd Army. In a series of set-piece attacks in September and early October, supported by massive artillery bombardments and aided by better weather, British and Australian forces edged forward and inflicted heavy casualties on the German defenders.

The air fighting above the battlefield saw the death of two notable aces. On 23 September Werner Voss, who had shot down forty-eight planes, was killed in an unbalanced fight against eight British opponents from an elite squadron, and on 25 September Georges Guynemer, who had fifty-three victories to his name, was killed in mysterious circumstances near Langemarck. Like the British ace Albert Ball, who had been killed back in May, these men were famous individualists, but the future of air fighting belonged to the hunting pack leaders, men like René Fonck, Edward Mannock, and above all Manfred von Richthofen.

In an attempt to divert British aircraft resources from the Flanders battle, the Germans had begun a systematic campaign of bombing against targets in southern England. Strategic bombing with large aircraft had been developed by all the combatant powers; the Russians had tried to launch raids as early as 1914 using a bomber built by Igor Sikorsky, a designer of genius. The Italians had begun to mount raids on Vienna in 1916 and the French had attacked cities in the Rhineland. But the German attacks on England were the first systematic and sustained air campaign. Starting with daylight raids in the summer they continued with night raids through to the early winter. The bombing aircraft being used were called 'Gotha', a name that proved deeply embarrassing to the British royal family who responded by changing their family name from 'Saxe-Coburg Gotha' to the unimpeachable 'Windsor'.

The bombing caused a certain amount of panic, and some of those who could afford to leave London moved away. Civilian misery was increased by lengthening queues for food. Shipping losses and the impact of convoying on port capacity had reduced the quantities of food imports, but shortages were perhaps more to do with panic purchasing than lack of supply. The strikes by workers in many industries during the summer had actually led to wage rises that fed demand. Indeed at the end of 1917 the best-paid working-class families were starting to outstrip the incomes of the lower middle classes.

Britain hadn't vanquished the U-boat threat by late 1917, but it had been contained. Convoying had significantly diminished the losses of shipping and had contributed to increased losses of U-boats, which were more easily found by escorting destroyers when U-boats were drawn to a convoy. In October the Germans lost twenty U-boats compared with only ten new ones commissioned. A massive mine-laying operation in the Straits of Dover forced the U-boats to go north around Scotland, limiting their range. Increased use of patrolling aircraft to spot and attack U-boats on their way through the North Sea reduced U-boat effectiveness, although only two were sunk by this method. But British shipping losses in the first half of the year had put serious pressure on imports, and although the United States was in the process of creating an enormous shipping industry almost from scratch (on 4 July 1918 the USA would launch ninety-five new merchant ships), this would not be available very soon. The most crucial element was making best use of the shipping available. The creation of the Allied Maritime Transport Council in November 1917 helped identify how to move key commodities most efficiently. There were also moves to increase domestic supply where possible. Britain reduced imports of timber, crucial for pit props in mining, by felling more trees at home, creating a Forestry Commission for the purpose.

Economizing shipping space alone was not enough: merchant ships needed crews. Neutrals were important, and Norway, which had the world's fourth-largest merchant fleet in 1914, lost 780 ships during the war and 2,000 of her seamen died. Generous recompense and favourable insurance terms bought Scandinavian assistance, although German threats to invade the Netherlands prevented the USA from a wholesale hiring of the Dutch fleet. The British Empire also made a crucial contribution: Newfoundlanders, Gujaratis, Bengalis, Jamaicans, Somalis, Chinese and every imaginable inhabitant of islands and coastlands served to man the ships. The coloured 'Lascars' faced harsh conditions, institutional discrimination, and occasionally racist violence, but without their contribution the supply of the war effort would have been curtailed.

The result of all this effort was that by February 1918 Britain was actually landing more imports than in April 1917. The introduction of rationing for meat and sugar in that month, which apparently had a magical effect on reducing queues, was important mostly as a psychological measure and in creating a sense of fairness. Not only was Britain maintaining its imports, it was also maintaining a major maritime effort in the Mediterranean. This was an area where losses to U-boats were still rising and as a result seventeen Japanese destroyers were summoned to help protect troop convoys.

The renewed interest in the Palestine campaign reflected Lloyd George's frustration with Haig and his anger at the bloodbath in Flanders. It was at least possible that victories in the peripheral regions would provide a bargaining chip in the event of a compromise peace. It was also the case that a victory in the Holy Land would feel significant to a population which was still quite biblically literate. General Allenby had taken his time to build up formidable forces in front of Gaza. At the same time the Turks were distracted by organizing the Yildirim Army Group under General Falkenhayn for an attempted counter-attack in Mesopotamia to retake Baghdad.

The 3rd battle of Gaza started on 31 October when the cavalry of the Desert Mounted Corps made the risky move around the Turkish left flank to seize the town of Beersheba and the water supplies that were vital to their horses. In a famous charge the Australian Light Horse managed to surprise and overwhelm the dug-in Turkish infantry. The Turks had been caught by surprise by a traditional cavalry attack and crucially had not protected their positions with barbed wire. Between 1 and 7

November infantry attacks, some aided by tanks and with strong artillery support, were mounted at various points along the line between Gaza and Beersheba. Finally the British broke through and forced a Turkish retreat. The pursuit was aggressive and the British Yeomanry were able to mount a traditional cavalry charge with some success. Some 12,000 Turkish prisoners were taken and the Ottomans suffered 25,000 casualties in total.

British forces were able to advance rapidly and capture Jerusalem at the start of December. Allenby chose to enter the city on foot, refusing to ride a horse where Jesus had ridden an ass. This was humility as propaganda, deliberately contrasting with the grandiosity of the Kaiser's pre-war visit to Jerusalem. Inevitably there was talk of Allenby as 'heir to the crusaders', but such talk was discouraged by the Egyptian Expeditionary Force (EEF) and the civilian authorities because tens of thousands of Muslims were fighting on the side of the Entente. Other religious ambitions were also engaged, and joining the EEF was the 'Jewish Legion' which had been raised for the British by the Zionist Vladimir Jabotinsky. The Legion was composed of volunteers from the British Empire and the United States, many of them emigrants from the Russian Empire, who had been persuaded that support for Britain was the best way of achieving a Jewish state.

On 2 November, as the offensive began, the British Foreign Secretary Arthur Balfour made an announcement that was to have profound consequences for the future of Palestine. The Balfour Declaration committed the British to support the establishment of a Jewish 'national home' in Palestine. Lloyd George had encouraged the initiative in part because it appealed to his own religious sensibilities. But the Declaration had many motives: it appealed to American Zionist opinion and it was hoped that it would also influence Jewish opinion in Russia. The President of the British Zionist Federation, Chaim Weizmann, was an industrial chemist who had worked closely with Lloyd George at the Ministry of Munitions. One secret act of support by Palestinian Zionists had also proved important: the Nili spy network founded by the Aaronsohn siblings had provided crucial intelligence for Allenby's campaign. Nili was uncovered by the Turks in October 1917. Sarah Aaronsohn managed to shoot herself after four days of torture; two other members were hanged in Damascus in December.

The Balfour Declaration was a very carefully-worded document. It did not promise a Jewish state and it explicitly noted that the rights of other inhabitants of Palestine were not to be compromised. Some British Jews were opposed to it, fearing that a homeland might tempt anti-Semites to pursue a policy of expulsion. Indeed, a certain amount of support for the idea of the Declaration was motivated by anti-Semitic sentiment arising from the paranoid suspicion that the Jews were working for the Germans; according to this view, Jewish opinion could be bought with a suitable bribe. Events in Russia were interpreted by some in this way.

Operations in Palestine had involved a very substantial investment of imperial troops: eight British divisions and two from Australasia. These were forces that could have been deployed in France. This was less true of the forces engaging the Germans in East Africa, but like that in the Middle East, this campaign required a significant commitment of shipping that was in short supply. The result was increasing pressure to conclude the campaign. The new commander, Jacob van Deventer, was more willing to engage directly with the German forces, perhaps because he was less concerned about casualties amongst his mostly black African troops. The result was a bloody repulse in October in the battle of Daiwa, resulting in more than 2,000 casualties for the Nigerian Regiment. But it was a pyrrhic victory for General Lettow-Vorbeck, who used up almost all his remaining ammunition and lost over 800 of his own Askari. He was forced to retreat from the German colony into Portuguese territory.

Lettow-Vorbeck's adventures could provide a small propaganda boost for Germany, but the imminent collapse of Austria was a much more significant affair. Taking advantage of the winding down of operations on the Eastern Front, the Germans transferred some elite units to the Italian front with the intention of mounting a limited offensive which would relieve the pressure. At 2 a.m. on 24 October the Austrians and Germans struck at the Italians. A heavy artillery bombardment destroyed many front-line positions and this allowed mountain troops to infiltrate forward through poorly-sited Italian defensive positions. On 25 October Erwin Rommel commanding a company of Württemberg troops ambushed and forced the surrender of over 2,000 men of the 4th Bersaglieri Brigade.

Rommel reported that on 27 October the defenders of Mt. Mrzli from the Salerno Brigade collapsed completely and that he was hoisted up on the shoulders of Italian prisoners shouting '*Evviva Germania*' in relief at the end of their war. An Italian officer who tried to prevent the surrender was shot down by his own men. By this point Rommel's force had advanced nearly 20 kilometres climbing elevations of 2,500 metres and had taken 9,000 prisoners and eighty-one guns in less than two days.

The collapse of the Italians near Caporetto now began in earnest; within a week 280,000 had been taken prisoner. This was the biggest mass surrender of the war. The experience of prisoners of war during the First World War was on average better than that of the Second World War. Some of the best-treated prisoners were the Germans captured by the Japanese at Tsingtao. Perhaps the worst treated were the British and Indian forces captured at Kut, the majority of whom didn't survive their captivity, although this was more a result of Ottoman incompetence and indifference than genuine malice. The Hague Conventions were generally respected, although certain provisions were often breached. Both the Germans and the French liked to parade their prisoners for propaganda purpose, leading to widespread abuse by civilians. At best conditions were generally harsh.

Bolstered and encouraged by the arrival of British and French forces, the Italian armies began to stiffen their resistance along the line of the Piave. The initial collapse was due to the tactical incompetence of the Italian commanders and the skill of their opponents, but after the first shock the Italian army fell into a more general crisis. Its commanders had relied for two years on brutal discipline alone to keep their troops attacking. Officially the Italians executed 750 soldiers during the war, compared to 330 executions by the British, 600 by the French, and to an unknown number of Russians—certainly fewer than 1,000. Officially only forty-eight German soldiers were executed in the war although the number was probably higher; while similarly in reality the number of Italian soldiers shot was probably in reality over 1,000. Cadorna once again tried to blame the ordinary soldiers for the disaster, but the government had finally had enough and relieved him of his command, replacing him with General

Diaz. The new regime in the Army still carried out executions but began to take the welfare of the soldiers seriously for the first time. The home front also showed signs of new resolve; now that the war was firmly on Italian soil it could be presented as a genuine war of national defence. An association of war widows was founded in Milan in November with the specific purpose of persuading the public to rally to the cause of the sacred dead. A serious domestic propaganda effort was mounted; Mussolini was amongst the editors involved. The British provided secret funding of £100 per week for his paper *Il Popolo D'Italia*—in effect helping to create the foundations of Fascism.

Despite the diversion of forces to Italy under the command of Plummer, Haig still wanted to make sure that the Flanders battle could make at least some claim to success, and he needed to capture Passchendaele Ridge in order to end the fighting in a position which would not still be fatally overlooked. The first attack on 12 October had seen the exhausted New Zealand division halted short of the ridge with 45 officers and 800 men killed or dying of their wounds, the worst single-day loss that the nation would suffer in the war. Haig asked the Canadian commander Arthur Currie if his men could take the ridge. Currie said that they could but only at a high cost in casualties. Haig told them to do it. In two battles supported by methodical artillery fire they pushed forward and finally took possession of the ridge on 12 November, having suffered more than 16,000 casualties, including 3,000 killed, during the battle. Canada was about to suffer another trauma. On 6 December the French munitions ship *Mont Blanc* caught fire after a collision in the harbour of Halifax, Nova Scotia. Halifax was the main winter assembly point for convoys in the North Atlantic and was crowded, perhaps overcrowded, with shipping from all along the east coast of North America. The subsequent explosion was the single greatest man-made explosion to date. More than 1,600 people were killed instantly and 9,000 injured, and most of the north end of the city was destroyed. Amongst the dead were twenty-seven children and the matron at the Protestant orphanage. To add to the agony a blizzard began on 8 December, hampering the relief effort which had brought a swift and generous reaction from other parts of North America. By population Halifax suffered by far the greatest loss in the English-speaking world of any community during the war and unusually, the majority of these dead were civilians.

Amid these grim circumstances Canada held a general election on 17 December. The main issue at stake was conscription, and the vote was given not only to soldiers but to the close female relations of men serving overseas. This was a strikingly explicit recognition that male military service was a sacrifice for their womenfolk as well. In the United Kingdom this argument was used alongside arguments about women's service to war industry to make the case for including women in the post-war electorate.

The Halifax explosion was a distant echo of a bad week for the British on the Western Front. Ironically it had followed a stunning surprise victory. On 19 November General Byng had launched a massive raid at Cambrai, spearheaded by 400 Mark IV tanks and a hurricane bombardment which utilized sound ranging and flash spotting to identify the German gun positions and neutralize them. The destruction of the enemy guns protected the British tanks which in turn allowed the infantry to get forward. The results were astonishing: a 10-kilometre frontage of the Hindenburg line was penetrated and 8,000 German prisoners were taken for 4,000 British casualties. Nearly everyone was caught by surprise, including Haig who had no reserves available to exploit the victory. Most of the British tanks were out of action by the end of the first day's fighting, as they remained mechanically unreliable. Cambrai gave a moment of cheer to a British public which was increasingly depressed by food queues, air raids, and casualties. Church bells were rung and some of the tanks were brought back to Britain where they were sent on tour in support of the war loans campaign. Celebrations proved premature: the British got bogged down in fighting near Bourlon Wood and on 30 November the Germans hit back. Using stormtroop units and supported by novel artillery tactics and by ground attack aircraft, the Germans sent the British reeling and ultimately captured more of the British front line than the British had taken on 19 November.

Some of these German attacking troops were newly arrived from the east, where recent events had released some German troops and promised to release many more. The Kornilov affair had cost the Kerensky regime the support of the army leadership and at the same time had strengthened the influence of the soviets. In addition to this, renewed and severe industrial strikes provided further opportunities for recruitment. In Moscow, where the Bolsheviks had traditionally been weak, the aftermath of an employers' lockout in the armaments industry saw a big increase in attendance at Bolshevik meetings. During September the Bolsheviks increased their influence, with the soviets gaining majority support along with their allies, the Left Social Revolutionaries, in some of the key cities, and by October the Bolsheviks were in a position to contemplate a seizure of power.

For a turning point in world history, the Bolshevik revolution was a low-key affair. The Central Committee of the Bolsheviks voted 10–2 on 26 October that the time was ripe to take control. The first Bolshevik uprising occurred in Tallinn in Estonia on 5 November. The uprising in Petrograd was allegedly signalled by a shot fired at 9.45 a.m. on 7 November by the gunboat *Aurora*, the Bolsheviks having gained the support of the majority of the sailors of the Russian Baltic fleet stationed at nearby Kronstadt. In reality the Bolshevik 'red guards' had already quietly occupied the majority of government buildings in the city during the early hours of the morning. The Bolsheviks easily seized power in Minsk on the same day. They faced more difficulties elsewhere. In Moscow it took until 15 November to overcome resistance and there was serious fighting in Kiev as some elements in the soviet opposed the Bolshevik coup. It took until 27 November to take control of Tsaritsyn in the south.

The Bolsheviks immediately implemented radical policies, nationalizing banks and industry and announcing their support for independence movements within the Empire. They also supported the holding of democratic elections on 25 November which the Provisional Government had finally got around to scheduling. These first fully democratic elections managed to achieve a roughly 60 per cent turnout amongst a universal adult male and female electorate and provided a clear result. The Social Revolutionaries received more than 16 million votes from their mass peasant base, easily outpolling the Bolsheviks, who were supported mostly by city-dwellers and by some of the Western Front soldiers and who received under 10 million votes. The Bolsheviks' allies, the Left Social Revolutionaries, received more than 2 million votes and various liberal parties somewhat less. Menshevik support had fallen to a little over a million, and most Mensheviks seem to have defected to the Bolsheviks by this stage. The Jewish Bund and various Muslim parties gained about half a million votes each. The expressed desire of the people for a Social Revolutionary government was clear. Lenin ignored it. The newly formed Constituent Assembly was simply dissolved.

As a political party the Bolsheviks never came close to majority electoral support, but their propaganda slogans of 'Peace, bread, and land' and 'All power to the soviets' probably did command support from a majority. What Lenin meant by these slogans would turn out to be very different from what was generally understood. The Bolshevik 'revolution' was the work of relatively small numbers taking control of symbolic sites. The Provisional Government collapsed for the want of any real supporters. In the midst of fighting a war the government had been unable to implement democratic elections (which was true in all the other major combatant states), and the economic chaos that had brought down the Tsar had continued and worsened. Perhaps the government should have firmly associated itself with the call for a negotiated peace, but this would probably have precipitated an earlier challenge from the right.

Without the war a Bolshevik seizure of power was inconceivable and without Lenin's leadership it would have been impossible. Lenin made tactical mistakes at times, but he had a strategic vision that was far more closely attuned to the circumstances of 1917 than that of any other Russian leader. He had wanted the war and he was able to exploit it because he was neither a nationalist nor a pacifist. He was apparently able to embrace the popular will in Russia in order to lead the population in a direction which would have been almost universally rejected had it been properly understood. Only a handful of people grasped the intention to transform the imperialist world war into an apocalyptic global class war. Lenin used the desire for peace to brandish the sword of class revolution.

By contrast Woodrow Wilson had reluctantly drawn the sword in his desire to impose peace. Wilson did not await the outcome of the negotiations between Germans and Bolsheviks to be held at Brest-Litovsk; instead he anticipated them by publishing his own views on the basis for a peace treaty on 8 January 1918. Wilson's Fourteen Points included general idealistic ones: open diplomacy, freedom of the seas, the creation of an international organization, discussion about colonies, reduction of armaments, and free trade. They included some territorial specifics: the return of Alsace-Lorraine to France, the redrawing of Italy's borders on the basis of nationality, and the establishment of an independent Poland. The proposals demanded that the armies of the Central powers withdraw from all occupied territory in both the east and the west, that they cease interference with Russia, and restore Belgian independence. With their emphasis on permanent peace and international order, and appeal to national self-determination and democracy, the Fourteen Points were a supreme act of propaganda, designed to appeal to Allied and enemy populations alike.

Wilson's proposals found favour with liberals and social democrats in France and Britain, who felt that these aims were more defensible than the cynical annexationist ambitions of their own governments which had been exposed when the Bolsheviks published Russian diplomatic correspondence. Lloyd George indeed anticipated Wilson in a speech to British trade unionists, on 5 January 1918: though privately Clemenceau mocked Wilson's earnestness, quipping that God had been satisfied with a mere ten points; but in public he emphasized the common ground.

Certainly there was also a vulnerability in the enemy population to ideas that might form the basis for a negotiated peace. The food supply situation in the Hapsburg Empire had deteriorated still more and this time it exploded into mass discontent. On 17 January 1918, 200,000 workers in Vienna went on strike and soviets were formed. Discontent spread to other cities in the Empire. By the end of the month they had been joined by 100,000 strikers in Berlin and 400,000 elsewhere in Germany. Although Germany and Austria had so far experienced far fewer strikes than Britain, these strikes were much more political in their intent and in that respect more reminiscent of those in Russia. The German military responded by invoking the Law of Siege on 31 January, imprisoning 150 trade union ringleaders and calling up 50,000 strikers for military service.

On the whole the events in the Hapsburg Empire do not seem to have been responding to Wilson's support for national self-determination.

The strikes began in the core German cities and only later spread to other nationalities. But the Hapsburg naval mutiny at Cattaro on 2 February was a partial exception. Some of the inspiration was clearly Bolshevik, as the mutineers raised the red flag and demanded an immediate peace, and some of the causes were similar to a less political 'mutiny' that had just happened at the nearby Pola base—specifically discontent with living conditions. However, it is also clear that South Slav sentiment was playing a role amongst the Slovene and Dalmatian sailors. The revolt was quickly suppressed by the local commander, but it was an ominous sign for the future, even though the mutiny was successfully kept secret.

These manifestations of discontent gave both sides at Brest-Litovsk an incentive to do a fast deal. For the Germans and Austrians they indicated the need for an immediate 'bread peace' that could relieve domestic suffering. For the Bolsheviks they raised the hope that a German revolution was imminent.

On 18 January the Germans presented their demands, which effectively amounted to a dismemberment of the Russian Empire. Lenin responded by urging acceptance as a tactical step; the Bolshevik regime was defenceless, and to survive it had to buy time to allow a German revolution to overthrow the military regime. Nikolai Bukharin called for a revolutionary war against Germany instead. Trotsky came up with a radical alternative, a unilateral declaration of peace without accepting German terms. When the German demands were renewed on 10 February, Trotsky ordered Russian troops to stop fighting. For a day or two the German high command were baffled by this policy of 'No war, no peace'. For the German generals this was not how the game was played. But the decision was taken that if this was how the Bolsheviks wanted to play, so be it, and the German armies started to advance on Petrograd and Moscow. Lenin now asserted his authority, telling the Politburo there was no alternative but to accept German terms, and on 3 March 1918 a peace treaty was signed at Brest-Litovsk.

The Bolsheviks had kept public opinion behind them whilst they consolidated power, had stalled the Germans whilst they themselves were defenceless, and had signed a peace that they believed to be essentially meaningless. The peace was humiliating and unacceptable for much of Russian opinion. It even alienated the Left Social Revolutionaries who were the Bolsheviks' only remaining political allies, and it rendered a civil war inevitable. It created hostility amongst the Entente powers and in the USA where there was a widespread belief, shared by his Russian enemies, that Lenin was a fully bought German agent. The prominence of men of Jewish background in the Bolshevik revolution, understandable given the anti-Semitism of the old regime, in turn fuelled a new wave of bigotry as suspicions that the 'Ashkenazi' Jews were hand in glove with the Prussian militarists were embraced by conspiracy theorists in the Allied camp.

But Brest-Litovsk had been carefully designed to apparently conform to the Reichstag Peace Resolution. Germany did not 'annex' Russian territory; instead it recognized the 'independence' of the Baltic states and Ukraine, the Bolsheviks having already recognized Finland as an independent state in December. Belarus also declared independence. Poland also was to be reunited and independent. In fact all of these new states were to be bound to Germany by economic ties and continued military occupation. The Ottomans did take Russian territory under the pretext of restoring territories lost in 1878. Likewise there were no 'indemnities' in the treaty, just simply-worded one-sided 'trade' deals and costs. These considerations allowed the German majority socialists a salve to their consciences whilst they also realized that opposing a treaty which would apparently bring a bounty of food to the hungry masses would be political suicide.

Brest-Litovsk underlined a decisive German victory in the east and therefore created a clear opportunity to negotiate a peace in the west from a position of strength. If Belgium were to be evacuated and Germany showed a willingness to talk about Alsace and Lorraine, it was highly unlikely that western populations would have been willing to continue the war in order to deny German dominance of eastern Europe. Germany stood to win the war at the negotiating table, a source of genuine worry to the leaders of Britain and France. On 8 March Clemenceau responded to the treaty and the obvious crisis of the war with a rousing speech in the French National Assembly: 'You ask me what my domestic policy is? It is to make war. You ask me what my foreign policy is? It is to make war.' In the speech he echoed Danton in

1792 calling for the total commitment of the nation in a life or death struggle. This was to be total war against an implacable enemy. But whether he could really have carried the long-suffering French people with him if a 'reasonable peace' had been offered was questionable.

The German high command saw a different opportunity beckoning. Transferring forces from the east had for the first time in the war given Germany a slight numerical superiority in the west. Including the return of forces from Italy, forty-four German divisions were moved to the Western Front by the start of March. The French and British armies had been worn down and perhaps worn out and the Americans would not arrive in strength until the late summer. German forces had crushed their enemies in Serbia, Russia, and Italy, and were confident that they had mastered the tactics of offensive operations. One last offensive could win the war completely. If the British could be driven into the sea the Allied coalition would collapse. The German leadership had come to the point of not believing that peace with the British was possible. The Kaiser in his inimitable fashion opined that either Germany or Britain must go under.

Stormtroop tactics had largely been developed in the west. Since early 1915 specialist German units had been trying out limited operations, most notably pioneer companies under the command of Captain Willi Rohr. Similar thinking had been developing in the French army, and indeed the Germans had captured and translated an innovative manual by André Laffargue. The British were slower to develop these methods, but the tactical manual SS117 in February 1917 had also stressed 'infiltration' and trench raiding had refined offensive methods in all armies.

These tactics were to be utilized on a much larger scale, combined with the operational doctrine developed by General Hutier's VIII Army in the east. This called for the leading units to bypass strongpoints and keep the advance moving with the intention of breaking through into enemy rear areas and paralysing the response. This was combined with artillery tactics developed by Colonel Bruchmüller: massive 'lightning' bombardments intended to stun and paralyze rather than destroy. Counter-battery fire based on silent pre-registration and extensive use of non-persistent gases were combined with a creeping barrage and the use of heavy mortars against specific targets.

Whilst German skill would be important in the attack, it was above all the scale of the offensive that distinguished it from British and French efforts. Seventy-six German divisions were concentrated in the assault area, supported by 6,608 guns and 3,354 mortars. The attacking divisions contained most of Germany's remaining soldiers below the age of thirty-five. The sheer concentration of artillery meant that the Germans would be able to fire a rapid devastating barrage over both a sufficient width of the front to avoid being held up on their flanks and in sufficient depth to crush the defences of their British opponents. This initial assault was codenamed Operation Michael; it was anticipated that more blows would follow in quick succession.

By contrast their opponents were not in good shape. The British army had undergone a reorganization reducing the size of each division. This was not foolish, as it increased the ratio of artillery to infantry, but it created a mood of uncertainty which was compounded by the attempt to adopt German tactics of defence in depth. The front-line infantry were uncomfortable about abandoning continuous trench lines in favour of a web of strongpoints and in fact the British had misinterpreted the German system, placing too many troops forward and not maintaining the strong counter-attack forces central to the German system. The commander of 5th Army, the main defenders on the Somme, was the unpopular Gough. Finally to compound the woe, the BEF had been pressured to extend the line it was holding and take over incomplete French positions on the right.

The dawn of 21 March 1918 saw thick fog descend at dawn as the German bombardment began to blow the British position apart with more than 3 million shells. Command posts were wrecked, telephone lines were cut and British artillery disabled by counter-battery fire including large numbers of gas shells. The fog hampered the attackers, but it was a death blow to the British defensive system which relied on good visibility allowing mutual support of positions. At 9.45 a.m. the German infantry began to advance, by which time perhaps 10 per cent of the British defenders were already dead or wounded and the rest were all to some extent in shock. Shielded by the fog, German forces often got right on top of British positions before their enemy knew they were there and were able to mop up resistance with hand grenades. British infantry in isolated forward outposts often gave up as soon as they realized they were surrounded, and the Germans took 21,000 prisoners on the first day. On average the German army had advanced 4 kilometres—an impressive result on the Western Front.

But the British had still largely held the 'battle zone' and the German army had also paid a high price—almost 40,000 casualties of which 11,000 were dead. The German advance, impressive as it was compared with other attacks since 1914, had been held far short of what Ludendorff had expected. It was the next two days that turned the battle into a crisis for the British and their allies. Gough lacked reserves and was unable to hold the battle zone. For once he made the right decision and ordered a retreat, a move that saved most of his army. Byng, commanding British 2nd Army to Gough's north, was therefore also obliged to fall back. By 23 March the Germans had taken 40,000 prisoners and captured 400 British guns, and had advanced as far as the Somme, about 25 kilometres. On that evening Haig admitted that the situation was serious. The Germans had added to the psychological pressure by opening fire on Paris with a massive 380mm railway gun, and even Clemenceau warned his ministers that they might have to evacuate the capital.

At a meeting at Doullens on 26 March the British requested that Foch be given the job of coordinating the Allied armies in defence of Amiens. The French politicians agreed, Clemenceau quipping that Foch now had what he had always wanted. Foch replied that he had been given a lost battle and told to win it. But by this point the German forces on the Somme were outrunning their own supplies; the devastated wasteland behind them was proving hard to negotiate and the army was undersupplied with both horses and trucks. This was exacerbated by a determined effort by British and French airmen to attack German supplies and reinforcements moving forward.

On 28 March 1918 the German army launched the long-prepared second stage of the attack, Operation Mars, aimed at the British forces near Arras. Stronger British defences in depth stopped the attack in its tracks with heavy casualties. Near Montdidier, French forces also checked the advancing Germans with a vigorous counter-attack, causing one German artilleryman, the usually optimistic nationalist Herbert Sulzbach, to admit that it had been a 'depressing' day. On 3 April at

Beauvais, Foch was given strategic command of operations as 'generalissimo' in the west and with the authority to direct the Italians as well.

The British scraped together forces from every source. Troops were brought back from the Middle East, where they were replaced by newly raised Indian forces. Indian recruiting had been a tremendous success story, assisted to some extent by the declaration in August 1917 by the Viceroy, Edwin Montagu, that Britain intended to move towards Dominion status for India.

Soldiers held back in Britain were released for the front, including, for the first time, eighteen-year-old conscripts. Then the conscription age was raised and exempted men were 'combed out' of industry. In order to make this palatable, previously exempt groups were dragged in. The British fatefully imposed conscription on Ireland, and also encouraged the Canadian government to enforce it in Quebec. The result of the latter was massive anti-conscription riots over Easter 1918 which helped invigorate *Québécois* nationalist opposition to the 'Prussians' of Ottawa; while the former hardened opinion in support of Sinn Féin and discredited the Constitutional Convention and the Irish Parliamentary Party who had failed to prevent this assertion of British dominance.

On 9 April the Germans mounted another massive offensive against the British in Flanders. The Portuguese forces holding the line generally had no great commitment to the war and, certainly neither trained nor equipped to hold off such a heavy attack, broke and ran. One exception was the machine gunner Anhibal Milhais who stayed behind to cover the retreat, holding back a full German battalion, and became a national hero when he rejoined his comrades days later. Haig, clearly somewhat unnerved, released an order of the day asking the British forces to fight on 'with their backs to the wall'. Although Plummer was forced to give up the gains of the Passchendaele battle, he was able to prevent a breakthrough and hold Ypres. Once again reinforcements were brought up from other parts of the front and deployed rapidly by truck.

On 21 April 1918, Manfred von Richthofen was shot down and killed. This was credited to a Canadian pilot, Roy Brown, serving in the Royal Air Force, which had been created by the merger of the army's Royal Flying Corps and the Royal Naval Air Service on 1 April. In fact it is likely that Richthofen was killed by fire from Australian troops on the ground. Having shot down eighty aircraft, Richthofen was the definitive air ace of the war, and his death was a propaganda blow to Germany. This was followed by another. On 23 April, St George's Day, the Royal Navy attacked the U-boat base at Zeebrugge, landing marines and sinking block ships in the harbour. Although the raid was a failure, it was presented as a success to boost morale. More fundamental was the check to the German armies, which again began to run out of impetus. The German army had now suffered half a million casualties in little more than six weeks.

The timely commitment of French reserves had twice rescued the British army. Ludendorff therefore calculated that the French army must by this stage be overstretched. A heavy attack might achieve a breakthrough, which could end the war in the west. On 27 May the Germans launched another huge offensive against France's 6th Army on the Chemin des Dames. General Duchêne had positioned his troops poorly, neglecting defence in depth, and a key sector was held by four shattered British divisions that had been sent to rest and recuperate in a 'quiet sector'. The result was catastrophic for the Allies. On the first day the Germans advanced 16 kilometres, crossing the river Aisne, and by 1 June the advance had covered 55 kilometres and reached the Marne; on that day Pétain wrote to Foch that seventeen divisions had been completely exhausted in the battle. About 100,000 French casualties had occurred in under a fortnight. Some members of the Chamber of Deputies demanded the sacking of Pétain and Foch, but Clemenceau won a vote of confidence on 4 June.

In Britain the mood of panic was inflamed by the Pemberton Billing libel case. This bizarre affair had begun in February 1918 when the MP and editor Noel Pemberton Billing had published an article in his journal *Vigilante* entitled 'The Cult of the Clitoris'. In it he had drawn attention to a private production of Oscar Wilde's play *Salome* in which the American actress Maud Allan had performed the dance of the seven veils in front of Margot Asquith, wife of the ex-Prime Minister. Effectively accusing Mrs Asquith and Allan of lesbianism, Pemberton Billing went on to suggest that the British Empire's war effort was being undermined by 47,000 highly placed 'perverts' who were being blackmailed by the German secret service. Allan sued Pemberton Billing for libel and after an extraordinary case in which a motley collection of borderline insane homophobic and anti-Semitic conspiracy theorists appeared for the defence, the MP was cleared to the acclaim of crowds outside the Old Bailey.

This moment of triumphant bigotry in Britain had parallels elsewhere at this decisive moment. In May 1918 the already severe provisions of the United States Espionage Act of 1917 were expanded into the Sedition Act, which effectively ended the constitutional protection of free speech for the duration of the war. Almost immediately the leader of the American Socialist Party, Eugene Debs, was arrested for making speeches against conscription. In June, Agnes Smedley, Taraknath Das, and Sarindranath Ghose were arrested in San Francisco. This was precipitated by the discovery of a letter from Smedley to Trotsky, but in reality was a response to their activities on behalf of the Ghadar independence movement, opposed to British rule in India. Interrogators tried to blackmail Smedley, over her sexual relations with Indian men, into betraying her colleagues. However, she stood firm. Official repression was paralleled by mob violence. In April whilst the police looked on, a German immigrant coal miner, Robert Prager, was lynched in Collinsville, Illinois, on suspicion of 'spying'. Some German-speaking Mennonites in Kansas were tarred and feathered after they refused to donate to the Red Cross. This was a frequent charge against the 'unpatriotic'. Dr Ruth Lighthall was arrested in Chicago in June after she refused to buy Red Cross stamps from the neighbourhood children, who denounced her to their parents. She was charged with attempting to cause 'insubordination or mutiny'. She refused to deny that she had criticized the Red Cross, choosing instead to challenge the law in defence of her right to free speech, including describing President Wilson as a coward. She was sentenced to ten years in prison.

The febrile mood in the USA preceded any great human loss overseas. By the start of June 1918 there were 650,000 American troops in France, but fourteen months after the American entry into the war hardly any of them had seen action. One who had was Private Henry Johnson of the 369th New York Regiment. He was the first American awarded the highest French honour, the *Croix de guerre avec palmes*, for his heroism in fighting off German trench raiders hand to hand on 15 May. However, although his actions were noted by Gerneral Pershing, Johnson received no medal from the US government. Johnson was black.

Pershing had aggressively defended the rights of American soldiers to serve under the command of their own officers as an American army, rightly suspecting that Haig and Pétain wanted to use his men simply as reinforcements for their own units. There was also a desire for the American Expeditionary Force to be equipped with US weapons, but the mobilization of American industry on the huge scale required was proving slow. In the crisis at the start of June, American sensibilities needed to be set aside. Pershing was persuaded to allow divisions and even regiments of US troops to go into action under Allied command and to prioritize the sending of infantry and machine gun units that could be dispatched straight into battle.

The first major battle fought by the Americans was a counter-attack conducted by 1st Division at Cantigny on 28 May 1918, with significant French artillery and tank support. This was quickly followed on 6 June by actions from two other 'regular' divisions, 2nd and 3rd, in the vicinity of Château-Thierry and nearby Belleau Wood. The latter saw the US Marine Brigade in action. Allegedly the Medal of Honor winner, Sergeant Dan Daly, goaded his machinegun section to advance with the challenge 'Come on you sons of bitches, do you want to live forever?' Casualties were serious: nearly 2,000 Americans didn't survive the week. But the Germans gave ground and 1,200 of them surrendered. Although inexperienced in the refinements of trench warfare, these regular US forces were generally skilled with their personal weapons and in the face of heavy losses retained a willingness to advance, which many British and French veterans now lacked. In the semi-open fighting on the Marne they did well. The German general facing them considered them to be 'shock forces'.

American forces also went into action on the British sector. At Le Hamel the Australians mounted a raid in force in the company of the American troops they were mentoring. Coordinating with tanks and aircraft which dropped ammunition to the advancing machine gunners, the Australians and the Americans celebrated 4 July with a sharp little victory.

The initial impact of the Americans—and the crucial one—was the psychological effect on both sides. Exhausted British and French units saw the Americans as a promise of final victory and were able to hold on a little longer. By contrast, for the Germans it was another new enemy and one that possessed an inexhaustible pool of fresh opponents. The Germans were also finding that their enemies seemed increasingly to anticipate their actions. Moving forward from their fixed positions the Germans had relied increasingly on radio communications rather than fixed telephone lines. In March they had introduced a new cipher system, the ADFGVX, the best that had ever been used up to this date, but by the end of May the brilliant French cryptanalyst Georges Painvin had broken this cipher sufficiently to be able to read German messages within a day of interception. This allowed one German attack in early June to be crushed almost before it started and gave a major advantage to the defenders throughout the summer.

Germany's allies had also undertaken offensive operations in the early summer. On 7 May 1918, Romania had been forced to sign the treaty of Bucharest which made territorial concessions to both the Hapsburg Empire and Bulgaria. This freed up forces for both these powers. On 15 June the Austrians attacked across the Piave, just north of Venice, in the hope of exploiting the German victories in France. They were held by British, French, and Italian forces and at the end of June driven back by a counter-attack. The Ottomans now took advantage of the Russian collapse to regain their lost territory in the north-east. The Ottoman III Army then pushed on into formerly Russian territory. In part this was in response to massacres of the Azerbaijani population carried out by Armenian Bolsheviks that had occurred around Baku in March, which had led to the Azerbaijanis declaring independence. The local Armenian forces managed to check the Turkish invasion at the end of May and this in turn led to the creation of an 'Army of Islam' consisting of both Turks and local Muslim volunteers. The contest in the Caucasus had become multi-sided, and the British had sent troops north from Iraq labelled 'Dunsterforce' to try to stop the oilfields of Baku falling into hostile hands. The Georgians meanwhile had begun to look to the Germans as protectors from the Turks.

Similar things were happening throughout the former Russian Empire as both alliances moved to protect their interests from each other and from the Bolsheviks whilst nationalist revolution played itself out. In newly independent Finland a vicious civil war was fought in March, with the Red Army supporting the left-wing forces and the German Baltic Division supporting the 'whites' led by General Mannerheim. The result was a 'White' victory and a wave of brutal repression, with nearly 5,000 'Reds' executed in April. Many more would die subsequently in horrific prison camps. In May the Don Cossacks who had been suffering under the 'red terror' rose up against the Bolsheviks with German assistance, finding an effective leader in Pyotr Krasnov. But an even bigger threat was from the enemies of the Central powers. In May the Czech Legion in Siberia, which was still loyal to the Entente cause, began to interfere with trains that were repatriating German and Austro-Hungarian prisoners of war who were being released under the terms of Brest-Litovsk. The Bolsheviks attempted to disarm the Czechs, leading to an outright rebellion at Chelyabinsk. The Czechs were the most effective military force left in Siberia and were quickly able to seize control of the main railway junctions including the city of Samara. Encouraged by this, the Russian democratic parties created a Provisional Government on 8 June. They immediately sought outside assistance. In July 1918 Woodrow Wilson was visited by Maria Bochkareva who had escaped the Bolsheviks via Vladivostok and who added her voice to those calling for intervention on behalf of the White Army. On 16 July 1918 the Tsar and his family were murdered by the Bolsheviks in Ekaterinburg fortress, as White forces, spearheaded by the Czech legion, approached the city. The Tsar had paid with his life for the Russian decision to go to war; he was one of the few major political figures to do so. But in April 1918 the young man who had fired the first fatal shots, the assassin Gavrilo Princip, had died of tuberculosis in an Austrian prison.

On 15 July the Germans launched another great offensive, to the east of Reims. But this time the French had captured prisoners who revealed that the attack was coming and as a result the French began a defensive bombardment before the Germans. The attack was called off with heavy losses. On 16 July another German attack did better, crossing the Marne and advancing 5 kilometres before French and American forces re-established the line near Château-Thierry. Foch refused requests from Pétain to release reinforcements that would weaken 10th Army, a powerful force of French, colonial, and American forces under the command of General Mangin and supported by more than 1,500 guns and 300 tanks. The French Renault tanks were lighter and faster than their British equivalents and afforded the possibility of an advance at faster than walking pace, if not exactly a lightning breakthrough. On 18 July, Mangin struck south-west of Soissons, attacking without a preliminary bombardment at dawn. The US 1st and 2nd Divisions spearheaded an attack which took 10,000 prisoners and 200 guns. Italian and British forces soon joined the attack, which became the second battle of the Marne. Haig was unhappy about the use of the four British divisions, fearing another German attack at Ypres. Ludendorff was indeed planning such an attack, but the deteriorating situation on the Marne forced a postponement. The German army slowly pulled back from the salient. Foch called a meeting with Haig, Pétain, and Pershing on 24 July. He had prepared a long memorandum that called for an abandonment of the defensive and the start of a general offensive. At this stage Foch still believed the war would last until 1919, but in the meantime the western armies would smash the German salient and clear the key railway junctions in a series of attacks.

Foch was the first to realize that the second battle of the Marne was a genuine turning point, but the war was far from over. At the end of July, Germany was still in control of vast territories in the west and in the east, and her allies also had large forces stationed on enemy soil. Ludendorff still believed the war was winnable. Within two months it would be lost.

CHAPTER 5
THE LAST YEAR 1918–1919: ARMISTICE AND PEACE

At the start of August 1918 the German army was still holding more ground than it had held at the start of March. Furthermore its positions were not the mighty defences of 1917, but improvised positions recently occupied. It was also holding them with far fewer troops. The casualties of the spring had reduced the strength of all infantry units, but particularly the best assault divisions. At this point the army fell victim to a plague. The 'Spanish' influenza saw disease return to its traditional place in siege warfare. The H5N1 virus probably crossed from poultry to humans in the base camps of the BEF in 1917. Unlike most influenza viruses, this bird flu had the diabolic effect of preying on the young and fit, because its impact was derived from the overstimulation of the body's own immune system. The influenza seems to have struck the Germans slightly ahead of their enemies in summer 1918 and its impact was greater on an army that was already holding too much ground and had no immediate hope of reinforcement.

Since May most of the BEF had been able to rest and recuperate and it was now ready to attack. The Australians deployed in front of Amiens had probed the weak German positions and the local army commander, Henry Rawlinson, had begun to develop a plan for a large 'set-piece' attack. Foch was enthusiastic, but insisted that the French army join the attack near Montdidier. Rawlinson's plan was dependent on surprise and the use of large numbers of tanks. The French, who had fewer tanks available, would need a longer bombardment, so it was agreed that they would attack after the British in order for the British attack to achieve surprise. The Australians would be joined in the attack by a British corps and by the Canadians.

The Canadian Corps was the single most powerful unit in the Allied Army. The four over-strength divisions were still quite fresh, having been kept out of most of the fighting in 1918 by the insistence of the Canadian government that it should be kept together. The officers and men were skilled and experienced and it was an all-volunteer force, conscription having been introduced only recently to Canada. It now moved in secret down from Flanders. The Cavalry Corps was also brought up to exploit any breakthrough. Tanks were moved into position using the noise of over-flying aircraft to cover their movements.

The Amiens attack was supported by nearly 2,000 artillery pieces including 684 heavy ones. A carefully calculated counter-battery fire plan meant that more than 500 of the 580 defending German artillery pieces were instantly brought under fire at the start of the attack at 4.20 a.m. on 8 August. This neutralization of much of the German artillery massively aided the advance of the 580 tanks. The attack was also assisted by dense fog.

By the end of the day the Canadians had advanced 13 kilometres and the Australians nearly as far. The British, supported by fewer tanks and assaulting tougher defences, managed only 4 kilometres. Overall a breach in German lines of nearly 25 kilometres in breadth had been created. Some armoured car units broke through into the German rear areas, overwhelming headquarters and supply columns.

Amiens remains the least known great victory of the British army. The British press, after years of disappointment, never quite understood what had happened, indeed British propaganda policy had been consciously playing down the army throughout the year. But this does not mean that the BEF won the war in the west single-handed in 1918: even Amiens was strictly speaking in fact an Allied victory, including the successful French attack on the flank at Montdidier.

These battles of Amiens-Montdidier were not cheap victories. The BEF and the French had suffered 44,000 casualties in four days. But they had taken 30,000 prisoners and had inflicted some 75,000 casualties in total. The high proportion of prisoners was significant. Ludendorff believed that the German army had been 'infected' by defeatist Bolshevik propaganda, and when he referred to Amiens as the 'black day' of the German army he principally had in mind alleged incidents such as the case where retreating troops jeered reinforcements as 'strike-breakers'. General Hutier was perhaps more realistic: he thought his men were simply worn out. The failure of the last offensives seems to have been a tipping point in the morale of the army; the hope of peace through victory had kept war-weary soldiers fighting for a while, but as Paris receded, this hope ebbed away. If victory could not be achieved, then the sacrifice of the soldiers and their families would be futile. Faced with overwhelming force on the battlefield, men began to consider that surrender was an acceptable and honourable option and for the first time significant numbers of junior officers agreed.

The British commander at Amiens had also presided over the disastrous first day of the Somme. But this was not a simple matter of 'learning'. Rawlinson's failure in 1916 had not been intellectual but moral: he had deferred to Haig's interference in his attack plan, with disastrous consequences. On 12 August 1918 he responded differently, when Foch put pressure on Haig to press on in the face of mounting casualties. Rawlinson met with his corps commanders. They expressed the view that it would be a waste of men to push on in the face of stiffening German resistance and Rawlinson passed this advice up the chain of command. Haig then informed Foch that he would attack with Byng's 3rd Army instead.

It was a crucial moment. The Canadian Arthur Currie and the Australian John Monash had given the view from the ground to their commanders and they had been heard. It may have helped that as commanders of Dominion forces they had more influence than most subordinates. But what now emerged was a new rhythm of war in the west, short sharp blows which were discontinued when resistance stiffened and quickly followed by new attacks elsewhere on the line. It involved overturning most generals' natural instincts; rather than following up the initial breach in pursuit of the elusive breakthrough, this was a 'lateral' exploitation. Once the Germans had committed their reserves to seal the breach, another attack would strike their weakened line. It allowed the Western Allies to exploit their greater resources and greater mobility. Large fleets of motorized vehicles could be used to move troops and supplies to the new attack points. In quick succession the British struck at Albert, the French at

Noyon, and the British again at Arras. In two weeks they recaptured most of the ground that the Germans had taken in March.

Throughout August the number of German soldiers taken prisoner continued to rise sharply. This was partly a consequence of more fluid conditions leading to units being cut off and surrounded, just as had happened to the British and French in the spring. A major propaganda effort was mounted by the Western powers to encourage surrender by dropping from aeroplanes leaflets promising good treatment; this included listing the rations that prisoners received. It may have helped some tired and hungry soldiers make their decisions, but was probably marginal; surrender after all was a risky business, with the killing of prisoners by enraged enemies quite common. It was much safer for units to negotiate a surrender en masse, led by their officers, and this became a more common pattern. At the same time and to some extent independently there was a 'silent mutiny' developing amongst German troops away from the front lines. Men in transit away from the battlefield slipped away from their units, soldiers in hospital prolonged their stay.

The turn against Germany in the west changed the balance of Allied strategy. In August various contingents of troops had been landed in Russia in order to secure war supplies against capture by the Bolsheviks, to assist the withdrawal of the Czechoslovak Legion, and to encourage the 'White' forces in the overthrow of the Bolshevik government which was nominally cooperating with the Germans. The hope was that this might bring Russia back into the war on the Allied side. The initial motivation for the intervention was much more practical than ideological. Some 3,000 American troops landed at Vladivostok in August and 7,000 Japanese troops were also sent to Siberia at President Wilson's request. The Japanese contingent would grow rapidly to 70,000 as the Japanese government began to pursue its own ambitions in the area. In September the anti-Bolshevik Russian forces in Siberia created a government at Ufa which reflected the outcome of the democratic election.

A small British force moved into Central Asia and a larger one landed at Archangel in the far north on 2 August. This force quickly became involved in direct combat supporting the White armies against the Bolsheviks and was pushed back to its bridgehead by the defeat of the Whites. Trotsky used harsh discipline to stiffen the resistance of the Red

Army on all fronts and the Bolsheviks utilized terror to maintain control behind the lines. This intensified when on 30 August a young socialist revolutionary, Fanny Kaplan, almost succeeded in assassinating Lenin. One of the most ruthless practitioners of terror was Josef Stalin who had been sent to defend the city of Tsaritsyn in the south of Russia. Stalin succeeded in this but in the process became involved in a personal feud with the equally ruthless Trotsky.

Whilst Russia continued to loom large in the deliberations of the Allied Supreme War Council, in practice it would disappoint both sides. By the end of August the German Foreign Office was thoroughly disillusioned by the double dealing and lack of real cooperation from Moscow. The army managed to get a 'supplementary' to the Brest-Litovsk treaty on 27 August, promising 6 billion marks in compensation and access to oil in the Caucasus. A secret clause allowed the Germans to move through Russia to act against the Allied intervention. Meanwhile the Bolsheviks continued to propagandize German and Hapsburg troops in support of the European revolution.

The Allies continued to plan offensives in all theatres, but despite some advocates of a peripheral strategy Foch could sense that the west was now fluid enough to take the lead. On 30 August he modified his strategic plan, prioritizing a major Franco-American thrust through the Argonne forest to capture the key towns of Mézières and Sedan. This would cut the major rail lines and limit the capability of the Germans to move reinforcements to contain breakthroughs. The Western Front would then collapse. General Pershing, who preferred the idea of an attack through Metz, was determined not to allow the American army to be subsumed by its allies and insisted on mounting an operation that would be clearly American. The resulting compromise was that the Americans would still be allowed to conduct their planned attack to reduce the St-Mihiel salient, already authorized by Foch. They would then be switched to mount a major offensive into the Argonne.

The American operation at St-Mihiel has been both overpraised and, in reaction, unduly criticized. The Americans completely eliminated the salient and took 13,000 prisoners at the cost of 7,000 casualties. A certain amount of chauvinistic nonsense, following Pershing's prejudices, has been written about how American troops demonstrated superior rifle skills and frontier spirit uncorrupted by the decadence of European generalship. In fact the truth was almost the opposite, because the best AEF divisions had learned an enormous amount during the summer and they now ignored the posturings of Pershing's headquarters in order to apply sophisticated 1918 trench warfare techniques: carefully planned artillery bombardments and systematic bite-and-hold advances. The attack was also supported by 1,400 Allied aircraft. The German command had realized the salient was untenable and had planned its evacuation, but they were nevertheless caught by surprise by the effectiveness of the American attack, and what had been intended as an orderly German withdrawal came close to becoming a rout.

This performance of the American forces had a psychological impact on Ludendorff which was quickly reinforced by another shock from an unexpected quarter. Franchet d'Espèrey had been transferred to command the Salonika front after a poor performance facing the German offensive. Inevitably nicknamed 'desperate Frankie' by the British, he was indeed driven to redeem himself and he set about doing it with panache. On 15 September French and Serbian forces, the latter including volunteer ex-Hapsburg prisoners of war (both Serb and Czech), attacked at Dobra Pole supported by a powerful artillery bombardment. Within two days they had broken through. It was a significant achievement, because contrary to subsequent German slanders, the Bulgarians were still tough opponents, as they demonstrated by defeating another Greek and British attack at Doiran on 19 September. It was only *after* the breakthrough that Bulgarian forces began to disintegrate into a full-scale revolt against their commanders. The Franco-Serbian forces mounted a ruthless pursuit. On 27 September some 4,000 mutinying Bulgarian soldiers joined with leaders of the Agrarian Party in declaring the monarchy overthrown and founding a republic. This persuaded the Bulgarian high command to seek an immediate armistice, which was declared on 29 September. On 4 October King Ferdinand abdicated in favour of his son, Boris.

The Bulgarian withdrawal from the war did have serious consequences for the remaining Central powers. Entente troops could now advance rapidly back into Serbia towards the Danube, outflanking the Austrian positions in Italy. Other units could advance quickly overland on

Constantinople. German soldiers and civilians would have their confidence further undermined. Ludendorff would claim in his memoirs that it was the Bulgarian capitulation, which he presented as an unexpected failure by Germany's ally, that first forced him to consider an armistice. This was misleading; Bulgaria's collapse was in part a reflection of the weakening of German support caused by Ludendorff's own defeats.

Further east the Ottoman Empire was independently facing catastrophe. The war and the campaigns of ethnic cleansing had brought the fragile economy of the Empire long past the point of collapse. By 1918 nearly a quarter of the agricultural land of the Empire was uncultivated and yield per acre had fallen 20 per cent. The Anglo-French blockade of the Mediterranean coast added to the problems of cities that had traditionally supplemented local supply with imports. As in other strained agrarian economies some peasant communities took to withholding supplies from the markets, and speculation and hoarding by middle-men drove up prices. The result was widespread malnutrition and even famine. More than 100,000 died in the area of Mount Lebanon alone.

The Germans and Austrians had by 1918 sent several thousand soldiers, mostly specialists, to bolster the Turkish forces in Palestine, but this was all that could be spared. The Turkish Army Group was now commanded by Liman von Sanders, defender of Gallipoli, and his principal subordinate was Mustafa Kemal, who now commanded VII Army. These were proven and able generals. But the long years of fighting and the effects of disease and malnutrition had ground down Turkish military manpower. By the end of the war more than 450,000 Ottoman soldiers had died of disease, exceeding combat deaths. Another 500,000 had deserted. In October 1917 a German general reported that one division which had been sent to Palestine had lost more than 60 per cent of its troops in transit either to desertion or sickness. Furthermore the Turkish government had been fatally tempted by adventures in Central Asia, sending some of the best remaining troops off to Baku. The result of this was that the defenders of northern Palestine in September 1918 were outnumbered almost 2 to 1 by Allenby's forces and almost 4 to 1 in mounted troops, still vital in this region. Their commanders chose not to retreat, less from confidence that they could hold out than from fear that the army would rapidly collapse if it left its positions.

Although victory was almost certain, Allenby's plan was still a brilliant one. With a well thought-out deception plan involving some of his mounted forces, he convinced his enemies that he intended to break through on the eastern flank. Once they had been diverted, he struck hard on the coastal side on 19 September, in fact breaking through the Turkish front line. He then thrust three cavalry divisions through a gap in the Carmel mountains on 20 September. Realizing he was in danger of being cut off, Kemal retreated from Nablus, but the retreat came close to becoming a rout as aircraft bombed and machine gunned the Turks. The use of airpower was a striking feature of the battle; it had begun with a heavy bomber raid on Sanders' headquarters and complete air superiority played an important role in limiting the casualties in Allenby's army to less than 1,000. The Turkish army in Palestine was effectively destroyed, some 30,000 men killed, wounded, missing, or prisoners. Arab villagers massacred cut-off detachments in retaliation for Turkish atrocities.

This battle of Megiddo (the site of the biblical Armageddon) involved Turks, Germans, Arabs, Britons, Sikhs, Pathans, Gurkhas, Maoris, Australians, Jamaicans, the Jewish Legion, and the Franco-Armenian Legion. If not 'all the nations of the earth', it felt near enough for some to claim the fulfilment of biblical prophecy of the end of times. The leader of the pacifist Baha'i faith living in Haifa thought so, and responded with admirable practicality by dispersing the sect's grain supplies to help relieve the famine in the vicinity, an act earning him a British knighthood.

Allenby's forces now moved rapidly into Syria. Australian cavalry beat Arab forces under T. E. Lawrence to be the first into Damascus on 1 October 1918, but on 3 October Prince Faisal entered the city and on 5 October he announced an Arab constitutional government, with Allenby's apparent blessing. The French, who expected to gain control of greater Syria under the terms of the Sykes-Picot agreement with the British, were unimpressed.

With the destruction of the Palestine Army Group and with the last remaining significant organized armed forces far away beyond the Caucasus, the Turkish government had no means to protect Constantinople when the Salonika Army advanced on the city. On 30 October the Turkish government signed an armistice on the Greek island of Mudros.

Allenby's glamorous campaign overshadowed a much more decisive achievement by the British army on the Western Front. At start of September the Dominion forces made the running as they pushed past the old Somme battlefields. The Australians launched a successful attack on Mont Saint-Quentin and the Canadians smashed through the Drocourt-Quéant position, forcing Ludendorff to abandon his hoped-for winter line and fall back to where he had started in March.

Foch now encouraged the BEF to join in a general attack that could support his main effort in the Argonne. The Canadian Corps reinforced further their reputation as the most powerful force on the Allied side by pushing across the Canal du Nord on 27 September, but by this time the entire BEF was rolling forward. On 28 September British, Belgian, and French forces attacked in Flanders. Further south, starting on 26 September, British artillery fired 750,000 shells in two days on a frontage of less than 10 kilometres. A bombardment of this intensity shattered the German defences. On 29 September the British 46th Division, men from the Midland counties of England, not in any sense an elite force, crossed the St Quentin canal in front of the main Siegfried defence line and broke in. By the next day they had smashed right though the Hindenburg position.

By contrast things had gone poorly in the Argonne. On 26 September American forces had advanced quickly up to the Kriemhild line where they had been stopped by well-positioned German defences. By 29 September six fresh German divisions had arrived and had counterattacked strongly. French forces had managed greater success in the more open territory to the left of the Americans. But for the next week the Americans took heavy casualties for negligible results whilst their supply system largely collapsed. Aided by his dynamic Chief of Staff, Maxime Weygand (who may have been the illegitimate grandson of Prince Metternich), Foch drove the Franco-American forces to maintain the pressure. Foch sent Weygand to Pershing with the suggestion that French troops be moved in to stiffen the attack, and that French commanders should take control of some American divisions. An angry Pershing sent Weygand back to his commander and ordered American troops forward regardless of casualties. In a week the Americans suffered 75,000, a rate of loss comparable with the worst suffered by any army in the war.

Foch's offensive was now in danger of resembling Ludendorff's, being dragged along by tactical success in one sector regardless of strategic significance. The British were doing best in terms of ground captured, enemy divisions met and defeated, and casualties inflicted. Haig appealed to London for bicycles and motor vehicles to help speed the advance; on 9 October the Canadian Cavalry Brigade even managed to mount an old-fashioned cavalry charge at Le Cateau. But it was also the case that the British army and the Belgian and French armies alongside them were advancing in the areas that the Germans could most easily afford to concede.

On Sunday 29 September Ludendorff announced to assembled military and civilian leaders that an immediate armistice was necessary. Remarkably even at this meeting prompted by the prospect of imminent defeat, Hindenburg stated that it was important that certain districts of France with iron ore reserves should be secured for Germany in the peace treaty, but Ludendorff dismissed this wildly irrelevant idea. The Kaiser then arrived for a second conference, at which Hindenburg passed on Ludendorff's recommendation that an armistice be sought. It was agreed that the government would need to be reconstituted to incorporate democratic elements. Chancellor Hertling resigned and Prince Max of Baden, thought to be a liberal figure, although in reality a strong supporter of aristocratic leadership, was asked to form a government which could approach President Wilson for an armistice and peace negotiations based on his Fourteen Points.

Prince Max was rightly suspicious of the motives of the high command and tried to get Hindenburg to commit to paper that the government was seeking an armistice at the request of the generals. He also sought to delay the approach to the Americans and try for a solution short of an armistice, but constant insistence from Ludendorff about the urgency to get a ceasefire before an imminent offensive forced his hand. On 4 October Max was finally able to form a new government which brought in the leading figures behind the Reichstag Resolution of the previous year: Philipp Scheidemann of the Social Democrats and Matthias Erzberger. The majority Socialists had been cautious about getting caught up in the wreck of the old regime, but the national interest had prevailed. On 5 October in a speech to the Reichstag, Prince Max publicly requested Wilson's aid in negotiating a peace. He stated that he did this on behalf not only of Germany but 'all humanity'.

All humanity was suffering a new catastrophe. October saw the influenza epidemic really expand into a global pandemic; it would eventually kill far more people than the war—in the region of 21 million. Because of its peculiar nature in over-stimulating immune systems, it was no less deadly in neutral countries than in the blockaded half-starved cities of central Europe. The prosperous USA was hit just as hard: 20,000 died in New York City. But wartime conditions undoubtedly helped it spread; troop ships and training camps were perfect incubators, and the movements of armies and refugees spread the disease more quickly. One in twenty of the population of the Gold Coast died in the autumn of 1918. The impact of the disease was worst in some of the remote places on Earth. In November and December it reached Western Samoa in the South Pacific, a German colony that had been seized by New Zealand troops without a shot in August 1914. The war had spared the island; disease did not. 7,500 Samoans died, 20 per cent of the population. Entire villages of Inuit died in the polar north.

Wilson's initial response to the German request was cautious. It was phrased as an enquiry rather than an answer. Had the Germans accepted the Fourteen Points? Were they prepared to evacuate all occupied territory immediately? Who exactly was the Chancellor speaking for? The leaders of the Entente powers who were meeting in Paris were worried that Wilson had omitted any military conditions from his note, and they suspected that the German generals might be playing for time. Clemenceau, Lloyd George, and the Italian Prime Minister Orlando sent a joint note to Washington insisting that any armistice be drafted by military experts in order to prevent the Germans resuming the fight.

Not for the first or last time the German navy now made a crucial and destructive intervention in the fate of the nation. On 11 October a U-boat sank the mail steamer *Leinster* with the loss of 450 lives, some of them American, 135 of them women and children. The news of this sinking arrived in Washington simultaneously with the largely positive German reply to Wilson's questions. American public and political opinion was once again outraged. Theodore Roosevelt expressed the view that government policy should be to demand unconditional surrender. Heavy losses at the front combined with the first signs of an American victory further hardened opinion.

The October fighting in the Argonne had continued ferociously. The US 1st Division suffered 9,000 casualties in the first ten days of the month. A battalion of the American 77th Division became a focus for national concern after being surrounded and cut off for six days. When it was relieved only a third of its original strength were still standing. On 8 October Corporal Alvin York won the Congressional Medal of Honor for capturing 132 German soldiers single-handed. A skilled rifleman from Tennessee, the intensely religious York had initially attempted to register his conscientious objection to his conscription, although he had later changed his mind. The mass surrender was perhaps also an indication that the will of the defenders was starting to break. General Pershing reorganized his forces for a new effort and aided by French advances on the easier ground to his left began a new assault on the Kriemhild position on 13 October. In this battle of Montfaucon, American forces finally managed to break through the line on 17 October. At the same time British, Belgian, and French forces finally fulfilled Haig's hope of a breakthrough in Flanders. Between 14 and 17 October they captured the key rail junctions of Douai and Lille, and on 19 October liberated Bruges and Zeebrugge.

As the German army retreated, it deliberately left devastation in its wake. Infrastructure and industrial assets were systematically destroyed in France and Belgium. This was presented as 'tactical' in that it was denying assets to the advancing enemy armies, but there is a strong sense that these actions, carried out when the battle had clearly turned against Germany, were a deliberate and malicious attempt to weaken France in the longer term. Advancing soldiers, particularly but not exclusively French ones, were angered by this behaviour. The British war correspondent Philip Gibbs reported that on the liberation of Valenciennes he was told by civilians that the Germans were 'bandits and brigands' who for four years had stolen and destroyed everything and had even burnt down houses on the night that they left. In some cases the reaction to liberation was exhausted indifference, but there were also instances of great rejoicing. In Lille the British and Australians under General

Birdwood were the first to arrive, but the first liberating French soldier was Carl Delesalle, the son of the mayor, causing popular delight. Clemenceau met an equally emotional response when he visited on 19 October.

This mixture of anger and growing confidence found expression in Wilson's response, which was received in Germany on 16 October. In it Wilson stated categorically that there would be no peace unless Germany abandoned its 'inhumane' warfare on land and sea, and that the 'arbitrary power' which had governed the German nation and led to war must be destroyed or at least neutered. In effect the demand now was for regime change.

On 17 October the German military and civilian leaders met to respond. Despite the developing string of defeats, Ludendorff now changed his tune, claiming everything was improving and if the home front could simply supply him with several hundred thousand men a month he would be able to hold out through the winter. Scheidemann was blunt: hundreds of thousands more men would not improve the morale of the army because the war had already broken the spirit of the people. The German population were disillusioned by the failure of the submarine war, by the defection of allies, and by the distress at home. Ludendorff then asked whether morale at home could be raised, to which Scheidemann replied, 'That is a question of potatoes.'

The central estimate of deaths caused by the blockade of Germany up until November 1918 is 424,000. Malnutrition struck many who did not die; ten-year-old boys in Freiburg were on average 2 centimetres shorter in 1918 than they had been in 1914. Not every area of the country suffered equally and the suffering was unevenly distributed through the population. This in many respects made things worse, as tensions between regions and between town and country had become severe. Farmers near Freiburg were charging 25 marks for 50 kilograms of potatoes when the official price was 9 marks. Urban populations had descended on the fields in 1918 simply to steal crops.

At the meeting Ludendorff had accused the civilian politicians of failing to deliver reinforcements and of failure to raise home front morale—they in turn were baffled as to why he now believed the army could hold out when he had not thought so three weeks earlier. Ludendorff may have convinced himself things had changed, but above all he was now positioning himself as the indomitable warrior who could not be held responsible for the defeat. He was constructing a story of betrayal, a 'stab in the back'. It was an idea guaranteed to resonate with the educated classes who were steeped in the music of Wagner: his portrayal of the German front-line soldier as Siegfried cast the civilian politicians as the cowardly Hagen. This was the view that would later be promulgated by Corporal Adolf Hitler, who was blinded by mustard gas in the British offensive on 15 October.

But the mood of most ordinary soldiers was not one of heroic immolation. Amongst the German soldiers killed in early October was the poet Gerrit Engelke, who died of wounds as a prisoner of the British on 11 October. He had served since 1915 at St-Mihiel, Verdun, the Somme, and in Champagne, and in 1916 had won the Iron Cross on the Yser. He had written little during the war but in 1918 he wrote *An die Soldaten des grossen Krieges* ('To the Soldiers of the Great War'):

> Come along! Comrades! For from front to front, from battlefield to battlefield,
> May the world's new holiday come to you all!
> Off with your steel helmets, caps, lay down your rifles
> Enough of this bloody hatred and murderous sense of honour.

Engelke had hoped that the war of peoples could be followed by a peace of peoples.

On 20 October the German government, after three days of fierce arguments, replied to Wilson that it agreed to suspend submarine warfare and stated that the new German government would be based on the representation of the people through equal, universal, direct franchise. Wilson's response on 23 October clearly reiterated the developing view that the military leaders of the Entente would need to agree the terms of an armistice. Clemenceau moved immediately to get Foch and Pétain to start drawing up detailed terms. Foch also consulted with Haig and Pershing. Haig was pessimistic as to whether the Germans were really on the point of collapse and spoke in favour of moderate terms. Pershing was confident that the Germans would soon be beaten down and indicated that if unconditional surrender was not pursued, then the armistice should be as harsh as possible.

In Germany the political crisis continued. The high command tried to distance itself from the government's reply, and Ludendorff, now apparently converted to the idea of a fight to the finish, was dismissed on 26 October. Germany now found itself facing the consequences of the destruction of its last ally. On 24 October, the first anniversary of Caporetto, General Armando Diaz, commanding the Italian army having replaced Cadorna, launched three Italian armies with British, French, Czechoslovak, and American support against the Hapsburg positions along the Piave river in northern Italy. Initially the attack was checked, but British forces under Lord Cavan managed to cross the river on 27 October and Diaz fed his reserves through the bridgehead. The defenders were cut in two and pockets began to be surrounded and to give up. The pace of surrender accelerated rapidly: by 1 November 100,000 prisoners had been taken and by 3 November this had risen above 400,000. The battle had been fought around the small town of Vittorio and it became known as 'Vittorio Veneto'. It was a major Allied victory and it went some way to restoring Italian pride.

Even as the battle was being fought the Hapsburg Empire was collapsing. As early as 24 October, Hungarian leaders had appealed to their soldiers just to return home and on 28 October the field commander Field Marshal Svetozar Boroević had communicated that only an immediate armistice could prevent anarchy. The new Foreign Minister Gyula Andrássy had agreed to accept Wilson's terms on 28 October, on the same day the Czechoslovak National Council had declared independence in Prague. A 'South Slav' council of Croats, Serbs, and Slovenes followed suit in Zagreb on 29 October. The 'Aster Revolution' in Budapest had already deposed the Hungarian government, the Emperor reluctantly accepting the new government formed by opponents of the war. On 31 October the former Prime Minister István Tisza was assassinated by communists in front of his wife, becoming another of the few leaders of 1914 who paid with his life for his failures. On 2 November the Emperor Karl authorized an armistice with the Italians which amounted to surrender: the army would surrender half its artillery and be reduced to twenty divisions (although it is questionable whether twenty even existed at this point), all Entente prisoners would be released, and the Entente would be allowed to move forces by rail through Austria against Germany.

The last fifty days of the war had seen genuinely decisive victories against three of the Central powers. Weakened by economic collapse and internal conflict as they certainly were, they were nevertheless still crushed on the battlefield. The German army had not quite suffered the same fate, but by the start of November it was only weeks, perhaps days away. French and American forces were now advancing rapidly in the Argonne, and on 6 November the French captured Sedan. The British attacked the line of the Sambre Canal on 4 November supported by a French attack on Guise. The battle is best remembered for the death of the poet Wilfred Owen, but it also saw the fall of the last organized German defence lines short of the Meuse. From this point the main problem for the advancing armies was the extent to which they were outrunning their own supply lines.

But the precipitating event in the final German collapse was the mutiny of the navy. The German Admiralty in a final and fatal decision decided to redeem the honour of the battleship fleet by ordering it out in a last desperate effort against the British, now reinforced by a large and powerful American contingent of modern battleships. The ordinary German seamen recognized this for the suicide mission it was. Morale in the battleship fleet had been deteriorating since 1916; bad rations and petty discipline had been exacerbated by the perceived gulf between ordinary sailors and their privileged officers. It is noteworthy that the U-boats, where officers and men had largely shared the risks and the conditions, remained entirely loyal despite the heavy casualties that had been suffered in that branch of the service. On 29 October the stokers extinguished the boilers and raised the red flag on three battleships; within days the revolt had swept through the entire fleet and by 6 November mutinous sailors controlled Kiel, Lübeck, Hamburg, and Bremen. The next day they began moving inland, spreading revolt through Germany. These mutinies were indirectly a triumph of the overwhelming superiority of the Royal Navy. After the war, conservatives would try to blame the mutinies on socialist subversion, but investigations indicated that the sailors' politicization followed their social grievances.

As the German collapse began, the Kaiser prepared to head to the army headquarters at Spa. This was partly in the hope of rallying the troops but also perhaps from a growing sense that he might not be safe near Berlin. The head of the Berlin police force provided a report on 29 October that the population now desired peace at any price and that they now looked to President Wilson for their salvation. The report claimed that the war had created immense social divisions in the city, as the munitions workers and profiteers had prospered at the expense of the solid middle classes. Murder, prostitution, and theft had soared above pre-war levels and the black market had corroded respect for law. The report ominously targeted 'eastern Jews' as a particularly dangerous group.

After the departure of the Kaiser to the front, Germany began to descend into the revolution precipitated by the navy. The news of the Austrian armistice and the naval mutinies accelerated the need to make peace quickly. In Munich on 7 November, Kurt Eisner of the militant Independent Socialist Party declared the monarchy abolished and an independent Bavarian Republic in front of a cheering crowd of more than 60,000 people.

The German armistice delegation which crossed the front line on 7 November was led by Erzberger. Foch was the main Allied representative. He aimed to secure a rapid evacuation of France and Belgium, to take control of bridgeheads over the Rhine, and to force the Germans to give up 5,000 artillery pieces, 2,000 aircraft, 30,000 machine guns, and 10,000 trucks to guarantee that they would be unable to resist any further advance. Significantly the British sent an admiral to the armistice negotiations. Admiral Wemyss was tasked to see that the German fleet, particularly the U-boats, was delivered into British hands. The Americans sent no representative. The Allied powers agreed that the blockade would be continued until Germany signed the final peace treaty. The German delegation was brought to a railway carriage in the forest of Compiègne to be told the terms that would be imposed for a ceasefire.

The German delegation were shocked by the conditions demanded. Erzberger pleaded that Germany was on the brink of Bolshevism, the blockade was contributing to social collapse, and the army required weapons to maintain order. Foch was implacable. Compiègne was not a negotiation.

In the meantime the German government that Erzberger was representing had indeed collapsed. The Kaiser had pleaded that he be allowed to lead his troops in a desperate attempt to restore his fortunes. General Groener with brutal lack of sentiment informed him that the army was no longer willing to follow him. On 9 November the Kaiser abdicated and the next day fled to Holland. The fall of the Kaiser was accompanied by the replacement of Prince Max by a republican government under the socialist Friedrich Ebert. The new government confirmed Erzberger's power to sign the armistice.

On the day that the Kaiser abdicated, the French soldier poet Guillaume Apollinaire died of Spanish influenza in Paris. He had been born Wilhelm Kostrowicki of Polish-Italian descent; on his deathbed he had heard the crowds in the street outside shouting 'death to Wilhelm' and wondered in his delirium why they hated him. Apollinaire was the most important modernist writer to die in the war. His *Calligrammes*, published in 1918, were perhaps the most radically innovative response amongst all the war poets.

Erzberger signed the Armistice under protest at 5 a.m. on 11 November. It went into effect at noon European time, 11 a.m. GMT. Some American generals deliberately scheduled attacks on the last morning of the war in full knowledge of the imminent ceasefire; the last soldier known to have died in combat on the Western Front was Henry Gunther from Baltimore, killed in the Argonne at 10.59 a.m. Part of the BEF ended the war at Mons; the first British soldier to die in battle is buried within yards of the last.

The news of the signing of the Armistice triggered massive celebrations on the streets of the main cities of the Allied powers. Popular relief was tempered with mourning for the dead. The British Empire had lost over a million men, the French 1,400,000. Wilfred Owen's mother received news of his death on the morning of 11 November.

Over the next few days British, French, and American forces crossed the Rhine bridges into Germany. French soldiers in particular reacted with anger to the German towns and countryside unscarred by conflict. There were numerous acts of petty abuse and some serious violence.

British forces on the other hand seem to have been much more concerned with the prospect of demobilization. Failure to discharge the longest-serving men led to a series of mutinies during the winter, the most serious being at Calais. This was not confined to bases in Europe; Australian forces mutinied in Egypt.

German demobilization was something of a haphazard affair. Many soldiers simply slipped off home. Later a mythology would develop that returning soldiers had been insulted and humiliated, but in fact the civilian authorities went out of their way to celebrate the achievements of the troops. Indeed it was the socialist politician Scheidemann who insisted on addressing them as 'undefeated in the field'. This rhetoric, understandable for a government nervous about the loyalties of returning troops in a revolutionary situation, would later be used as further evidence for the idea of a stab in the back.

Germany had technically not surrendered, but the acceptance of the armistice terms was a clear admission of complete defeat. The military quickly disassociated themselves from the Armistice, but it had been the military leadership that had compelled the representatives to sign. The German defeat in 1918 was simultaneously military, economic, and political; indeed it could not be otherwise. For four years Germany had been juggling its limited resources between maintaining its armies in the field, sustaining the civilian population and therefore the political order at home, and supporting its weak allies. If it failed in any one of these vital tasks, then defeat would quickly follow. All three had to be kept up and in the autumn of 1918 all three efforts failed almost simultaneously. Defeat on the battlefield in the west discouraged civilians and allies, the grinding down of the domestic war economy discouraged the army and prevented the provision of resources to allies, the collapse of allies discouraged the military and civilians alike. By late September there were no reasons to hope for success and the inevitability of failure set off the search for an end to the conflict.

Similarly the victory of the Western powers was a military, economic, and political victory. It was hard won. It is easy to look at the imbalance of population and industry and decry the inefficiency of the war effort in taking four years to defeat the Central powers. But this is to miss the point. The Central powers had initiated war in 1914 because they believed their martial qualities would give them a reasonable chance of victory against the economic odds. The Austrians had proved deluded on this score, but the Germans had reason for their belief. The slow process by which the armies of Britain and France became a match for their opponent did not really reach full fruition until late 1918. At sea, however, the picture was different. The German navy showed some real tactical qualities, but strategically it was a mismatch; the superiority of the British navy was unchallenged from late 1914 onwards. As a result German ambitions for a 'world war' were largely constrained to Europe and parts of the Near East, and the Entente was able to build on its initial economic advantage.

In 1914–15 Germany was able to expand its economic base with the capture of territories in the east and west. Contrary to the widespread view of liberal economists before the war, plunder of resources could be carried out to the benefit of the German economy. But by contrast the British control of the seas which allowed access both to the tropics and to the 'neo-Europes' of the British Dominions, Latin America, and above all the USA was much more significant. The British economy was protected from contraction and the global division of labour established by the 'empire of free trade' was allowed to operate in a relatively uninhibited fashion. This in turn allowed the French to recover from the shattering losses of resources of 1914. By contrast the 'autarkic' Central powers were increasingly forced to improvise on the basis of constrained resources, unavoidable but far less 'efficient'. To some extent this was also at the root of Russian failure. The expensive British investment in naval power killed very few Germans in uniform but it nevertheless won the war. It finally did so because the growing economic entanglement between Britain and the United States provoked Germany into a reckless policy of confrontation with the latter. But this was not only an economic clash. In the end British and American forms of 'liberalism', an ideology driven by a shared vision of global capitalist trade, were united by a desire to protect the nineteenth-century order of things, including peace, representative government, and gradual reform. As the war continued they were able to wed this to a pragmatic accommodation with the idea of national self-determination, at least for Europeans, which would be mediated through international law embodied in a new form of transnational organization. National self-determination plus a League of Nations was a winning political formula, something that even Matthias Erzberger came to recognize in 1918 when he wrote a pamphlet endorsing the proposal.

By contrast Germany never really found a political objective to the war beyond self-aggrandizement and the destruction of the existing order. Anti-colonial rhetoric did have an appeal, resentment against the British, French, and Russian empires was real enough, and some of the forces unleashed by Germany in wartime would gather strength in the aftermath of the conflict; but it became all too apparent that German anti-colonialism was being bound in service to the creation of a German Empire. Similarly German flirtations with 'state socialism' as a war ideal could not hide the reactionary 'DNA' of the regime. Hapsburg thinking was even more reactionary, although perhaps a little more benign; it really was trying to put the clock back to an imagined happy multi-ethnic family under paternalistic Imperial rule. Indeed the Hapsburg war against nationalism climaxed with a concerted effort to persuade the Serbian population that the Empire was their protector against nationalist 'bandits', with the aim of turning the Serbs into grateful Hapsburg citizens after the war. Meanwhile the Empire as a whole saw itself in practice being reduced to little more than an appendix of Germany, with the result that the existing national minorities more than ever felt the need to break with Vienna.

Similarly the Turks never really worked out what their ultimate goals in the war were. Early appeals to global Islam faltered in the short term, although they would be the wellspring of a powerful subterranean current in twentieth-century history. The last year of the war saw the pursuit of a strange and impractical 'Pan-Turanian' dream in which the Turks would seek back their destiny on the steppes they had left 900 years earlier. In fact the ultimate victor would be a limited nationalism under Mustafa Kemal, who would become the 'father' of a new compact and largely ethnically unified Turkish nation.

Although France, the United States, and the British Empire would all later commemorate the end of the war on 'Armistice Day', the war did not end at 11 a.m. Greenwich Mean Time on 11 November 1918. Indeed in many places even the fighting had not ended. In the north of Russia,

British forces found themselves heavily engaged with the Bolsheviks even as the Armistice went into effect. But even the Armistice with Germany gave little immediate indication of what peace would look like or when it would come. Germany might reject the final peace terms and choose to resume fighting, even if the Armistice had been designed to make such a choice difficult bordering on suicidal. Germany could cease to exist as a unified entity or descend into such complete chaos that it would be hard to know who to make peace with. Germany might succumb to a Bolshevik revolution and join with the Soviet Union in a renewed apocalyptic class war. Or the victorious powers might themselves collapse into squabbling, and seek individual settlements with whoever could be found to negotiate. Over the next six months all of these outcomes appeared close to realization at times.

One last formal armistice with Germany still needed to be implemented. Lettow-Vorbeck only discovered the news of the Armistice a week after the ceasefire on the Western Front, ending the war on the soil of the British Empire in Northern Rhodesia. He returned to Germany to acclaim as an 'undefeated hero', but his prolonged campaign had achieved nothing militarily. British Imperial casualties in combat were tiny compared to those in Europe and the Middle East, and the war in Africa remained strategically a 'sideshow'. But it had cost the lives of almost 100,000 African porters on both sides and many more civilians caught up in the predations of the armies. It would take generations for parts of East Africa to recover; the wealth of wildlife in the region in the mid-twentieth century was not a sign of pristine nature, but a product of the devastation of the human communities.

An even greater human disaster continued to unfold within the Russian Empire. On 18 November Admiral Kolchak overthrew the legitimate but ineffective government in the city of Ufa. This began a clear turn towards the White struggle becoming purely reactionary. The Russian Empire was torn apart by a conflict between two brutal anti-democratic forces, multiple other factions, and invading foreign armies. The anti-war protests of 1917 which had brought down the Tsarist regime and the Provisional Government had not ended the war: they had unleashed anarchy.

But any attempt to restore the old dynastic global order was doomed to failure. On 11 November the Hapsburg Emperor Karl had declared that he was withdrawing from exercising power and that he would accept whatever constitutional arrangement his peoples made. On 12 November a German Austrian Republic was declared and on 16 November a Hungarian Republic. In fact Karl had deliberately refused to abdicate the Austrian throne and soon reiterated his claim, resulting in a stalemate not broken until eventually he fled to Switzerland. The Austrian Parliament then passed a law in April 1919 specifically deposing the Hapsburg family, ending the career of the world's longest-ruling major dynasty.

By contrast the newest dynasty, the House of Windsor (est. 1917), was less threatened by the transition to democracy. The United Kingdom held a general election in December 1918 under the terms of the recently passed Representation of the People Act, which expanded the electorate by removing previous residential and property restrictions and rendering almost all men over twenty-one eligible to vote. One exception was conscientious objectors who were temporarily disenfranchised for having exercised their legal right, a clear indication of the importance of military service in this extension of democracy. Propertied women over the age of thirty were also enfranchised in part to counterbalance the feared radicalism of younger men. Lloyd George was re-elected as Prime Minister of a coalition which was in reality mostly the Conservative Party. This 'khaki' election had heard a great deal of rhetoric about 'making Germany pay', and this would haunt the British government during the peace negotiations. The Labour Party, now for the first time fully committed to a socialist platform, made gains at the expense of the Asquithian Liberals, who were almost wiped out. So were the Irish Parliamentary Party who were comprehensively defeated by Sinn Féin in most of Ireland. Amongst the Sinn Féiners elected was Constance Markiewicz, the first ever woman MP, although like all her Sinn Féin colleagues she refused to take her seat in Westminster and was instead a founder of the Dáil Éireann, an Irish parliament that began to sit in Dublin from 21 January 1919. The new self-proclaimed Irish government would attempt to participate in the peace conference, to the considerable embarrassment of Woodrow Wilson, who did not intend this particular interpretation of 'self-determination'.

Wilson had decided to take an active and personal role in the peace negotiations. The first President ever to leave American soil whilst in office, he crossed the Atlantic and landed in France on 13 December 1919. His arrival in Paris was met by rapturous crowds. Wilson had become a popular hero in wartime Europe, supported by trade unionists and moderate socialists who saw him as the embodiment of a peaceful and progressive future.

Moderate socialists found themselves confronting radicals in Germany and in doing so they allied with the most reactionary elements. On 4 January 1919 the Reich government dismissed the self-proclaimed head of the Berlin police, the Independent Socialist Emil Eichorn. This precipitated an uprising of the most militant wing of the socialists, the Spartacist group led by Karl Liebknecht. The government used the army and right-wing paramilitary volunteers, the *Freikorps*, to savagely put down the uprising. Liebknecht and Rosa Luxemburg were captured and murdered on 14 January. Government sponsorship for the *Freikorps* created a permanent breach between the SPD and the emergent German Communist Party. The satirical artist George Grosz produced a print of a *Freikorps* officer, complete with monocle, drinking the blood of the workers. He entitled it 'Cheers, Noske' in reference to the socialist politician who had authorized the action.

The first election of the German Republic was on 19 January 1919. It saw a turnout of more than 80 per cent, with women, enfranchised on a basis of equality, voting for the first time in similar numbers and ways to men. The largest single party was the SPD with 38 per cent of the vote (the Independent Socialists obtained just over 7 per cent). The parties that had joined the SPD in the 1917 peace resolution, the progressive Democrats and the Catholic *Zentrum*, each got about 20 per cent. A clear majority of adult Germans had voted for moderation and for democracy. Many of the voters hoped that this would send a clear signal to their former enemies that the nation had genuinely embraced Wilsonian ideals and that this would influence the nature of the peace treaty. Unfortunately, by their actions the old establishment were sending a very different signal. Remarkably, elements of the military were even at this point attempting to secure a victory in the east, as if the gains of Brest-Litovsk could still be maintained after the Armistice. In Courland, General von der Goltz was plotting to use the *Freikorps* ostensibly against the Bolsheviks, but in reality to overthrow the new governments of the

Baltic states. In Paris, the Polish leader Roman Dmowski warned the Allies that Germany was Janus-faced, making peace in the west whilst waging war in the east. Local Germans and the retreating army were committing atrocities against the Polish population and the Poles were also threatened by Ukranian nationalists and the Bolsheviks.

The peace conference officially opened on 19 January. Lloyd George and Wilson wanted to engage with the Bolshevik regime, if only to win the propaganda battle, but Clemenceau did not. In part this was because France had been Russia's main creditor and the Bolsheviks had repudiated these debts. In the end the Bolsheviks were invited to meet with their Russian opponents on an island off the Turkish coast. The 'White' Russians refused. The conference set up a commission on the proposed League of Nations. Wilson vigorously supported this, but the principle blueprint came from Jan Smuts. Smuts wanted a League that would reflect the interests of the white Dominions of the British Empire; like Wilson he tended to see non-whites as childlike people to be paternalistically ruled, certainly not suited to self-determination. A major part of the business of the new League would be disposing of the German overseas empire and the non-Turkish parts of the Ottoman Empire. The suggested solution was 'mandates': periods of tutelage which would lead to self-rule when peoples were finally ready for it. In practice these League of Nations mandates seemed suspiciously similar to the imperial ambitions of wartime diplomacy.

The Japanese stirred up a great deal of trouble by arguing for a racial equality clause in the League charter; this of course was based on their own irritation at their citizens being discriminated against rather than any genuine belief that other people were equal to the Japanese. At the same time the Japanese government was insistent on its share of mandates in the Pacific, which quickly became imperial possessions.

The return to France of the lost provinces of Alsace-Lorraine was endorsed. The population was not consulted, but Lorraine, birthplace of Joan of Arc, was clearly French. Alsace was German speaking, but the experience of German rule since 1871 had been unhappy and the population were probably content to be returned. Another German nineteenth-century conquest, Schleswig, was returned to the neutral Danes. More contentiously, Germany would lose territory in the east to newly independent Poland. Most of it was clearly and obviously inhabited by Poles; in Silesia there would be referenda over contested areas. Although German nationalists would complain bitterly about these 'mutilations', hardly any of the territory surrendered was primarily inhabited by ethnic Germans. The more reasonable grievance and a clear breach of self-determination was the clause preventing union with German Austria. The reason was cynically pragmatic: such a union would leave Germany more populous than it had been in 1914, and for that alone it was completely unacceptable to France.

Throughout the conference Clemenceau tried to pursue French future security. Germany was to be permanently disarmed as far as possible. The German army would be limited to 100,000 men, the navy reduced to a coastal defence force; Germany would not be allowed tanks, aircraft, or U-boats. The Germans would not be allowed to station forces in the Rhineland. In the immediate aftermath of the war none of this seemed anything but obvious to anyone other than the Germans. The more idealistic hoped and the conference hinted that this forced disarmament would be the first stage of a more general process of disarmament which would eventually embrace the victors as well as the vanquished.

France also sought to bolster its security by the creation of friendly powers to the east. The loss of the Russian alliance, which had been the bulwark of France up until 1914, led to a search for alternatives. This did not always prove easy. The French wanted a strong Yugoslavia and the nucleus of this existed in the state that had been created on 1 December 1918 when the ex-Hapsburg South Slav Council had decided to join with Serbia. But the Yugoslavs clashed with the Romanians, who wanted to annex the ex-Hungarian Banat, and Yugoslavia was also in conflict with Italian ambitions in Dalmatia and Slovenia. Italian irritation at what they saw as a betrayal of the wartime promises they had been made led to their withdrawal from the conference at the end of April, although their Foreign Minister would ultimately return to sign the treaty. A more outright betrayal was the decision to simply 'award' the tiny Kingdom of Montenegro to the new Yugoslavia, despite it having been a wartime ally.

Although Czechoslovakia was later derided as a product of Versailles, the Czech leadership had already created the state by February 1919; what was decided in Paris were the frontiers. Significant numbers of Sudeten Germans found themselves within the state in order to give it 'secure' borders, as were significant numbers of Magyars. This helped precipitate a crisis in Hungary, and on 21 March the Hungarian government under Count Károlyi was forced to resign after the French had ordered further withdrawals of Hungarian troops from disputed territory. He had tried to implement social reform, including land redistribution, but was haunted by the increasing pressure of the Czechoslovaks, Romanians, and Yugoslavs, all of whom were involved in incursions to grab territory before a final peace treaty. Károlyi, who had had wartime contact with the Entente, hoped to be treated as an ally; instead Hungary was subjected to blockade and invasion and he lost the confidence of all parties. Communists seized power, releasing their leader Béla Kun from prison. Kun, who had been converted to Bolshevism whilst a prisoner of war in Russia, nationalized all large businesses and landed estates, abolished titles of nobility, forced the clergy to work in hospitals, and instituted sex education in schools. The Hungarian revolution alarmed the allies in Paris that the Bolshevik revolution was on the point of overwhelming central Europe. Lloyd George imagined a 300-million-strong Red Army under German officers sweeping west. Clemenceau, encouraged by Foch, wanted to unleash the Romanians to crush the revolution. Instead, Jan Smuts was despatched to talk to the Hungarian communists in the hope of opening a new channel of communication to Lenin.

Lenin's hoped-for European revolution appeared to have begun. In Bavaria, Eisner had been defeated at the polls and then murdered by a right-wing fanatic in February 1919. Left-wing militants now rallied to the communists and on 6 April the communist writer and war veteran Ernst Toller seized power and declared a Bavarian Soviet Republic. But the social basis of his power was very limited, and a counter-revolution was quickly organized by the *Freikorps* who overthrew the Soviet on 3 May. Counter-revolutionary violence was widespread in Germany. The *Freikorps* acted pre-emptively in Berlin in March, slaughtering in cold blood more than 1,000 left wingers including many of the sailors who had mutinied the previous year. The *Freikorps* presented themselves as war veterans but many of them were actually recruited from those who were slightly too young to have served. The vast majority of German war veterans showed little interest in either politics or street fighting but simply wished to resume their civilian lives.

Within Russia the Bolsheviks were experiencing mixed fortunes: from the end of April they were able to start to drive Admiral Kolchak back through Siberia, but they were still losing ground in the south to the forces of General Anton Denikin (a protégé of Kornilov), which had been aided by the French intervention at Odessa. Trotsky's efforts in creating a disciplined Red Army were starting to bear fruit, and ultimately the atrocities committed by reactionary White forces against workers and peasants meant that the Red armies got enough tacit support to win, despite peasant hatred of the grain requisitions of 'war communism'. Fear of Bolshevism had become a global obsession. There was a massive disturbance as far away as Buenos Aires where more than fifty died and the government responded by interning Russian agitators. Workers in Johannesburg seized the town hall, and in New South Wales striking miners and seamen brought the state to near collapse. In Winnipeg a general strike in the spring caused nervousness throughout North America. In Britain, Basil Thomson, the head of Special Branch, was convinced that Bolsheviks were behind the growing industrial militancy; in Glasgow, paralysed by a general strike in February, there was a certain amount of revolutionary rhetoric, but Lloyd George was able to get the main trade unionist leaders negotiating through the spring. In Italy the growth of militant socialism provoked the formation of Mussolini's *Fascio milanese di combattimento*, sponsored by the small businessmen in the city. Its inaugural meeting on 23 March was guarded by a squad of armed blackshirted *arditi*, former stormtroops of the Italian army. By the middle of April groups of fascists had been founded in most of northern Italy. The United States was also facing a militant surge: there would be 3,600 strikes in 1919. But what terrified the respectable public was a letter-bomb campaign and the riots in Boston, New York, and Cleveland on May Day. Ex-servicemen were prominent in the attacks on socialists in New York; by the end of the year the American Legion would play an important part in anti-socialist repression. Black ex-servicemen on the other hand were perceived by the authorities as part of the problem. At least ten black veterans were murdered by white mobs in the South with the collusion of the police. Many black leaders tried to get to Paris in the hope of adding a racial equality clause to the peace conference, but the State Department refused passports to most of them. The Attorney General Mitchell Palmer believed that the Bolsheviks were behind black militancy and that their leaders were 'seeing red'.

The limitations of a Wilsonian world fit for democracy in the face of the red scare and racial prejudice were starkly illustrated in British India. Terrified of the prospect of Bolshevik subversion, the British had introduced the 'Rowlatt' Acts which allowed extensive detention without trial. Popular protests against these measures, which seemed to insult India's wartime contribution, had united the Indian National Congress, now lead by Mohandas Gandhi, and a growing Khalifat movement, which feared for the loss of Muslim influence if the Ottoman Caliph was deposed. A mass protest in the Punjab city of Amritsar was met by disproportionate violence by Indian Army troops under the command of General Dyer on 5 April 1919. The British admitted to killing 379 protesters; the INC claimed that more than 1,000 had died. Less noticed in the west was another anti-colonial uprising inspired by Wilsonian rhetoric: on 1 March 1919 a group of Korean students declared independence from the Japanese, inspiring massive protests in the peninsula. These too were bloodily repressed in March and April: the Japanese admitted over 500 civilian deaths, Korean sources claiming more than 7,000. In response Korean exiles formed a provisional government in Shanghai. Egyptians who had been under effective British rule for decades also appealed to Wilson for self-determination and mounted mass protests; the British responded with martial law.

Many hopes would be frustrated in Paris. Amongst those in the city was the Vietnamese revolutionary Nguyễn Ái Quốc, later to become known as Hồ Chí Minh, who petitioned Wilson for the end of French rule in Indochina. He was ignored and this reinforced his growing conviction that the liberation of his country could only be achieved by Leninist anti-imperialism. Wilson had no desire to upset the British and French over the issue of empire, not least because there were sufficient tensions and divisions over the peace with Germany.

Reparations were to be imposed on the defeated power by the victors, but they were not a fine for losing, unlike the indemnity that Germany had demanded of France in 1871. Nor were they an attempt to make

Germany pay for the burden of fighting the war. They were recompense for damage done, to force the German taxpayer to carry the cost of rebuilding and replacing the civilian property destroyed by the actions of the German forces. Because Germany had been only briefly invaded the physical damage to the country had been minimal, and it did not seem unreasonable to most non-German observers to expect Germany to pay this bill. But there were two related problems: one was defining what were the reasonable limits to German liability for 'war damage', and second was the moral basis for the claim. After all, if Germany had simply been acting in self-defence in August 1914, then the fact that the war had been fought on foreign soil was an unfortunate outcome of its own military skill for which it should not be held responsible. On the other hand if Germany had deliberately unleashed the war on its innocent neighbours, then it could be argued that morally it was responsible for all the damage done, including the human cost.

Wilson wanted reparations defined as narrowly as possible. Lloyd George, worried that the bulk of reparations would go to the French and that the British would lose out, wanted a much wider definition that would help cover the costs of the war, as the electorate had been promised and as the Conservative press still demanded. Clemenceau knew that it would be difficult to get everything his public wanted, but was determined to secure German payment for the rebuilding of northern France, a task which would be beyond the French taxpayer unaided. Clemenceau initially also favoured a narrow definition of war damage. It was the British who pushed for the broader definition. Ingeniously Jan Smuts suggested that 'damages' should also include the cost of pensions for widows, orphans, and the disabled, a definition which had an obvious appeal in the British dominions distant from the battlefields. Billy Hughes, the virulently anti-German Prime Minister of Australia, stated that the costs to the bereaved families in his nation were every bit as real as destroyed houses in France. The seriously wounded in the British and French empires numbered in the millions. Some of their injuries were horrendous; men survived who would probably not have done in earlier conflicts. The American sculptor Anna Coleman Ladd had come to France in 1917 to make masks for men whose faces had been completely destroyed. By 1919 she had made 195 wonderfully detailed masks, based on photographs of the men before their maiming, but there were an estimated 20,000 such men. The dead had also left a burden: in the United Kingdom there were 192,678 widows and 355,211 children eligible for pensions.

The decision to include these costs would eventually drive up the reparations bill to a level which was likely to damage the economies of both Germany and the victors if it were ever paid, because excessive reparations would devalue the German currency to such an extent as to make German exports too cheap to compete with. Only by permanently excluding Germany from global trade could this be countered, and this in itself would damage the world economy. But it should be noted that the new German government was instituting a level of pension provision for its own 'war victims' that would be considerably higher than that in most of the victor countries. The real burden on the German state after the war was not reparations, which were barely ever paid and then only on a very long repayment schedule, but its own war-related expenditure.

The most radical alternative suggestion came from John Maynard Keynes, an economic advisor in the British conference delegation. He wanted all war debts cancelled; this would remove the burden of payments from governments struggling to deal with reconstruction. General cancellation would make France and Italy net winners, Britain would lose out slightly, and the United States would take a loss of £1,688 million. But as the USA had confiscated German property worth many times this amount it would be a nominal loss. This cancellation of inter-allied debt would make space that would allow the victorious powers room to reduce or even remove any claim for reparations. The Americans disliked the idea of cancelling the loans whilst being sympathetic to the idea of limiting reparations as they had suffered no major losses. The French liked the idea of cancelling the debts, but still felt Germany needed to pay for the devastation inflicted on France.

What caught the Entente powers by surprise was the intensity of German reactions to the clause justifying reparations, the so-called 'war guilt clause'. Article 231 stated that the German government bore the primary responsibility for the outbreak of the war. For the German right, some of whom were aware of how uncomfortably close to the mark this was, the clause was an insult to national honour. For the German centre and left this was an unfair burden to place on a new government which had rejected the old order.

On 8 May Friedrich Ebert announced a national day of mourning in response to the Allied terms; Scheidemann called them a sentence of death. Perhaps 200,000 gathered outside the Reichstag to protest on 15 May. On 31 May Walter Rathenau published an article entitled 'The End'. Rather than sign the peace treaty he argued that the government should simply dissolve itself and force the Entente powers to take over the government of Germany. They would soon recognize the impracticality of permanent occupation and would be forced to re-establish a German government on better terms. But Erzberger argued in cabinet that the actual result of intransigence would be that further delay would see the break-up of Germany and even greater loss of frontier areas. Groener, commanding the army, agreed with this; the military could do nothing to prevent occupation in the west and needed to be able to defend the east and maintain domestic order. If Germany signed the treaty it could buy time that would allow the hostile coalition of enemies to fall apart and allow a chance to renegotiate later.

Through the continuing blockade, the Entente powers were using hunger as a weapon to force Germany to capitulate. An estimated 100,000 Germans died of hunger after the signing of the Armistice. The maintenance of this blockade was becoming increasingly controversial. Herbert Hoover wanted it lifted, partly driven by humanitarian motives, but he was also seeking to sell the substantial supply of over-produced American pork to the desperate Germans. In the end about one month's supply was allowed through. In the United Kingdom reports from British soldiers about civilian suffering around Cologne had begun to soften attitudes. The Quaker Dorothy Buxton formed a lobbying group 'Fight the Famine', which in April 1919 became 'Save the Children' and which would go on to organize famine relief in central Europe and Russia. In the meantime the blockade powerfully added to the sense of grievance in Germany.

For the long run of world history there was another angry response to the proposed peace treaty that was perhaps even more significant than that in Germany. China had been an Allied power, albeit an essentially non-combatant one, and thousands of Chinese labourers and merchant seamen had aided the Allied effort. China's reward was to see the German colony of Tsingtao in northern China handed over to the Japanese and further economic concessions made to Japan. This was rightly seen as outrageous and led to a great protest by students and intellectuals in Tiananmen Square on 4 May 1919. The Chinese government joined those other states refusing to sign the treaty.

On 15 May 1919, 20,000 Greek soldiers landed at the city of Smyrna on the west coast of Asia Minor. Smyrna had an ethnically mixed population including many Greek speakers. Although this was claimed to be justified as a purely military measure under the terms of the Armistice of Mudros, it was clearly intended as a precursor to annexation of the coastal area and the establishment of a 'greater Greece'. The Greek occupation led immediately to inter-group violence and some 100 Greek and more than 400 Turkish civilians were killed, most of the latter by the occupiers. In response to this invasion Mustafa Kemal, now a senior Ottoman commander, sponsored the 'Amasya circular' on 22 June, which warned that the territorial integrity and independence of 'Turkey' was under threat and called for resistance. Reprimanded by the Sultan, he took a leave of absence rather than respond to the summons to return to Istanbul. This marked the beginning of what became known as the Turkish War of Independence. Kemal had been encouraged in his actions by clandestine contacts with the Bolsheviks, who would later provide arms for the Turkish resistance as a 'second front' against their enemies.

This was the context for the court martial in absentia in Constantinople of key leaders of the previous regime. The Ottoman government had been placed under pressure by the occupying forces to hold the Young Turk leaders to account for the massacre of the Armenians and others. On 22 July the court martial brought in a guilty verdict. These trials were an unprecedented attempt to establish culpability for a massive violation of human rights; they were also highly dubious in procedure and conducted under foreign pressure. The reliability of this proceeding remains a matter of enormous historical controversy between Armenian and Turkish nationalists. It was Armenian gunmen who carried out the death penalty in the form of street assassinations on several of the men found guilty.

Only a few individuals would be tried in Germany for war crimes, but for Germany as a nation the reckoning approached. The German delegation at Versailles objected to Article 231, the possible scale of reparations, the potential territorial losses, and the scale of disarmament. On 29 May they made a set of counter-proposals based on their interpretation of Wilson's Fourteen Points. These came close to splitting the Council: the French were furious, but members of the British and American delegations were becoming critical of the French who they saw as inhumanly vengeful and territorially ambitious. An abortive separatist uprising in the Rhineland was widely seen as the result of French intrigues. But in the end the 'Big Three' stuck together and on 16 June the Germans were informed they had three days to accept the treaty, although the deadline was quickly extended to 23 June.

On 21 June the German High Seas Fleet which had been anchored at Scapa Flow in the Orkney Islands was scuttled by its crews to prevent its handover to the British and their allies. Although the Germans cheered this act of defiance, it was these sunk German battleships off the Scottish coast rather than the inconclusive action at Jutland that was the real measure of British naval victory in the war. The one force that could genuinely threaten the survival of the United Kingdom had been destroyed and Britain's major war aim was achieved. Privately the British leadership had actually wanted to sink the German fleet, as deciding who should have it had become a point of contention amongst the victors.

Germany really had no choice. Hindenburg stated that he preferred honourable defeat to shameful surrender whilst at the same time informing the politicians that military resistance was impossible. On 28 June, five years to the day since the momentous assassination in Sarajevo, the German delegation, under protest, signed the Treaty of Versailles in the Hall of Mirrors where the German Second Reich had been proclaimed. The German delegation were made to enter the hall past four French sentries who had suffered severe facial injuries. The German Assembly ratified the peace treaty on 9 July. The passage through the Reichstag was contentious and the final vote close.

On 19 July London and Paris celebrated Peace Day. The centrepiece of the British celebrations was a temporary structure designed by Edwin Lutyens. Named the Cenotaph, Greek for 'empty tomb', this stark modernist monolith symbolized the dead of the British Empire. It produced such a powerful public response that the government commissioned a permanent copy. By contrast the French temporary Cenotaph, which had been displayed on Bastille Day, was a more figurative affair and was despised by public and critics alike, Clemenceau dismissing it as '*boche art* of Munich inspiration'. That night the newly married Lady Diana Duff Cooper fell through a skylight whilst watching the fireworks on her roof, breaking her thigh, an inauspicious start to her married life and to the peace. Equally inauspicious was the boycott of the Peace Day celebrations in Dublin by thousands of Irish ex-servicemen. In Luton in southern England disgruntled ex-servicemen burnt down the town hall.

Back in the United States, Wilson had spoken to Congress in support of the peace treaty, including the creation of a League of Nations, on 10 July, but through the summer and autumn he faced mounting opposition whilst his health deteriorated. In November after a failure to reach a compromise on the wording establishing the League of Nations, the treaty was rejected. Meanwhile the French Chamber of Deputies ratified the Versailles Treaty in September. Many felt that the treaty was too lenient, that it had failed to guarantee French security. Clemenceau addressed them, 'What you are going to vote for today, is not even a beginning, it is the beginning of the beginning... enter it well into your heads that this treaty is a set of possibilities.'

Those possibilities would shape the world through the twentieth century and beyond. Stalin and Hitler tried to change the verdict of both the war and the peace, but the Europe that finally emerged at the end of the twentieth century was the product of the democratic and nationalist revolution of the war years. Despite the racist limits of the Wilsonian vision it was a revolution that would spread far beyond Europe. The British Empire began its rapid transformation into a vague 'commonwealth'. German leadership in Europe when it finally came would be consensual and benign in a way unimaginable in 1914. The United States would discover, for good and ill, that once it had acted militarily in the world beyond the western hemisphere it would never be able to withhold its influence again. The uncontrollable costs, human and material, of this war of peoples did not end all wars, but in its destructiveness it demonstrated why ultimately war itself must end.

HISTORIOGRAPHY: HOW HISTORIANS HAVE INTERPRETED THE WAR

The modern historiography of the First World War begins in the early 1960s. There are four major reasons for this. The first is that the 1960s saw the deaths of the last major military and political leaders (for example, Paul von Lettow-Vorbeck in 1964, Maxime Weygand and Winston Churchill in 1965, and Alexander Kerensky in 1970). By the 1980s even the vast majority of ordinary veterans had died, with the last handful surviving until the second decade of the twenty-first century. This began to free historians to treat the subject as 'ordinary' history as well as ending the generation of new first-hand accounts.

The second is that from fifty years after the event previously closed archives became available. This reduced the reliance on published material. The fall of communism between 1989 and 1991 may have resulted in the last big archival opening—including not only Russian material but also material captured by the Russians during the Second World War. This process is now largely complete; although there are probably still some papers in private hands which might have an impact on the larger analysis, it is likely that historians are close to having access to nearly everything important that will ever come to light.

The third is changed perspectives. The 1960s and 1970s saw the processes of decolonization and western European union fundamentally altering the contemporary perspectives in which the history of the First World War was written, whilst the 1990s with the collapse of the Iron Curtain and the bloody break-up of Yugoslavia provided a further shift in the understanding of the war which refocused attention on central and eastern Europe. It is probable that the centenaries of the war will witness further reconsiderations.

Finally there was a change in those writing about the war. The vast majority of those mentioned below are professionally-trained historians with no personal (even childhood) memories of the First World War (and increasingly none of any personal involvement in war at all). Fritz Fischer, the oldest of the pioneers below discussed, was born in 1908, John Terraine in 1921, Paul Fussell in 1924, Jean-Jacques Becker in 1928. The historiography of the war is now firmly in the hands of a generation born after the end of the Second World War.

The works mentioned here are a fraction of those that have influenced this book. I have almost certainly left out friends and colleagues who ought to be mentioned here, for which I can only apologize. There are also some books and articles that do not fit obviously with the eight thematic strands below and which I list separately at the end. The discussion below is heavily weighted towards the historiography in English on the assumption that this is more accessible to the readers of this book. But where books initially published in languages other than English have influenced this historiography, they are noted.

Key works and their heritage since 1960

1. Fritz Fischer, *Griff nach der Weltmacht* (1961), translated as *Germany's Aims in the First World War* (1967)

Fritz Fischer, a professor at the University of Hamburg, began the modern historiography of the First World War with this study which translates more literally as 'The Bid for World Power'. Paying detailed attention to the high-level discussions of German politicians, generals, opinion formers, and industrialists from September 1914 onwards, Fischer rejected the idea that Germany had been forced into a war of self-defence, but argued instead that the First World War was a deliberate attempt to attain global dominance through conquest. Fischer effectively argued that Article 231 of the Versailles Treaty, which had assigned primary responsibility to Germany, was correct and that in important respects Imperial Germany prefigured the Germany of Hitler in its territorial ambition. This view caused enormous controversy in the Federal Republic of Germany and was widely condemned by conservative German historians.

Fischer responded to his critics with an even more monumental work, *Krieg der Illusionen* (1969), translated as the *War of Illusions* (1975), which argued that the war was a product of an attempt by the German ruling class to forestall the internal challenge posed by socialism. This was the so-called 'primacy of domestic politics'. Some of Fischer's ideas had been anticipated by the historian Eckhart Kehr, who had died tragically young in 1933, and in some respects he was renewing a critique that had been widespread amongst German socialists and liberals in the first quarter of the century. Fischer's contribution was to bring to greater attention little-known documentation which strengthened the case for the war as an outcome of deliberate policy. This stress on conscious decision making is illustrated by works such as Keith Wilson (ed.), *Decisions for War, 1914* (London, 1995). This includes an essay by Fischer's student John Röhl which states even more directly the claim of German responsibility. A more structural approach, reflecting Fischer's later work, can be seen in James Joll, *The Origins of the First World War* (London, 1984).

Fischer's writing raised profound questions about the ultimate meaning of the war. If the ambitions of the German Second Reich were really as far reaching as he suggested, then it follows that the war which was fought against those ambitions could not be dismissed as futile. A good example of this conclusion is the massive study of Britain in the First World War by Trevor Wilson, *The Myriad Faces of War* (Oxford, 1986). This perspective, along with other parts of the historical consensus, was strongly challenged by Niall Ferguson, *The Pity of War* (London, 1998). In a contentious argument Ferguson suggests that German ambitions in 1914 were essentially a prefiguring of the European Union rather than the Third Reich, although this may say more about Ferguson's poor opinion of that organization than about the intentions of the German leadership in 1914. Recapitulating a classic neutralist argument, Ferguson argues that Britain was profoundly mistaken in opposing this ambition. Although this part of Ferguson's argument has not gained wide support it is a useful corrective to the oversimplified view of German villainy. Certainly Ferguson's argument that Germany went to war because of its mistaken sense of a deteriorating position in comparison to France and Russia, rather than because of overwhelming ambition, seems plausible. A rather different understanding of the war's meaning can be found in the first volume of Hew Strachan's definitive history of the war, *The First World War: To Arms* (Oxford, 2001). Whereas Fischer had emphasized the reactionary nature of the German state, Strachan points to the radicalism of much German thinking, for example its embrace of anti-imperialism and anti-capitalism.

Monographs continue to build our sense of war plans and policies. Vejas Gabriel Liulevicius in his book *War Land on the Eastern Front* (Cambridge, 2000) suggests a specifically 'military utopia' in eastern Europe, providing a linkage to future German thinking. Isabel Hull in her book *Absolute Destruction* (Cornell, Ithaca, NY, 2004) looks back to the colonial practices of pre-war Germany to suggest an obsession with wars of annihilation, with ominous overtones for the future. The study by John Horne and Alan Kramer, *German Atrocities: A History of Denial* (New Haven, CT, 2001), looks at German military behaviour in 1914 and the later controversies about atrocity propaganda to understand the emotive issues around the idea of a German *Sonderweg.* Alan Kramer takes this argument much further in his book *Dynamics of Destruction* (Oxford, 2007). Jonathan Gumz in *The Resurrection and Collapse of Empire in Habsburg Serbia* (Cambridge, 2009) provides a further twist—he claims that the Habsburg army pursued a deliberate policy of de-politicization of the conflict from 1917, looking back to the nineteenth century rather than forward to the totalitarian states. The two Central powers had begun to move in completely opposite directions. Most recently Sean McMeekin, *The Russian Origins of the First World War* (Cambridge, MA, 2011), has attempted to turn Fischer on his head by arguing that the real cause of the war was a Russian southward drive for empire at the expense primarily of the Ottoman Empire, an ambition that came tantalizingly close to fulfilment by the end of 1916. This is a thesis that has found little scholarly support amongst specialists, but then neither did Fischer when he first published.

2. John Terraine, *Douglas Haig: The Educated Soldier* (London, 1963)

The author of this work was a freelance historian who would shortly come to greater prominence as the main writer for the massive BBC television series *The Great War*, produced to mark the 50th anniversary of the outbreak of the conflict. There was nothing particularly revolutionary about this biography; in many respects it restated the case of earlier Haig biographies and did not use any particularly new sources. Terraine argued that Haig was a conscientious professional given to careful consideration of the novel problems of the war. The defence of Haig in the book is quite measured and relies largely on emphasizing the unprecedented scale of the challenge of command on the Western Front in the face of so much new and untested technology. The implications of this go far beyond the narrow question of Haig and the British army. It was written at a time when the reputation of British generalship during the war had become extraordinarily low. In 1961 a scurrilous account of the British generals in 1915, Alan Clark's *The Donkeys*, had helped establish a view of the commanders as spectacularly self-serving and incompetent, an impression that would be reinforced when this work was used as source material for the highly successful anti-war musical theatre production *Oh! What a Lovely War*, which was first staged the year that Terraine's book was published. Terraine's subsequent books refined and expanded his case. *To Win a War* (London, 1978) specifically considers the campaigns of 1918 and claims that Haig and the British army played the primary role in the ultimate victory.

But in the short term the critique of British generalship continued to develop. Norman Dixon, *The Psychology of Military Incompetence* (New York, 1976), suggested that the problem with command was not so much intellect as such but that the army was predisposed to favour 'authoritarian' personality types who were inflexible and unimaginative. Tim Travers, *The Killing Ground: The British Army and the Western Front 1900–1916* (London, 1987), used a wealth of archival material to renew the indictment of British command in a new way, considering the army as a culture wedded to tradition. It was followed by *How the War was Won* (London, 1992), which examined what Travers saw as a limited shift to a technological paradigm. Denis Winter, *Haig's Command* (London, 1991), was the most intemperate and controversial attack, although one which has been severely criticized on methodological grounds. Robin Prior and Trevor Wilson, *Command on the Western Front* (Oxford, 1992) and *Passchendaele* (New Haven, CT, 1996), were critical studies of British generalship which fundamentally reframed the problem. The former, a study of Sir Henry Rawlinson, emphasized that the problem was a failure not of intellect but of implementation, whilst the latter showed the degree to which the uncertainty of political direction allowed the debacle to develop. The Royal Navy has largely been spared the same critical attention, but Andrew Gordon's *The Rules of the Game* (Annapolis, MD, 1997), an extraordinary forensic study of tactical failures at Jutland, is an exception.

Terraine helped influence a younger generation of British military historians and was honoured with a fellowship of the Royal Historical Society in 1987. A good example of work in this tradition is Gary Sheffield and Dan Todman (eds), *Command and Control on the Western Front* (London, 2004). Paddy Griffith, *Battle Tactics on the Western Front* (New Haven, CT, 1994), is polemical in its challenge to the notion of the British army as conservative, arguing instead for intelligent adaptation. Gary Sheffield, *Forgotten Victory* (London, 2001), is in many ways a restatement of Terraine's fundamental argument. It also introduced the idea of a 'learning curve' on the Western Front—to the author's subsequent regret!

The arguments about the battlefield competence or otherwise of the generals seems not to have obsessed French and German historians to the same degree. The Second World War created political contexts which tended to overshadow the purely military dimension and meant the trauma of casualties in the First World War was not seen as so unique and aberrant. Guy Pedroncini, *Pétain: general en chef 1917–1918* (Paris, 1974), was a determined attempt to rescue its subject's military achievements from the oblivion threatened by his collaboration in the Second World War. Holger Afflerbach, *Falkenhayn* (Munich, 1994 [in German]), was much less sympathetic.

American historians have shown greater interest in the tactical performance of the German army. Bruce Gudmundsson, *Stormtroop Tactics* (Westport, CT, 1989), was a pioneering work on the way that tactical improvements were developed and institutionalized, and Martin Samuel, *Command or Control?* (London, 1995), compares the British and German armies in a way that is damning towards the former. Terence Zuber, *Ardennes 1914* (London, 2007), makes an even more unfavourable comparison between the tactical capabilities of the French and the Germans at the start of the war. By contrast Robert Foley, *German Strategy and the Path to Verdun* (Cambridge, 2005), and particularly David Zabecki, *The German 1918 Offensives* (London, 2006), acknowledge German tactical strength but are much more negative in their view of German strategy. The Eastern Front has been much less well served; Dennis Showalter, *Tannenberg: Clash of Empires*, is refreshingly iconoclastic. Edward Erickson, *Ordered to Die* (Westport, CT, 2000), is appreciative of the performance of the Ottoman army. Mark Thompson, *The White War* (London, 2009), is the only full-scale study of the whole campaign on the Italian Front in English; it is massively damning of the Italian high command.

The British debate can sometimes seem exceptionally insular. William Philpott, *Bloody Victory: The Sacrifice on the Somme and the Making of the Twentieth Century* (London, 2009), significantly shifted the ground in understanding that crucial battle by more fully considering the French context. Michael Neiberg, *The Second Battle of the Marne* (Bloomington, IN, 2008), is a properly international history of the most important battle of the war. Robert Doughty, *Pyrrhic Victory* (Cambridge, MA, 2005), has brought to an Anglophone audience a massive study of the French army (ultimately more important than the British). As the title suggests, Doughty's overall verdict is that the French army did modernize its thinking during the war, but slowly and at great human cost. Bill Rawling, *Surviving Trench Warfare: Technology and the Canadian Corps* (Toronto, 1997), charts the 'learning curve' of what became the finest force on the Allied side, and Mark Grotelueschen, *The AEF Way of War* (Cambridge, 2007), does something similar over a shorter time span with his divisional level study of the Americans.

The debate around Haig rumbles on. Paul Harris, *Douglas Haig and the First World War* (London, 2008), renews many of the criticisms of Haig's failings, whilst Gary Sheffield, *The Chief: Douglas Haig and the British Army* (London, 2011), is on balance favourable. But it is perfectly reasonable to suggest that the obsession with Haig is disproportionate to his actual significance. There have been far fewer studies of Foch, a much more important figure, but Elizabeth Greenhalgh, *Foch in Command* (Cambridge, 2011), makes up for this neglect.

A half century of polemics and investigations into military performance have provisionally created the following conclusions. Firstly, that the methods and philosophies of pre-war training did give German armies a significant tactical advantage in the early months and years of the war. Secondly, that all armies entered the war with a level of command professionalism that was high by the standards of any previous war and that this in itself was part of the problem for attaining any form of decisive victory. Thirdly, that all armies were to some degree surprised by the onset of prolonged positional warfare, but perhaps none of them were completely surprised by it and all of them continually adapted to the conditions, in terms both of offensive and defensive operations. Fourthly, that the most important level of adaptation was below the level of army command—from corps right down to platoons and sections, and that as the war went on practical decision-making had to be delegated downwards. This in turn created a mismatch between strategic goals and tactical possibilities which was never fully overcome by any commander, with the result that even the supposed 'masterpieces' of the war—Tannenberg, the Brusilov offensive, Caporetto, and the Michael Offensive—turned out to be strategically sterile and even self-defeating.

3. Gerald Feldman, *Army, Industry and Labor in Germany, 1914–1918* (Princeton, NJ, 1966)

Prior to Feldman's book the general tendency had been to admire the efficiency of the German war effort. Feldman argued instead that the German war economy was the field of an ongoing faction fight. Feldman contended that from 1916 the military in conjunction with allies in heavy industry pursued unrealistic goals in armaments production at the expense of civilian well-being. This chimed in well with Fischer's view of the German Empire as driven by unrealistic reactionary politics.

Feldman's view was reflected and expanded in Norman Stone, *The Eastern Front* (London, 1975). In this more radical work of revision Stone demonstrated that the Russian war economy did not fail in production of armaments, but that the ultimately successful effort to equip the army in the field came at the expense of the civilian economy. Some aspects of Stone's theses have been modified but not overthrown by Lewis Siegelbaum, *The Politics of Industrial Mobilization in*

Russia, 1914–17 (London, 1983), and Lars Lin, *Bread and Authority in Russia, 1914–1921* (Berkeley, CA, 1990).

The question of civilian well-being was at the heart of Jay Winter, *The Great War and the British People* (London, 1985). Winter used demographic evidence to argue that the war had a positive impact on the living standards of the poorest segment of the British population because their bargaining power was increased by full employment. It was argued that heavy industry and the military did not dominate the political system to the same extent in the Entente powers. John Godfrey, *Capitalism at War* (Oxford and Providence, RI, 1987), focusing on France, and Kathleen Burk (ed.), *War and the State* (London, 1982), which dealt with Britain, apparently showed that despite errors in detail the way in which the civilian governments of these powers managed to rein in both capitalist and military interests was for the public good. Richard Wall and Jay Winter (eds), *The Upheaval of War* (Cambridge, 1985), represented the climax of the tendency to explain the outcome of the war in terms of the superior responsiveness of the more democratic powers. Winter used demographic data to show that while the poorest section of the population in Britain and France actually improved their living standards during the war, German civilian health went into serious decline.

Ferguson in *The Pity of War* mounted a powerful challenge to all of this. He argued that if the definition of 'war economy' is inflicting 'maximum slaughter at minimum expense', then the Central powers spent less and so killed their enemies much more cheaply and were therefore more efficient. For Ferguson civilian living standards were irrelevant in the pursuit of victory, and the fact that Germany allowed them to decline even to the point of marginal members of the population (such as illegitimate children and the elderly) dying of malnutrition showed a ruthless focus on what really mattered; the idea that domestic collapse preceded battlefield failure was simply the myth of the stab in the back. It should be said however that Ferguson's alternative explanation of Germany's defeat is notably vague, as he doesn't seem to believe the German *army* was defeated either.

It is certainly true that in the aggregate the Entente and associated powers spent vastly more than their opponents, but when disaggregated these figures look much more suspect. The most efficient war economy by Ferguson's chosen measure was the Ottoman Empire and the least efficient was the United States, a definition of economic efficiency which is to say the least counter-intuitive. It is striking that 'efficiency' by this measure is generally inversely correlated to per capita wealth and because in aggregate the Central powers were poorer they tended to have less to spend. Furthermore the definition of war economy that Ferguson uses was derived from Bertrand Russell, a passionate pacifist who believed the war was a futile error. Moreover the real objective of war was not to kill soldiers but to *win*, or at least survive. By that measure the Romanov, Hapsburg, Hohenzollern, and Ottoman empires all failed *completely*—even if they spent less money in their failure. In fact if the purpose of expenditure is seen not so much as killing the enemy but saving the lives of one's own citizens and subjects, the profligate United States, which suffered relatively few casualties in achieving its objectives, spent wisely, whereas the Ottoman Empire, which suffered catastrophic human losses, did very poorly despite the resilience of its soldiers.

The comparative political economy perspective has been restated by Peter Gatrell, *Russia's First World War* (London, 2005). The Russian case remains the strongest argument for the impact of domestic economic failure preceding battlefield collapse. But the relationship in Germany in 1918 is probably a very subtle and complex one and cannot be reduced to a simple dichotomy. Nevertheless Ferguson's critique has diminished the confidence of the 'Whiggish' view that democracies handled their war economy better. In the end all of the combatant powers seem to have allowed military expenditure a largely free hand, and the similarities are greater than the differences. The Entente powers and the United States spent more because they *could*, and access to the global economy outside Europe ultimately decided the war.

4. Paul Fussell, *The Great War and Modern Memory* (Oxford, 1975)

This was not the first important book to consider the literature of the First World War; that distinction belongs to Jean Norton Cru, a Franco-American veteran who wrote a classic critical study of war memoirs entitled *Témoins* in 1929. Fussell, a Professor of English Literature specializing in the elegant ironies of the early eighteenth century, was similarly a veteran, of the American army in the Second World War, and much of *The Great War and Modern Memory* is in fact a consideration of American writing about the Second World War. It was also a book published in the immediate aftermath of American defeat in Vietnam and very much reflects the powerful anti-war sentiment of its time and place. The book was both critically acclaimed and controversial, and it remains central to discussions of the cultural meaning of the war.

Fussell's central argument is that the war demonstrated to its participants their helplessness in the face of machine-made death and destruction. Because of both the sensibilities of the time and the existence of literary censorship the

British soldier writers were largely unable to express their feelings in print with obscene language appropriate to the obscenity of war. Instead they used the available language in an ironic fashion in both poetry and prose, exploiting the gap between expectations and reality in order to expose the meaningless horror of the war. This anti-heroic sensibility was for Fussell the essence of modernism and in turn the war helped create a world receptive to modernist writing.

Some British military historians, notably John Terraine, took great offence at what they saw as Fussell's recycling of false old myths about the 'donkey' generals, but the lasting significance of Fussell was in generating a new interest in the cultural meaning of the war.

Regarding literature, visual arts, and the memory of war in Britain, Samuel Hynes, *A War Imagined* (London, 1990), is a more nuanced and historically contextualized study than Fussell's. Rosa Maria Bracco, *Merchants of Hope* (Oxford and Providence, RI, 1993), demonstrates that the bestselling literary works of the post-war period were more conventionally patriotic than those by Fussell's literary giants. Hugh Cecil, *The Flower of Battle* (London, 1996), and Martin Stephen, *The Price of Pity* (London, 1996), similarly suggest that the literary memory of the war was more diverse than those by Fussell admits. Trudi Tate, *Modernism, History and the First World War* (Manchester, 1998), tackles modernism much more directly than Fussell ever did. Brian Bond, *The Unquiet Western Front* (Cambridge, 2002), and Dan Todman, *The Great World War: Myth and Memory* (London, 2005), consider the process of historical memory in Britain over the long run. Both argue that the British myths of the war were constructed by later political developments rather than being straightforward reactions to experience.

John Cruickshank, *Variations on Catastrophe* (Oxford, 1982), suggests conclusions about French war writers that have some similarity with Fussell's, although it also embraces greater variety in formal response. Frank Field, *Three French Writers and the Great War* (Cambridge, 1975), was more interested in the way that war writers shaped political ideologies. This perspective was taken up in Modris Eksteins, *The Rites of Spring* (New York, 1989), and George Mosse, *Fallen Soldiers* (Oxford, 1990). These books approach the issue of war and modern memory in very different ways. *The Rites of Spring* is a diffuse and sometimes maddening meditation on modernism before, during, and after the war, which sees Germany at the centre of the story and even makes the case for Nazism as a modernist perversion. By contrast Mosse's work looks back into the Romanticism of the nineteenth century and sees the cultural response to war as more purely reactionary.

Kenneth Silver, *Esprit de Corps: The Art of the Parisian Avant Garde and the First World War* (Princeton, NJ, 1989), produced a more ambiguous picture about the relationship between art and modernity. In certain respects the war years saw a retreat from the vigorous experimentation of the pre-war period, although the emergence of surrealism in the 1920s was a powerful legacy of a wartime loss of faith in 'reason'. Jay Winter took this rejection of the link between war memory and modernity much further. Examining public ceremonial and memorials as well as art and literature, he argued in *Sites of Memory, Sites of Mourning* (Cambridge, 1995) that the impact of mass bereavement meant that Europeans tended to seek comfort in tradition in understanding the war. Far from supporting modernist rejection of old values, the war reinforced them. Winter's argument has been expanded by his student Stefan Goebel, *The Great War and Medieval Memory* (Cambridge, 2007), which studies comparatively the commemoration of the war in Britain and Germany.

It is possible that the modernism versus tradition argument is a false dichotomy. Artistic modernism was a multifaceted movement and was not always the same in different places and in different art forms. Furthermore modernist fascination with psychology and the 'deep past' meant that modernism was itself sometimes backward looking.

Leonard Smith, *The Embattled Self: French Soldiers' Testimony of the Great War* (Ithaca, NY, 2007), shows how the idea of the war as defined by futility was a contested process and one tied to the problem of the moral meaning of 'witnessing'. Perhaps for now the final word on the memory of the war should go to Jean-Yves Le Naour, *Le soldat inconnu vivant* (Paris, 2002), translated as *The Living Unknown Soldier* (London, 2005). The story of 'Anthelme Mangin', an amnesiac soldier who became the focal point for the hopes of dozens of families of the 'missing', this micro-history traces the long afterlife of this story as a powerful myth of the war.

5. Jean-Jacques Becker, *Les Français dans la Grande Guerre* (Paris, 1980), translated as *The Great War and the French People* (Oxford and Providence, RI, 1985)

Becker set out to understand the resilience of the French people in the face of German invasion in 1914. Based on an extraordinary mastery of primary sources, he argued that robust civilian living standards (see section 3 above) combined with a high level of 'self-mobilization' by opinion formers allowed France to win a war of national defence in sharp contrast to the shattering of national unity in 1870 and 1940.

Simultaneously, in a book that won the Pulitzer prize, David Kennedy, *Over Here: The First World War and American Society* (Oxford, 1980), considered the construction of consent for the war in the progressive-era United States. Gerard DeGroot, *Blighty* (London, 1996), understood British wartime society as being centrally defined by conservative values and deference. By contrast John Horne, *Labour at War: Britain and France 1914–1918* (Oxford, 1991), emphasized the extent to which the working class found their own values within the war effort, particularly in their support for Wilsonian democratization.

W. Bruce Lincoln, *Passage Through Armageddon: The Russians in War and Revolution* (New York, 1994), was more focused on political history but gave a good sense of the limits of Tsarist credibility, whilst Roger Chickering, *Imperial Germany and the Great War* (Cambridge, 1998), was centred around the polarization that developed from 1917. Hubertus Jahn, *Patriotic Culture in Russia during World War 1* (Ithaca, NY, 1995), showed both the possibility of commitment to the war effort in Russia and its limitations. George Robb, *British Culture and the First World War* (London, 2002), showed a society with a stronger patriotic consensus.

Stéphane Audoin-Rouzeau and Annette Becker, *14–18: retrouver la guerre* (Paris, 2000), translated as *14–18: Understanding the Great War* (London, 2002), took the idea of a war by consent further by emphasizing the idea of 'war culture' in which opinion formers helped mobilize popular passion toward the utter destruction of the enemy. This work also owes much to Mosse, *Fallen Soldiers*, in its perception of the war as a process of 'brutalization'.

A powerful challenge to this comes from Benjamin Ziemann, *Front und Heimat* (Essen, 1997), translated as *War Experiences in Rural Germany, 1914–1923* (Oxford and Providence, RI, 2007). In the preface to the English edition, Ziemann demonstrates a great deal of scepticism about the idea of war culture, arguing that ordinary Bavarians hated and resented the war. Recent works on the United States, such as the contentious polemic by Thomas Fleming, *The Illusion of Victory* (New York, 2004), have tended more than Kennedy to stress the role of repression and coercion on the home front. Brock Millman, *Managing Domestic Dissent* (London, 2000), similarly claims that the British government from 1917 was heavily focused on the revolutionary threat at home.

The multi-authored collections compiled by Jay Winter and Jean-Louis Robert, *Capital Cities at War: Paris, London, Berlin 1914–1919* (Cambridge, 1997, 2005), were an ambitious effort to utilize metropolitan history as a method of understanding the progress and outcome of the war on the home front; urban history was also the focus of Maureen Healy, *Vienna and the Fall of the Habsburg Empire* (Cambridge, 2004). Roger Chickering, *The Great War and Urban Life in Germany: Freiburg 1914–1918* (Cambridge, 2007), is a monumental achievement bordering on the 'total history' of a small town at war. Very different, but equally impressive, is Martha Hanna, *Your Death Would Be Mine* (Cambridge, MA, 2006), a moving account based on the letters of Marie and Paul Pireaud from the rural south of France, which provides powerful backing for many of Becker's concepts. Adrian Gregory, *The Last Great War* (Cambridge, 2008), consciously follows Becker in many respects in trying to understand the general support for the war in Britain, but is cautious about endorsing a strong view of 'war culture' and brutalization.

Any account of any society during the war must recognize that some degree of popular support and legitimacy was vital to the war effort. But it must also acknowledge that both old systems of authority and new systems of bureaucratic subordination and the manipulation of consent by propaganda had a role to play. This is a view that also needs to be extended to the armed forces.

6. Tony Ashworth, *Trench Warfare 1914–1918: The Live and Let Live System* (London, 1980)

The social history of armies during the war had been gathering pace since the late 1960s. A monument to diligent scholarship was the work of a talented amateur, Martin Middlebrook, who conducted 555 interviews with veterans to produce his oral history, *The First Day of the Somme* (London, 1971). Bill Gammage, *The Broken Years* (Victoria, 1974), used both oral history and extensive contemporary documentation to recover the devastating experience of ordinary Australians at war. What set Ashworth's work apart was the ambition of trying to understand the fundamental sociological forces that allowed men to endure the war for so long. Ashworth contested the view that soldiers were powerless victims and argued instead that by covert methods they managed to gain some degree of control over their circumstances. Ashworth's argument owed a debt to Guy Pedroncini, *Les mutineries de 1917* (Paris, 1967), which showed the extent to which the 'collective indiscipline' in the French army was a strike against the tactics of the commanders.

Stéphane Audoin-Rouzeau, *Les combattants des tranchées* (Paris, 1986), translated as *Men at War 1914–1918* (Oxford and Providence, RI, 1992), used the trench journalism of French soldiers to argue that 'national sentiment', a fundamental belief in the necessity of defending French soil, was key to explaining their endurance. John Fuller, *Troop Morale and Popular Culture in the British and Dominion Armies* (Oxford, 1991), uses similar sources but explains the endurance of the British more in terms of the persistence of civilian culture in the BEF.

Leonard Smith, *Between Mutiny and Obedience* (Princeton, NJ, 1994), is an important study of the French 5th Infantry Division through the entire war, which centres on the constant negotiation of behaviour between soldiers and their commanders, informed by the soldiers' sense of themselves as citizens. Alex Watson, *Enduring the Great War* (Cambridge, 2008), stresses junior leadership and individual psychology as central to endurance in both the British and German armies. In part this follows arguments first developed for the British by Gary Sheffield, *Leadership in the Trenches* (London, 2000).

Not all historians have seen the endurance of armies as primarily explained by popular consent. Julian Putkowski and Julian Sykes, *Shot at Dawn* (London, 1989), was a campaigning book designed to expose the injustice of British capital court martials. Nicolas Offenstadt, *Les fusillés de la Grande Guerre* (Paris, 1999), extended the argument internationally. Bernd Ulrich and Benjamin Ziemann, *Frontalltag im Ersten Weltkrieg* (Frankfurt am Main, 1994), translated as *German Soldiers in the Great War* (London, 2010), also emphasized military discipline and various forms of resistance. Christopher Pugsley, *On the Fringe of Hell* (London, 1991), is a careful examination of the interaction of morale and discipline in the New Zealand Division. Helen McCartney, *Citizen Soldiers: The Liverpool Territorials in the First World War* (Cambridge, 2004), extends this to investigate the way in which morale and discipline interacted with men's civilian identities.

It is now generally accepted that the armed forces cannot be treated independently of consideration of the societies from which they were recruited, but that at the same time the challenge of industrial warfare created important similarities in response in soldiers from diverse national backgrounds. Certainly soldiers can no longer be considered simply as pawns moved around the battlefield without wills of their own.

7. Margaret Higonnet et al. (eds), *Behind the Lines: Gender and the Two World Wars* (New Haven, CT, 1987)

This volume responded to the developing fashion for gender history by rethinking the idea that the war had improved the position of women. Borrowing the image of the 'double helix', it suggested that if women made progress during the war this was counteracted by the extent to which exclusively male military service excluded women from the most central wartime concept of valuable citizenship. Thus whatever value was placed on women's wartime contribution was 'trumped' by an increase in male prestige that was at least as great.

Gail Braybon, *Women Workers in the First World War* (London, 1981), and Deborah Thom, *Nice Girls and Rude Girls* (London, 1998), are key studies of women's war work in Britain. Margaret Darrow, *French Women and the First World War* (Oxford and Providence, RI, 2000), considered work as part of the wider experience. Ute Daniel, *Arbeiterfrauen in der Kriegsellschaft* (1989), translated as the *War from Within* (Oxford and Providence, RI, 1997), is a thorough exploration of the lives of working-class women in Germany during the war, which also began a serious reconsideration of the historical meaning of 'emancipation' in the German case. Belinda Davis, *Home Fires Burning* (Chapel Hill, NC, 2000), concentrates on women's agency in food protests in Germany. Raymond Jonas, *The Tragic Tale of Claire Ferchaud* (Berkeley, CA, 2005), is an intriguing study of a single controversial figure in wartime France.

Kathleen Kennedy, *Disloyal Mothers and Scurrilous Citizens* (Bloomington, IN, 1999), is a powerful study of women war resisters in the United States. Susan Grayzel, *Women's Identities at War: Gender, Motherhood and Politics in Britain and France during the First World War* (Chapel Hill, NC, 1999), turned its particular focus to the stress on the rhetoric of motherhood as women's wartime duty and the many complex ways this interacted with lived experiences. Nicoletta Gullace, *The Blood of our Sons* (London, 2002), considers the political implication of 'sacrificial' motherhood, arguing that this rather than work was the key to the franchise in the United Kingdom. Lisa Budreau, *Bodies of War* (New York, 2010), focuses on the aftermath of wartime and the experience of the Gold Star mothers who lost their sons. Susan Grayzel, *Women and the First World War* (London, 2002), is a fine overview of the state of this topic.

There has also been a burgeoning of studies of masculinity, particularly in the British army. Studies include Joanna Bourke, *Dismembering the Male* (London and Chicago, 1996), Santanu Das, *Touch and Intimacy in First World War Literature* (Cambridge, 2005), Jessica Meyer, *Men of War* (London, 2008), and Michael Roper, *The Secret Battle: Emotional Survival in the Great War* (Manchester, 2009). Lois Bibbings, *Telling Tales about Men* (Manchester, 2009), considers ideas of masculinity in relation to conscientious objectors. Janet Watson, *Fighting Different Wars* (Cambridge, 2004), brings together the ways in which British men and women understood the war through the categories of masculinity and femininity.

It is likely that gender will be a key category in future understandings of the war. It is also increasingly clear that the picture is not easily established. For women in most countries the war produced both progress and backlash. It did acknowledge important recognition of their role as citizens but also an increased emphasis on their biological identity. For men the celebration of the warrior ethic often proved transient in the face of impersonal mechanized slaughter. For both men and women wartime separation created an intense desire to re-establish domestic normality.

8. Avner Offer, *The First World War: An Agrarian Interpretation* (Oxford, 1989)

Written by a distinguished Israeli economic historian, this is a work brimming with ideas, transnational in scope and interdisciplinary in execution. The book is a thoughtful examination of the British blockade of Germany, of British and German naval grand strategy before and during the war, and the global context of British imperial expansion in the transoceanic neo-Europes that determined the outcome of the war and helped shape the peace. The peculiar genius of its author means that it has had no real successor, but it does point to the way in which the war might be imagined 'transnationally'.

John Morrow, *The Great War: An Imperial History* (London and New York, 2003), is an ambitious attempt to reimagine the war through an explicitly imperial frame. To some extent it privileges extra-European imperialism over the issue of imperialism within Europe, but it is certainly thought provoking. Margaret MacMillan, *The Peacemakers* (London, 2001), is a lively work of popularization by a distinguished diplomatic historian. As well as arguing that the Versailles Treaty was not in itself doomed to failure, it extends consideration of the process well beyond its German dimension. This idea is extended in Erez Manela, *The Wilsonian Moment* (Oxford, 2007), which pays particular attention to the way that the Paris Peace Conference was perceived outside Europe and argues that the origins of third-world nationalism owe a great deal to reactions to both the promise and failure of Wilson's democratic rhetoric. Lawrence Sondhaus, *World War One: The Global Revolution* (Cambridge, 2011), argues that the war itself unleashed these forces.

William Storey, *The First World War: A Concise Global History* (Lanham, MD, 2009), deals innovatively with two themes sometimes neglected in overviews (including this one): technology and the environment. Tammy Proctor, *Civilians in a World at War 1914–1918* (New York, 2010), is an invaluable corrective to the surprisingly common view that the war was really only experienced by soldiers. It is also global in its scope.

A final mention should be made of Peter Englund, Secretary of the Swedish Nobel Prize committee for literature, sometime war correspondent and both academic and popular historian. In 2008 Englund published in Swedish an extraordinary work drawn from twenty personal accounts of the war, which was translated into English in 2011 as *The Beauty and the Sorrow: An Intimate History of the First World War*. Englund describes it as an anti-history concerned not with why things happened but how they felt to those who were there. His participants, including a German schoolgirl, a middle-aged French civil servant, a Venezuelan soldier of fortune in the Ottoman army, and a British governess serving as a volunteer nurse on the Russian front, provide an episodic narrative where the viewpoints occasionally connect with the recognized historically significant events, but just as frequently follow their own personal logic.

It seems likely that the approaching centenary of the war will produce a flurry of new works. Major contributions are likely regarding Russia and Austria. The centenary of the foundation of dozens of states in 1918–19 is likely to produce further new perspectives. At the same time the growth of global history has produced new challenges. The difficulty of integrating the dual perspective of a European catastrophe and a global turning point with the requirement to capture the more human and intimate dimensions of the war will challenge historians for decades to come.

ACKNOWLEDGEMENTS

We are grateful for permission to reprint the following material:

Lines from a poem by Vladislav Petković Dis translated by Bernard Johnson, and from 'An die Soldaten des Grossenkrieges' ('To the Soldiers of the Great War') by Gerrit Engelke, translated by P. Bridgewater in Tim Cross (ed.), *The Lost Voices of World War 1: An International Anthology of Writers, Poets and Playwrights* (Bloomsbury, 1988, 1998); reprinted by permission of Bloomsbury Publishing Plc.

'Today on Earth' by Zinaida Gippius translated by Jana Howlett from the original Russian in *Poslednie Stikhi* (Peterburg, 1918), and lines from 'Quieter' by Zinaida Gippius translated by Jana Howlett from the original Russian in V. V. Uchenova (ed.), *Tsaritsy Muz. Russkie Poetessy XIX-nachala XX vv* (Sowremnik, 1989), in Jana Howlett, 'We'll End in Hell My Passionate Sisters: Russian Women Poets and the First World War' in Dorothy Goldman (ed.), *Women and World War 1: The Written Response* (Palgrave, 1993); reprinted by permission of Jana Howlett.

Extract from a soldier's song translated by Mark Thompson, in Mark Thompson, *The White War: Life and Death on the Italian Front* (Faber, 2008); reprinted by permission of the publishers, Faber & Faber Ltd. and Basic Books, an imprint of the Perseus Books Group. Although every effort has been made to trace and contact all copyright holders before publication this has not been possible in all cases. If notified, the publisher will rectify any errors or omissions at the earliest opportunity.

I would like to thank the Master and Fellows of Pembroke College, Oxford and my colleagues in the University of Oxford History Faculty. I'd particularly like to thank Sir Hew Strachan whilst mentioning that he has no responsibility whatsoever for any errors of fact or interpretation in this book. I would like also to thank the community of scholars who have made the International Society for First World War Studies so stimulating. I thank all those at Oxford University Press who have helped to steer this book through production. This book is dedicated to Theodore Reginald Cohen.

INDEX